**PULL IT
OFF
THE PAGE!**

PULL IT OFF THE PAGE

"Experiencing the God whom we sing,
preach and read about"

Leslie Bishop-Joe

XULON PRESS

Xulon Press
2301 Lucien Way #415
Maitland, FL 32751
407.339.4217
www.xulonpress.com

ISBN-13: 978-1-6628-1725-0

I'm grateful to the Lord for His timing in allowing me to bring this book forward. Many thanks to my husband, Clarence, and my family for your ongoing support in all of my endeavors.

To all of my ministry partners here in the United States and abroad, I greatly appreciate you.

This book is also dedicated to those who, like me, have a burning desire to know the God of the Bible and to experience His presence and power in the way that we read about but seldom see. There are many who yearn to move beyond programs and rituals to an authentic relationship with a true and living God. My hope and prayer is that you will be inspired to intentionally seek our God with renewed passion and an appetite that only He can satisfy.

Contents

Introduction: Pull It off the Page!

"Experiencing the God whom we sing, preach and read about"

To say that I am grateful to the Lord for allowing me to once again share through writing that which He has placed in my heart is certainly an understatement. I'm a firm believer that the Lord is stirring His people and causing us to reject lifestyles that reflect an acceptance of "going through the motions" with no real zeal for our abundant lives in and through Christ. Our time of gathering for fellowship and worship can so easily move away from a spontaneous response to His powerful, sweet presence. Before we realize it, we may find that we have allowed ourselves to become comfortable with a very controlled time of worship, with others telling us when to lift our hands, when to shout unto the Lord, when to praise Him, when to tell Him that we love Him, and so on.

Ironically, before sending this book for print, I have had to come back and add to the foregoing statements regarding "controlled time of worship" as we have now come outside of the four walls of the church due to the COVID-19 pandemic. While we continue to mourn the loss of our loved ones and acquaintances during this pandemic, in my opinion, the church at large has experienced a reset as it pertains to our relationship with Christ and our need for intimacy with Him. We've been pulled out of our comfort zone of the four walls and have had to confront what the Bible has always stated, and that is simply that God's people, not the building, are the church.

As I have had the opportunity to move in and out of various Christian circles, it has become apparent to me that so many believers have an earnest desire for more of God's presence, for more of a reality in their walk and experience with Him. If you are one of those who has been crying out to the Lord from this place of yearning for more, then you are certainly not alone. Like you, there are many others who want to pull from the pages of the Bible and begin to experience this great God, this supernatural God of our faith. He is our Deliverer, our Lord, and our King! Our heart's cry has become, "Lord, we know that there has to be so much more. Lord, please give us more!" Until we come to grips with what our souls truly long for, we will continue to "go through the motions" of church work, conferences, and living lives that are simply facades that reflect very little of what we really desire deep inside. For so many of us, what our souls truly long for is not the *things* that the Lord provides but rather an encounter, a faith-filled life with Him. This cry unto the Lord is for lives that reflect the power that we read about and preach about from the pages of Holy Scripture.

The Bible is not like our history, English, or literature books that we read in school, but it is Spirit and it is life. Through the Bible, we connect with the heart of God, we learn His will for our lives, and we become familiar with His character. It is through His word that believers begin a journey, a faith walk, while still in this present world. That is exciting!

Hence the writing of this book. In it I will share messages that are intended to stir, encourage, and challenge you to take a journey with me as we seek the Lord and ask Him to show us how to take His written word and "pull it off the page" and into our everyday lives in a greater way. I will seek to encourage you by any means necessary. We're living in a time of great spiritual adversity, so we must become reacquainted with the God who we read, preach, and sing about. I challenge you now to make the commitment to apply all that the Lord impresses upon your spirit as we embark upon our journey together to delve into His word and to "pull it off the written page" and into our lives in a real way.

Commit to a Fresh Start

Hello, my friend. I'm grateful that you've picked up this book and have decided to move forward with a life of applying the word of God daily and experiencing more of what we read about in the scriptures. In order to experience a fresh start, there must be a commitment to show up and be present for your life each day from this day forward. No more sleepwalking. Many of us have not obtained what God has revealed to us simply because we have halted between two opinions and haven't made up our minds to believe Him.

Live with expectation! Trust God's favor! Know that He is faithful and that He has an expected end planned for you. Know that He has preceded you in every situation. Wherever He's leading us, He's there before we arrive on the scene. We speak of praising Him and thanking Him in advance of our blessings or the answers to our prayers, but in reality, we can't thank or praise Him in advance because there is no way to get ahead of Him. He is already in our tomorrows. So, the psalmist said it well: "I will bless the Lord at all times, His praises shall continually be in my mouth" (Ps. 34:1). A life of expectation warrants continual praise.

I have no way of knowing how you generally start your day, but I want you to consider what your life might be like if each day you started by simply thanking the Lord for the gift of life—your life. Before the cares of the day can begin to encroach upon you and cloud your thoughts with what needs to be done and what may not be working well, allow your mindset to shift to beginning this day with a focus on a new chance at life and new opportunities to make right or try again those things that didn't work out so well a day ago, a week ago, a month ago, or even last year. What would be different if you decided to start today to make a conscious effort to be fully present in the now and to begin to live, really live, with a focus on only those things that truly matter? In the grand scheme of things, many situations and circumstances that call for our attention really don't matter. In the grand scheme of things, after all is said and done, some things don't deserve all of the time and attention that they take from us because they constantly pull us away from our goals and our focus on destiny. When we seek the Lord for His will and purpose for our lives, and commit to following His plan to fulfill that purpose, He will help us every step of the way.

That is my challenge to each and every one who picks up this book. The challenge is to see God's word as a reality that is more real than anything that we could ever experience with our human senses. In order to see the word of God come off the written pages and become a reality in our lives, we must stand in agreement with what He has said and make a decision to truly allow Him to be Lord of our lives. We don't hear much anymore about making Jesus the Lord of our lives, but God has not changed His position regarding His relationship with man. Yes, He is a friend, a Confidant, a Healer, a Deliverer, and we can go on and on as we think about the wonderful facets of our relationship with Jesus. He is all of these things and so much more; however, He requires that if we truly desire to follow Him, that we allow Him to be Lord of our lives.

Most of us don't have a problem speaking of Him being "Lord of the Harvest," "Lord of the breakthrough," "Lord of the Sabbath," etc., but He is also "Lord of all," and He still requires that His disciples make the decision to place Him on the throne of our lives and yield to His ordained purpose without any hidden agendas. In order to do this, we must make a conscious effort to daily conquer those things that hinder and impede our progress and that cause us to place "self" and its contrary desires on the throne of our life.

Let's face it: giving up the control of our lives is not such an easy task. From the time that we were able to walk and talk, our task has been to become independent and to operate on our own. If you've ever been around a toddler as they go through what's called "the terrible twos," they constantly lay claim to their independence as they see it, by saying things such as, "No, I do it!" In other words, "I don't need or want your help; I can do this all by myself." Of course, we know that they can't, but in their little minds, they have everything all figured out and the adults around them are simply getting in the way. These little ones simply want their parents or caretakers to allow them to walk on their own, go their own way without the assistance of holding hands and being told what to do or when to do it. They quickly and adamantly protest, as they are oblivious to the danger that they place themselves in as they take off on a course of their own, apart from the watchful parent, because they are driven by their desire to be independent. Mind you, this desire for independence is natural and healthy.

As teens, we can't wait to get out on our own and do things our own way. Many of us can recall the times when we said, "When I'm on my own, I'm never going to do x, y, z like my parents did." So the struggle for independence and self-reliance starts very young and is very much a part of our makeup, our tools for survival in the worldly system. Again, I'll say that this is actually healthy, and having healthy independence and interdependence will serve as strong anchors as we make our way through the pathways of the Kingdom.

You and I are being challenged to accept a daily mission that will allow us to take our lives, our emotions, our ambitions, and our dreams off "hold" and to begin to live—not for tomorrow, next week, next month, or next year but for today. I am confident that as we learn to trust and to walk hand in hand with the Lord, He will help us to realign our priorities and to see the people and things in our lives that really matter and those that don't. This life is not a rehearsal. We are not here on vacation or by some freak accident or explosion that happened in the universe. You and I are here because of the great plan of God, the true and living God who is the Savior of all men. It's time for us to stop "going through the motions" and to begin to live in accordance with the plan and purpose of the King.

It's my hope and prayer that as you allow the Spirit of the Lord to minister to you through the pages of this book, you will be challenged to do some soul-searching, to take risks, to move out of your comfort zone, to dust off some old dreams and ambitions and to get reacquainted with the "you" that may have gotten lost in the shuffle of life. You may accept this challenge alone or with a friend, your Bible study group, book club partners, or whomever you choose. It might be a good idea to go through a week of challenges, then gather with friends to discuss what it was like and how each of you was affected. Each person who accepts the challenge will have time designated for introspection and assessing the impact, so whether your debriefing and reflecting is done alone or with a group, the outcome should not be significantly altered. However, sharing in a group setting affords the opportunity to hear the input and perspectives of others in relation to specific life challenges, which, of course, can be very beneficial.

It's time to make a fresh start!

No matter how close you may believe that you are in your relationship with the Lord right now, or how distant you may feel from Him, the reality is that there is a more intimate place to experience with Him a deeper and more intimate relationship that awaits each of us. Our God is all-wise, meaning that His wisdom is infinite. He is all-knowing, meaning that there's nothing that takes Him by surprise or that He can't figure out. He is all-powerful, His power is limitless and insurmountable, and He's everywhere present, meaning that there's simply nowhere that you and I could ever go, retreat to, or run to where His presence does not exist.

Each of us must decide how closely we want to walk with this supernatural God of our faith because the reality is that He desires close communion with us, and there's always more intimacy, knowledge, and power to experience with Him and to derive from Him as we determine that we will live from a place of greater grace, power, and love by applying His living word to our lives. Allow the Lord to speak to you; allow Him to reveal those areas of your life where He wants to show up in a greater way. You will begin to see that the challenges in your life are only opportunities for the Lord to show Himself strong rather than situations that the enemy can use to discourage you, distract you, and pull you down.

Wherever you are right now, just take a moment to say this short prayer of commitment to the Lord. If you're with someone else and you're committing to this together, you may certainly pray together. This is just a starter prayer, so feel free to add anything to this prayer that will positively affect your commitment to be present in your life from this day forward.

Dear heavenly Father, I come to you in the Name of Jesus asking that you would forgive me for all of the times that I have doubted you and your plan and purpose for my life. I realize now that all of the time that I have wasted walking in anxiety, fear, and unbelief has only been a distraction and a testimony to my lack of faith and trust in you. From this day forward, I commit myself again to you, to the leading of your Spirit, and to bringing glory to You by actively participating in each day of my life and viewing it for what it is--a special gift from you. With your help, I am making a commitment to a fresh start. I choose to forget the unfruitful things that are behind me and press forward to the life, the abundant life, that lies ahead. Lord, please fill me with your joy and let your glory be revealed in and through me. This is my prayer in Jesus's name. Amen.

Going Through The Motions

Now that you have committed to a fresh start, it's time to do some introspective work. Let me start by asking you a simple question. Why are you doing what you're doing with regard to your relationship with the Lord and your Christian walk? That question may seem rather strange to you, but I really want you to stop now and think about your life as it is today. If we're honest with ourselves, many of us would have to admit that oftentimes we're just going through the motions. The problem with that is that when we're just going through the motions, we're not really present in the moment. We have gotten into a pattern of behaviors and actions that have become our "normal" mode of approaching our lives. Have you ever felt like you were just operating on "automatic" with no real zest or enthusiasm in your life? For example, have you ever been driving along, and all of a sudden you look around and wonder how you got to where you are? There's just a total disconnect between where you started and where you are now. You were on "automatic" and your mind was somewhere else in the process of getting from point A to point B.

When we get into living life in a routine, it can become hard to remember the time (if there ever was a time) when we were really excited about living—not necessarily excited about anything or anyone in particular but just living with expectation and excitement about life. It's easy to get to a place where we find ourselves just doing what we do with no real rhyme or reason. It's just what we do, it's what we've always done—at least for a reasonable period of time. What a tragedy to get up day after day and go through monotonous, boring routines with no excitement, joy, wonder, or expectation. Yet I'm sure that most of us can attest to being in this space in our lives at some point in time.

Each day is a gift from God, and to see it and respond to it as anything less than that must certainly be an insult to Him. The psalmist declares in Psalm 118:24, "This is the day which the Lord has made; let us rejoice and be glad in it." The American Standard Version gives the last part of the verse as "we will rejoice and be glad in it." I like that. That seems to be the proper response to each new day regardless of what our circumstances dictate. Each day is made by God; therefore each day is good, and we're given the choice daily to either complain about what we feel is not right in our lives or to rejoice in the day. We can choose to rejoice!

I realize that many of you may be dealing with major obstacles, illnesses, losses, and various pitfalls of life.

However, the point that I am making here is that the routines of life sometimes hinder us from realizing that our God has a plan for each of us and that His desire is that we would live our lives in the joy, peace, and abundance that He alone can give. None of these (joy, peace, and abundance) is a direct product of our circumstances, although it's easy to assign these as by-products of what we're experiencing or going through in our lives. In other words, because things are going well for me, I have peace; because I have a new car, new house, I now have joy. We can yield to our circumstances at any given time, thus allowing them to have control over our emotions and the manner in which we relate or respond to the world around us. It is vital that we recognize the fact that our circumstances are not to dictate our response to the world around us. We must learn the necessary steps for cultivating the habit of focusing on the things that matter and dismissing the irrelevant distracters. You alone must determine what really matters in your life and to what you will assign relevance.

We can cultivate the habit of rejoicing "in spite of," although I'm not going to suggest that it will be an easy task. We all know that old habits are hard to break and cultivating new ones can sometimes be even harder, but we have to start somewhere. In order to get different results, we have to do something different, and sometimes we have to do a lot of things differently. Let me offer four simple steps for starters. These have more to do with our mindset, because I'm a firm believer that until things change with our outlook, what we see in our actions won't change much. These are some changes that you can embrace immediately, and soon you may find yourself adding more steps in order to move yourself closer to being one who rejoices "in spite of." It's all about perspective and having a determination to view life from the perspective of being an overcomer (that's who we are) and one who walks in agreement with the word of God. We can't agree with what we don't know, but as we draw closer to the Lord and fall in love with His word, we will begin to realize the many reasons that we have to be glad and to rejoice throughout each given day. Try these suggestions just to get started and to get your mindset moving toward gratefulness.

1) **See each day as a gift.** Most people who I know enjoy getting gifts. I certainly do. Can you imagine someone receiving a gift, casting it aside, or throwing it away without even taking the time to see what is wrapped inside? Why would anyone do that? What an insult to the giver of the gift, who no doubt had some anticipation of seeing how pleased the recipient would be after opening and seeing something that was carefully chosen and wrapped just for him or her. Yet in a sense, that's what we do when we fail to realize that each day is a precious gift from God. Too many of us start each day with our own agenda and "to-do" list without giving thought to what might be on the Lord's "to-do" list for us during the waking hours that lie ahead. Let's start each day by thanking God for the

gift of waking, breathing, and having the privilege of communing with Him before we take on the first task of our day.

2) **Face each day with anticipation.** None of us has any idea what we will encounter during any given day. Anticipation is a feeling of expectation or excitement about something that is going to happen in the near future. Let me take this opportunity to remind you that as a child of the King, you are an Ambassador here on earth, and each day you have a Kingdom assignment. Once we make up our minds to put Kingdom first, we can live in great expectation of what the King will do in and through us as we yield our lives to Him and His purpose. We are here to effect change in the earth, and that can't be done through our own agendas or devices. It's time to get excited not only about the word of God but about God Himself and what He's doing in and through His people! We've been called and set apart for such a time as this.

3) **Cultivate an attitude of gratitude.** Consider that everything and anything that is affecting your life right now, whether you consider it to be positive or negative, has to all work together for your good if you love the Lord and have been called according to His purpose (Rom. 3:23). It's easy for us to find numerous things that we could be displeased or upset about at any given moment on any given day, but an

attitude of gratitude has to be cultivated. We have to make a concerted effort to bring our thoughts and inclinations under subjection. When we could complain, we have to make a habit of thanking the Lord. I can't even count the times that I've cheated the Lord out of my sincere praise because my focus was on what wasn't going right in my life. I was caught up in my emotions and distracted from the things of God. No, we're not living in a bubble, and yes, there are some very unpleasant circumstances that each of us will have to face in this life. But we have so much to be thankful for! Remember that being grateful is a choice. Thank God that things aren't as bad as they could be.

4) **Treat your time like money.** On many levels, I think it might be fair to say "Treat your time or manage your time better than you treat or manage your money." I would venture to say that many of us are very undisciplined when it comes to managing our money, so we must make a conscious decision and effort to do better with our time management when we compare the two. Make a decision to stop squandering your time and refuse to let others misuse it. If there isn't enough time in your day for prayer and reading at least a daily devotional or passage of scripture, then your day is much too cluttered. Separate distractions from necessities that demand chunks of your time. Necessities warrant time and energy, distractions don't; therefore, they often deplete us and rob us of

critical time that could have been used for personal, professional, and spiritual opportunities for growth.

Each of us is only given a certain amount of time. We each get twenty-four hours in a day, and no matter how anointed we might be or how many titles or degrees we may hold, that fact will not change. We have to determine to stay focused and to spend our time wisely, because once it is spent, we can't get it back. As with money, it's important to invest your time wisely; only share it with those who can appreciate it and won't waste it. In short, place a value on your time and require that others do the same.

Going through the Motions: Get off the Merry-Go-Round

There is no reason for a child of God to get stuck on what seems to be a merry-go-round of life that has no specific direction. There are too many who are taking that ride day after day, and although most of us have experienced that rut at some point in our lives, there's no need to stay there. We must be deliberate and determined with regard to our desire to move forward. There are people who hang around the church and who appear to have fulfilling Christian lives, but emotionally and spiritually, they have actually checked out a long time ago. They're simply showing up physically but otherwise are just "going through the motions." Putting it simply, the fire in their Christian experience has gone out. You might be one of those individuals, and perhaps that is the very reason that the Lord has led you to read this book. He knows your inner longing to lay hands on the sick and see them recover, to prophecy with the assurance that what God has spoken will surely come to pass, and to live a life of faith and excellence on a daily basis. This life in Christ is ours to have today. The word of God has declared it; therefore, we need not doubt that it is the will of God for us to experience it.

The Bible is not just an ordinary book filled with stories of people, places, and times long ago. The Bible declares that the word of God is spirit and life; it is sharp and more powerful than any two-edged sword (Heb. 4:12). What other text do you know that can bring life to dead situations, circumstances, and people who are struggling in valleys with seemingly no way up or out? What other text do you know of that can cut to the very core of our being and show us who we are in our human frailty while at the same time reveal to us an all-powerful, all-knowing God who not only can, but will, save, heal, and deliver us if we will but ask Him? He stands with arms wide open waiting to receive all who will come to Him. We must come to Him believing that He is and that He will reward us for our diligence in coming to Him (Heb. 11:6). God responds to our faith. The merry-go-round of a pointless life stops when we throw up our hands and surrender to the true and living God who holds our purpose and destiny. There is a plan for you! There is no time for going around in circles, seeking our own way or, even worse, following the whims of those around us who think that they know what's best for us when the reality is that they don't even know what's best for themselves.

If you find that your life seems to be going in endless circles with no satisfaction or evidence of growth, then it's time to make a change. You have a choice. You absolutely do not have to go around that same revolution that leads to nowhere and nothingness again. Pray and ask the Lord for direction and make up your mind to follow the inclinations and leading that He places within your spirit. Many of you have received instructions from the Lord prior to this moment, but you have refused to act upon what He told you or what He showed you. That is the reason for your stagnation and frustration at this time in your life. It can stop right here, right now! Choose to obey. Choose to pursue purpose and to live with a God-given sense of direction. Believe that it's yours to have for the asking today.

In order to successfully pull from the written pages of God's word and apply it to our lives, we must be willing to honestly confront those areas of our lives where we find ourselves dealing with the same issues and circumstances repeatedly with seemingly no change in the results. We seem always to wind up right back where we started the last time that this concern arose. In order to stand against this area of stagnation in our lives, we are going to have to search the scriptures for words of instruction, encouragement, and principles that we can adhere to in order to change the pattern of behavior that has kept our life in an unending cycle of "sameness" rather than a consistent pattern of moving forward. There will be times when our progression and forward momentum will go at a slower pace, but the key is that we want to remain steady in a mindset and determination of having forward motion. Some keys to remaining in this posture of forward momentum are:

> get focused
> refuse to live life out of habit
> be deliberate about choices, decisions, and actions on a daily basis
> think things through rather than simply going with the flow and doing what you've always done

What area of your life is your merry-go-round connected to? Be honest with yourself. Does it have to do with relationships? Perhaps you continue to connect with people who really have no vision, and therefore they are unable to support your movement toward vision. Rather than help you to move to the next level, they coach you to stay where you are sometimes because it feeds their own comfort level and refusal to change. This may not be the concern in your relationships, but if you think that your merry-go-round is connected to relationships in some way, pray and ask the Lord to reveal how that area of your life prevents you from moving forward, growing and becoming the person that you sense God intends for you to be.

The area of connections as it pertains to our choice in relationships is very broad, and in order to be released from anything that is unprofitable, we must be willing not only to seek God for guidance but also to make the moves that He directs us to make even when those decisions make us feel uncomfortable. Remember that change can be difficult.

Refuse to wallow in condemnation. Although we are not to willfully take part in those things that are displeasing to the Lord, none of us is going to live a flawless life. We will not dot every *i* or cross every *t*, yet the Bible has declared in Romans 8:1 that "There is therefore now no condemnation to those who are in Christ Jesus who walk not after the flesh but after the spirit." God, our Father, sees us through the shed blood and sacrifice of the Lord Jesus Christ. If this were not the case, we would all live lives of utter defeat and frustration because our righteousness will never be enough to justify us in the sight of God. Thank God for grace, amazing grace, which is revealed in our lives day after day!

You may be burdened about something that you've done that you know is displeasing to the Lord, but just stop for a moment and think about the fact that His mercy has been extended toward you. If you have repented for whatever it is that continues to show up and take root in your life as a source of condemnation, then it's time for you to agree with the word of God in Romans 8:1: "There is therefore now no condemnation to them which are in Christ Jesus, who walk not after the flesh, but after the Spirit."

Understand that this has nothing to do with how you feel. Agree with the Word and your feelings will have to line up with your spirit. This may not be an instantaneous change with regard to how you feel, but what I am saying is that you can make a conscious decision to speak to yourself when you begin to experience those feelings of condemnation. For example, you can speak aloud or say within yourself, "I have repented of _____, God has forgiven me, and I refuse to walk in condemnation."

Remember the phrase that author Joyce Meyer coined years ago, which is also a title for one of her many books: "the battlefield of the mind." So many of our battles are waged in the mind, where we war alone and keep our struggles hidden from others, or so we think. Often after we have repented and sought after our new life in Christ, many of us are battling thoughts, memories, and other assaults that take place in our minds unbeknownst to others around us. What we fail to realize is that others may not have a clue what is driving us or what is actually going on, but they can see the impact that the attack on our minds is having on our actions, our relationships, and our approach to life in general. That's why I mentioned earlier that we may *think* that our mental battles and challenges are hidden, but the reality is that they affect not only how we think but how we feel and, subsequently, how we behave and respond. Those around us are affected. There is a way of escape, and that is to begin to feed the mind with what the word of God has said about us and make it a point to remind ourselves of those powerful truths when negative thoughts and accusations try to surface.

Someone may be reading this and say, "Well, I haven't repented of the works that continue to surface in my life to condemn me, so on some level, I should be condemned." If you have not repented, simply ask the Lord for forgiveness and believe what the scripture speaks to us in 1 John 1:9: "If we confess our sins, He is faithful and just to forgive us our sins and to cleanse us from all unrighteousness." This passage of scripture was written to believers. Why do you think this was written? It was simply written because Christians, the children of God, have always found themselves in situations that require pardon and forgiveness from a just but loving God. That's why verse 10 of that same chapter goes on to say, "If we say we have not sinned, we make Him a liar, and His word is not in us." We can thank God that His mercy intercepts His justice, because if we received what we deserve, we would be destroyed and a sentence of death would rest upon all of us.

As Christians and children of the Most High God, we certainly do not continue to *practice* sin as we did before coming to Christ, yet I'm convinced that one of the primary reasons many believers experience the stronghold of condemnation is because we've learned within our circles to act as if we have it all together when, in reality, we may be coming apart at the seams. That sort of mindset opens the door to suffering in silence and gives endless opportunities for our adversary, our enemy, the devil to keep us in a paralyzed state. Let's face it—when we're operating from a place of condemnation, we feel inadequate to contribute to situations and relationships as we otherwise could. We're locked into seeing ourselves as "less than," "failures," and "unworthy of contributing to the healing of others" simply because we've fallen short in some area of our lives. We spend so much time beating ourselves up for mistakes that we've made but that we can do absolutely nothing about.

Living under condemnation is a choice to live in the past and to reject the forgiving power of a true and living God who desires to transition us from glory to glory and faith to faith in our walk with Him. Have you ever considered the fact that nothing has taken the Lord by surprise? Whatever the fault, the mistake, the sin that brought you to the place that you find has paralyzed you, none of that surprises Him. Did you grasp that? You and I may wonder how in the world we could have gotten ourselves into some of the "pickles" that we've experienced in this life, but the Lord is never caught off guard. He knew where we would be before we got here. There's absolutely nothing that you've thought, said, or done that has taken the Lord by surprise. The enemy's trick is to make us feel ashamed and to cause us to turn and run away from the Lord, but the scripture proclaims in Proverbs 18:10, "The name of the Lord is a strong tower; the righteous run to it and are safe." Run to Him! Whatever it is that has caused us so much hurt, shame, and despair will never cause the Lord to turn away from us. He loves you and me with an ever-lasting love.

That kind of love is what we long for but can never quite wrap our heads and emotions around, because it is supernatural. Shame, condemnation, and conviction are not the same. Shame and condemnation come to hinder your walk with Christ. Conviction is a work of the Holy Spirit of God, and it takes place in our hearts in order to lead us to repentance. People talk about loving "unconditionally," but the unconditional love that man seeks to give on his own, apart from God, is flawed. We may say that we love unconditionally, but the truth is that we generally extend such love to a select few while omitting others. The Lord loves saint and sinner alike. He loves the murderer, the liar, the cheater, the backbiter, the fornicator, the adulterer, and on and on. Yes, He loves all of us, but the requirement for us to truly experience this great love is simply to admit our need for a Savior and to repent of our wrongdoing; otherwise the love remains one-sided. The word of God is very clear about the fact that while we were yet sinners, Christ died for us and that is all because of His great love, His unconditional love for us (Rom. 5:8).

The reality is that in our society, many struggle with the concept of submitting to God and repenting of our wrongs. We're held captive by condemnation when pride prevents us from admitting that we need the Lord and that we can't pick ourselves up and place ourselves on the right path that leads to our destiny. We must release pride in order to experience the power of forgiveness in our lives.

Embrace transformation. Some responses of the carnal mind to the things of God are, "I've got this," "I don't need anybody," or "That church stuff, religion, is for the weak ones who can't stand on their own two feet." To live for

Christ is an ongoing process of being transformed from the inside out, not just making a decision to do the right thing. Let's face it—we've all stubbornly held on to the reins of our lives at times even after being saved. Simply put, there are just some things about us that we consider to be the essence of who we are, and it's those things that are hardest to let go of. We excuse them by making statements such as, "That's just the way that I am" or "I can't help the way that I am; take it or leave it."

My friend, our minds must be renewed, and the only way for this to happen is through the transforming power of the Word of God. Romans 8:6–8 declares: "For to be carnally minded is death; but to be spiritually minded is life and peace. Because the carnal mind is enmity against God; for it is not subject to the law of God, nor indeed can be. So then, those who are in the flesh cannot please God." Okay, so what is this saying in a nutshell? In other words, there is no way that our flesh is going to conform to the things of God. We're deceiving ourselves when we think that we can just decide on our own to do what is right in the eyes of God, because our flesh—our carnal side—will always oppose the move of God in our lives. Our carnal, selfish mind, deliberately and on all levels, is set against God, no matter how good or sweet we or others may think that we are.

Being saved is not a ticket or pass to a "mistake-free" life. Quite the contrary, it is an opportunity for sinful man to come to grips with just how amazing the grace of God truly is. If we were perfect, we would not need a

Savior or the grace that He so freely gives. A part of what Jesus said in Matthew 9:12 is, "They that be whole need not a physician, but they that are sick." He spoke these words in response to a question that the Pharisees asked of His disciples regarding why He would eat with publicans and sinners. He simply shared the truth of why He came, which was to bring wholeness to those who recognize their great need for the Chief Physician.

God continues to cover and to forgive our sins and our flaws by the shed blood of Christ, and this is truly amazing. This is Amazing Grace! It's truly amazing that God continues to use men and women who are so messed up, torn up, and jacked up, but He does. Why? Because the truth of the matter is, we're all like that. He could have just said, "Forget it, none of them will ever measure up!" But in spite of our shortcomings and because of our inability to please Him otherwise, the Father sent Jesus to take our place. Jesus pleased the Father in every way as He walked this earth in the flesh. Refuse to accept any other demonic teaching that states otherwise. Jesus pleased the Father, lived a sinless life, and now He is the propitiation or perfect sacrifice for not only our sins but our sinful nature. We can't escape our sinful nature, but we can be born again and become endowed with the power to place that nature under subjection by the power and authority of God.

There is no need for the child of God to walk in condemnation. Jesus has come to set the captives free. That includes you, me, and anyone else who will accept deliverance. Romans 8:1 states, "There is therefore now, no condemnation to them who are in Christ Jesus who walk not after the flesh but after the Spirit." What was the dilemma that Paul was speaking of before he came to this conclusion? He was speaking of the struggle that takes place within all of us.

When you read Romans chapter 7, you will find that Paul is sharing a glimpse into the struggle that occurs between the flesh and the spirit man. What he said in Romans 7 probably sounds quite familiar to most, especially early in our Christian walk, but this struggle is not to be associated solely with those who are babes in Christ. Paul was not a babe when he shared his struggle in Romans 7, yet he wrote, "The things that I desire to do, I do not and the very thing that I choose not to do, that's what I find myself doing." Have you ever been there? Well, you're not alone. The key is that the Lord wants you to realize that you don't have to stay there in that place where the enemy can beat up on you with guilt, shame, and condemnation. Our Advocate with the Father is the Lord Jesus Christ, and because of His finished work on the cross, there is no room for condemnation in your life. He has taken it! Walk in the newness of life and refuse to be brought under a yoke of bondage because of things that were wrought in your old life or during times of weakness or just by living life. There are areas in our lives where we will daily fall short and not measure up, sometimes because we've set unrealistic expectations for ourselves.

The truth is that you and I are victorious. The enemy, Satan, wants us to forget this and to operate from a position of learned powerlessness that was ours before we were born of the Spirit of God. We have been redeemed, empowered, and justified. Grab hold of this truth, speak it out loud if you have to whenever you're faced with condemning thoughts, and watch the power of God begin to take a more prominent place in your thought life and consequently in your actions as you choose to embrace the transformation that is continually taking place in your life. Transformation is an inward process that manifests externally.

Repent and keep moving forward. Be quick to repent, and then move forward. Rejoice in the fact that God still has purpose for you and He wants to use you for His glory. If that's not amazing, then I don't know what is! Grace is not easy to understand or to explain, yet it is to be exemplified daily through the life of the believer. You and I are living testimonies of the matchless grace of God. How so? Our lives are a constant reminder, first to ourselves and then to others, that none of us can ever be good enough to earn God's favor or to deserve the blessings that are loosed to overtake us daily. Being aware of the fact that the Lord has provided everything that we need for each waking day can be encouraging and uplifting when our circumstances can cause us to become disheartened. Take courage and allow your strength to come from a place of knowing who God is and knowing that He is faithful. His word never fails.

Sometimes we have to encourage ourselves. Stop waiting for others to validate you and pat you on the back, because nine times out of ten that just won't happen, and certainly not at the time when you think you need it most. God wants us to find in Him our strength and will to persevere. That comes by trusting Him and experiencing Him coming through for us time and time again, even when others have forsaken us or have given up on us. Through meditating upon the word of God and making a conscious decision to apply it to our lives in a real way, the truth and power of the word will come off the printed page as the Lord intended. God's will is that His word would be applied to our lives in such a way that our walk and experience with the Lord will begin to look more like what we read about in the Scriptures. The word of the Lord is Spirit and life, and it is intended to take root in us and to become the very foundation of our lives. His word has come to set us free. So you might be asking, "What does applying the word of God look like? What am I supposed to do?" Applying the word of God starts with agreeing with what it says, then expecting and decreeing the results that His word promises.

Refuse to be under bondage of any sort and allow the Lord to use you in whatever way He chooses despite opposition. Note that I mentioned bondage of any sort. When we think of bondage, our minds typically go to some type of "sin" that we may be committing. Bondage can be anything that keeps us from freely responding to the Spirit of God. So just be aware that the journey to being free in Christ can be ongoing, but with each level of freedom, you will find that the voice of God and the tug of His Spirit become more pronounced. You have been empowered for the journey that God has ordained for your life, so begin to walk into it with confidence. This is a new day, and if you have accepted the Lord Jesus as your Savior, your past is forgiven. Now it's time for you to move forward in the power, courage, and confidence that are given to you by the Spirit of the living God for such a time as this.

Know in whom you have believed and whom you serve. We serve the God of the Bible. He has not and will not change. This is what He declares in His word (Mal. 3:6). He also declares that besides Him, there is none else—there is no other God (Isa. 43:11, 45:51, 46:9). He is the true and living God. The Christian has to be very clear about this because throughout this walk of faith, there will be times when God seems distant or nonresponsive. Whether He seems to be *doing* anything in our lives or not, it is vital that we know His promises and His character. It is totally unscriptural to think that as children of God, we will be up and never down or that we will have a clear understanding of trials that we may be confronting at any given time. However, the benefit of a relationship rather than a religious experience affords us many opportunities to build our trust in Him and to know His love and care for us. The Lord will never have a bad day. When we approach the throne of grace in our time of need or even when we just want to get into His presence to praise and thank Him, we will always find grace and mercy there. He will not shun us or turn us away.

I want to put to rest the false assumption that some have that the Lord is mad at them or doesn't want to hear from them because of mistakes that they have made. Listen, get into the word of God for yourself, read it, and get to know the One in Whom you believe. He does chastise us, He does correct us, and just as we have experienced with our natural parents, we are aware of those times when He is displeased with choices that we've made or actions that we've taken. But unlike our natural parents, He chastises us not for His own pleasure but for our profit because He knows us better than we know ourselves. Hebrews 12:10 reads, "Our fathers disciplined us for a short time as they thought best, but God disciplines us for our good, so that we may share in His holiness." And "For whom the Lord loves He reproves, even as a father corrects the son in whom he delights" (Prov. 3: 12).

Unless we were victims of an abusive childhood, we knew that our parents loved us even when they saw fit to discipline us. We had that understanding simply because we had a trusting relationship with them that caused us to know that they really had our best interest at heart. Having worked for more than thirty years in the field of child welfare and interacting with children and families where abuse is part of their narrative, I can say that the Lord is more than able to help those who have endured the pain of various traumatic events in their lives. There are countless testimonies of those who have had horrific starts, yet they are now on paths that are in stark contrast to where they or anyone else ever thought that they would be. Some of you reading this book have the testimony that your current life looks absolutely nothing like what you've been through.

So step away from religious rituals and the ideas of others as it pertains to what your relationship with the Lord should look like. Each of us has a unique relationship with Him just as every child in a family experiences their parents differently although they come from the same home environment. The next time that you're inclined to ask, "Where is this God of the Bible?" remember that He is as close as your next breath, and like you, He is anticipating a closer, more intimate relationship for the two of you. Reach out and touch Him now. He's only a prayer away.

Prayer: Father, in the Name of Jesus, I choose to interrupt the cycle of "going through the motions" in my life. Reveal to me those areas in my life where I have neglected to obey you. I declare that I am a doer of the word and not a hearer only. Renew my mind and restore my joy. My desire is for a more intimate relationship with you. This is my prayer, and by faith, I count it done. Amen!

Inspiration Break

Life teaches us many lessons, and one thing is for sure: we won't get another chance at this journey that we're on now. There is no time to continuously circle the same mountains or to do the same things that we've always done while expecting different results.

All of us can make a decision to be present and accounted for in our own lives. It's time to take a long, hard look at our lives and make a determination that we will play an active role in the good plan that the Lord has for us.

Declare today that you will no longer get caught in the vicious cycle of revisiting past mistakes and things that can never be undone.

Accept God's good plan for you to prosper, to walk in freedom, and to explore new areas of this abundant life that have been prepared for you.

Declare that fear of the unknown will no longer have a place of authority in your life as God calls you out of the ordinary to the extraordinary and from sameness to new heights that propel you beyond your wildest expectations.

Get acquainted with the God who is able to do exceedingly and abundantly above all that you could ever ask or think.

Lord, Is That You?

When is the last time that you really thought about the scripture that says "My sheep know my voice, and I know them, and they follow me"? Think about that. "My sheep know my voice." That seems to imply that the Lord speaks to all of His sheep, because there was no specification given in this scripture regarding certain sheep being spoken to. The message is that all of His sheep know His voice. This scripture becomes more of a reality in our lives when we expect the Lord to speak to us and when we trust that we will recognize His voice when He speaks. All too often we read scriptures, memorize them, quote them, and even preach from them, but the reality is that when it comes to applying the word to our lives, we often come up short.

You know that the Lord speaks. I'm sure that you have no doubt about that, but the question is, do you believe that He speaks to you? Do you hesitate to move on His instructions due to a need to check and double-check to see if it's really His voice that has spoken? I must admit that I've been guilty of this even to the point of wanting to "fleece" God in a sense. I've said things like, "Lord, if that was you, or if you're leading me to do this, please let this or that happen." It may sound ridiculous, but it's true.

That's known as fleecing God, and the fact is that many have done it at some point in their Christian walk. I'm not suggesting that this is how we should handle our prayer life or our relationship with God, but that's just a snapshot of where I've been, and the bottom line is that God has a way of meeting us where we are. He shows up and He answers prayers.

In Judges chapter 6, we read about Gideon fleecing God. Now many say that he was out of order for doing so or that he certainly lacked faith. Both of those positions may be true, but the reality is that God responded to Gideon from his position of faith or the lack thereof. Gideon humbly asked of God because his true desire was to see the people of Israel victorious. He just wasn't quite sure that he was the one that God really wanted to use in the process. Gideon asked God to make a fleece of wool wet with dew and the ground around it dry on one morning and then to make the fleece totally dry on the next morning and the ground around it had to be wet.

This is where we get the term "fleecing God." The fleece was to serve as a sign that God would definitely rescue Israel from the Midianites. Because of their disobedience, God had allowed the heathen nations to come in and rob the Israelites of food that grew in their fields and vineyards. The Israelites had become afraid of these people who would come in and take their crops, housing, and everything that they had time and time again. Gideon feared them as well. As a matter of fact, he was so afraid that the scripture tells us that he was down in a wine press threshing wheat, something that should have typically been done out in the open on a threshing floor. Being in this circumstance and operating with a fearful mindset, it was hard for Gideon to receive the word that came to him, describing him as a mighty man of valor. He did not see himself as a mighty man of valor by any stretch of the imagination, and he wanted God's pledge that He would deliver Israel once again from her enemies. God revealed Himself to Gideon as Jehovah-Shalom, the Lord is Peace. The truth is that although Gideon may have started out insecure and weak, he learned to trust and to obey God. Fear comes to oppose our faith, so we may often have to push past the spirit of fear in order to follow the leading of God and what He has spoken. God will deal with the fear as we move in obedience.

We know that the Lord spoke directly with His disciples when He physically walked with them on the earth, and He was always very clear with them that His sole purpose was to do the will of his Father. Jesus promised that although He was returning to the Father, His disciples would never be alone because He would send them another comforter, meaning the same as Himself, in the person of the Holy Ghost or Holy Spirit.

The Christian faith, which we embrace, is set apart from all others because we have a Savior who walks with us, talks with us, and leads us, for He is very much alive. Each day is filled with new mercies, new opportunities, and the chance for each of us to view our circumstances and situations from a fresh new perspective. Gaining a fresh perspective requires that we pull from the pages of scripture and apply what the Lord is speaking into our present experience. Understand that a major part of the advantage that we have as spirit-filled Christians is that we have a counselor, the Paraclete (who is the Holy Spirit) who has been called to walk with us and to lead us into all truth. He will only speak what He hears, so we know that we can trust Him (John 16:13). God the Father, God the Son, and God the Holy Spirit always operate as One. Our responsibility is to agree with the word of God and what is being shared with us by His Spirit. If what is being impressed upon your spirit does not agree with the word of God, then leave it alone, reject it. When you're unsure about whether or not God's word supports the inclinations of your spirit, search the word and pray until you are confident of His leading. Until you are sure, stand still, wait. The Bible is very clear when it says, "My sheep know my voice." In fact, these are words that Jesus spoke.

You might ask, "Well, how can I be so sure that I'm actually walking out His will and plan for me?" While visiting the church of my very dear friend, Lisa Silver, I heard a very inspiring message that focused on the Lord directing our paths, our steps being ordered, and the need to move in spite of fear. The message that I'm referring to pointed out how so many times, we as Christians waste so much time begging and pleading for the Lord to come down and tell us which path to take when the reality is that the Lord will bless the choice that we make in faith.

Consider Abram in Genesis chapter 13 when he and his nephew, Lot, came out of Egypt. Abram was very rich in livestock, silver, and gold according to the scripture, and Lot had flocks, herds, and tents. Because their possessions were so great, the land was not able to support both of them. They were not able to dwell together because they had so much, and somewhere along the way, the herdsmen of the livestock of these two men had a disagreement and Abram in his wisdom felt it was best that they part ways. Abram said to Lot, "Please let there be no strife between you and me, and between my herdsmen and your herdsmen; for we are brethren. Is not the whole land before you? Please separate from me. If you take the left, then I will go to the right; or, if you go to the right, then I will go to the left" (Gen. 13:8,9).

Abram seemed not to consider whether or not he would be giving up his blessing or giving up what appeared to be the "best" part of the land, but he gave Lot first choice regarding which portion of the land he preferred as a dwelling place. Lot chose the vast, green, plain of Jordan for his people and animals. Lot chose what appeared to be the best portion of the land. When we read the scripture surrounding this story, we find that Abram settled in the land of Canaan and built an altar unto God there, which indicates that he worshipped. I'm inclined to believe that a part of his worship may have been thanking God for peace with his relative and provision of the dwelling place.

Abram was blessed, although he did not seem to have the best portion. The reality is that the blessing of the

Lord rested upon him regardless of the portion of the land where he would ultimately reside and call his own. God instructed him to lift up his eyes and to look in every direction for as far as he could see. He was to walk the width and length of the land and to believe what the Lord God spoke to him, "For all the land that you see, I give it to you and your offspring forever" (Gen. 13:14–15). The point to be made here is that no matter which direction Abram had gone to pitch his tent and to establish a dwelling for his wife and others, the resident power and blessing of the Lord was with Him because he acknowledged God and he made wherever he was a place of worship to God. His environment had to yield to the blessing that God had already ordained for Abram's life—and not only his life but that of his descendants. Abram's innumerable descendants were a part of the blessing. God changed his name from Abram, which means "exalted father" to Abraham, which means "father of many nations." We as believers are Abraham's seed. Verse 16 reads, "And I will make your descendants as the dust of the earth; so that if a man could number the dust of the earth, then your descendants also could be numbered."

You might say, "How does this apply to me?" The truth is that we're blessed in the city and in the field. We're blessed no matter where we may choose to dwell when the hand of the Lord is upon us. Live a life of worship, trust what the word of God says: "acknowledge Him and He will direct your paths." Make a choice! Life is full of choices, and God has given the believer all things to enjoy with the understanding that we must seek Him in all things. He just wants us to make a choice and to trust that He will cause our situations and circumstances to line up with what He has already ordained for our lives. Wherever Abraham went, he was blessed and the place was blessed because of his presence. God dwelt with him. The key is to seek God and to acknowledge Him in all things, and He will bring to pass those things that we never even thought to ask of Him simply because of our trust and faith toward Him. Do you walk with God? If you're a born-again believer, then the answer is a resounding "Yes!" He is the One who causes our way to prosper, our dreams and desires to be fulfilled while His will and favor are released in and over our lives.

A faith walk is about moving toward what has been impressed in our spirits based on the fact that we know that we have consulted the Lord regarding our decisions. I was impressed in my spirit to start a ministry that came to be known as Women in Ministry—WIM. It started with me inviting several women to join me for what would be considered a mini retreat at a time share that my husband and I owned. These women and I had been leaders over our Young Women of Excellence ministry at the church that we attended. Well, the invitation was extended to these ministry leaders several times, and each time I was disappointed until finally one sister agreed to pull away with me to the beautiful Shenandoah mountains of Virginia for a Getaway at the Massanutten Ski Resort, which would later become the meeting place for several of our initial Getaways for Women in Ministry.

I will never forget sharing with this sister the vision that the Lord had given to me regarding ministering to and with other women of God. She became excited, and if you've ever had anyone become excited about a dream or vision that you're carrying, you know exactly how that made me feel. We prayed together for the seed of faith that the Lord had planted inside of me, and I felt such a sense of relief, release, and encouragement as we then turned our attention to enjoying the rest of our weekend away. There's something so very powerful about finding someone who can catch the vision that the Lord has given to you and who will agree with you in prayer concerning the manifestation. In those times where two can agree as touching, before anything manifests, the power of God begins to work out all of the details, and although everything seems the same, there's just a *knowing* that everything has changed.

The following year, I reached out to those same sisters again, but when the response was slow and I began to get somewhat discouraged, the Spirit of the Lord impressed upon me to ask women outside of the church I was attending. Now, understand that this is not an indictment against those women who seemed to be unresponsive, but what I want you to understand is how the Lord was leading me to embrace what had been His vision and intention from the start. The women who were to benefit from the ministry were not only those who were a part of the place of worship where I attended but Christian women from various denominations who also had a love for God and a desire for a deeper relationship with Him. It was when I began to reach outside of the four walls of the church I attended that the response was positive, and with an initial group of eight to ten women from various Christian denominations who loved the Lord, Women in Ministry—WIM was born.

For twelve years we convened for an annual Getaway—as they were referred to in our ministry group—where women from various Christian denominations across the US came together with a desire to get away from the distractions of daily life and to devote time to minister to the Lord and to one another, building one another in faith and basking in the Lord's presence. Each year afforded us an opportunity to meet new sisters and to experience a great outpouring of the Lord's Spirit. Women whom I had never met would hear about our Getaway and would come to take part in this time of great outpouring, fellowship, and spiritual renewal/refreshing.

While we were away at our thirteenth annual Getaway, the Lord impressed in my spirit that we were no longer to convene once a year in a specific location as had been our practice. The Lord had been faithful to us and had given us a strong foundation. That year, as the Getaway was coming to a close, I shared with the women what the Lord had impressed in my spirit. We were to begin taking the ministry to various locations and "connecting" with women in different states who would not otherwise know about us or be able to join us. The vision was that we were to "connect" with other ministries with the intent of "empowering and equipping" women to walk in their God-given purpose.

I asked everyone who was in attendance at that particular Getaway to pray about this next move, and the following year we began our two-day Connecting for Empowerment Conferences with three conferences in the first year. Time and time again, as we connected with women in various states, those women, their ministry leaders, and some of their spouses would subsequently share with us how their lives had been greatly affected and significantly changed in a positive way due to the gatherings. Each of these Connecting for Empowerment Conferences has been so dynamic and we have witnessed the power of the Lord as attendees have been encouraged and empowered to return to give greater service within their respective families, communities, and ministries. I have had men come to me after our conferences and say to me, "I don't know what you all are doing in your conference, but my wife has come back a changed woman." Others would talk about the renewed outlook that their wives had upon returning home from the conferences. This is a testament to how the Lord was so very faithful in meeting us whenever we would come together.

A walk of faith is primarily about moving and allowing the Lord to give landmarks along the way. We simply can't wait for all of the ducks to be in a row. That's not a move of faith. Why do we believe or hope for what we can already see? When the Lord is leading us, He will speak to us in a way that we can recognize, whether it's an unction from within or an impression or vision that just won't leave us alone; or maybe He will allow someone to speak a word into our lives that brings confirmation. We cannot neglect to read and study the word of God, the Bible, because it reveals the very heart and mind of God. It is His love letter and road map to the believer. Like Gideon, we may start out being taunted by fear because of the plots and schemes of the enemy, but remember that "greater is He that is in you than he that is in the world" (1 John 4:4). God will give you boldness to execute every facet of the dream and vision that has been placed in your heart!

We seldom start out with the entire story because if the Lord showed us everything, we would likely decide not to move forward. I'm sure there are many situations that you can attest to in your own life where you could say that if the Lord had shown you everything that was going to come against you from the beginning, you never would have moved forward with what He was leading you to do. That being said, if you did in fact take that move of faith, you must admit that the Lord has been faithful toward you. In order for the word of God to come alive for us that says, "Thy word is a lamp unto my feet and a light unto my path" (Ps. 119:105), we must be willing to step out on the path and move forward with the God-given vision. Light is given as we walk. As we trust in His word, our way is illuminated and the path that we must take becomes more distinct. The Lord will not fail you, nor will He leave you hanging!

I challenge you to cry out to the Lord from wherever you are. If you have allowed the fire and zeal in your life to grow cold for whatever reason, confess that now and declare that you are ready to start anew. Breaking free from the monotony of life is not a long, drawn-out process. It is a radical, intentional move toward those things that bring new life, zest, and meaning to this journey. Draw nigh unto God and He will draw nigh unto you (James 4:8). Being close to God is a decision on our part that must be followed up with purposeful action. You will find new meaning and purpose in life as you anticipate and yield to the direction that the Spirit of the Lord will begin to share with you.

Having a relationship with Christ is not something mystical or hard. People sometimes tend to make it seem so hard or out of reach, but just start each day speaking a prayer, honestly opening your heart, and stating those things that are inside (the Lord already knows what is within us, but the relationship is about sharing and trusting). Think of prayer as talking with God, sharing with Him (because He has things that He longs to share with you as well). Handle your relationship with the Lord with care, and remember that you can talk with Him as often, as long, and as candidly as you want. Refuse to allow anything or anyone to come between you and your Savior. Make time to commune with Him in prayer and then trust that He has heard your prayers. This is how faith takes root.

Prayer: Lord, thank you for speaking a good plan over my life. Forgive me for the times when I have not acknowledged you regarding the paths that I have chosen to take. There have been many occasions when I have wrestled with accepting your voice and direction for my life. Right now I agree with your word and declare that as your child, I know your voice and a stranger I will not follow. I am who You say that I am and I can do what Your word declares that I can do. Thank you, Lord! I trust You by faith. Amen.

Scriptures for meditation: Psalm 119:11 "Thy word have I hidden in my heart that I might not sin against you"; Psalm 119:105 "Thy word is a lamp unto my feet and a light unto my path"; John 10:5 "Yet they will by no means follow a stranger, but will flee from him, for they do not know the voice of strangers" (NKJV); 1 John 4:4 "You are of God, little children, and have overcome them, because He who is in you is greater than he who is in the world."

Vision, Direction, and Wisdom

(Frustration is often the result of moving without clear instructions or vision, in the wrong direction, or without wisdom. —L. Bishop-Joe)

While reading a devotional by the late Dr. Myles

Munroe titled "Daily Power & Prayer," I came across a wonderful analogy of vision as it pertains to our Christian walk. He gave an example of signage that is placed at construction sites to notify the public of what may be coming but is not yet built in that particular location. We've all seen those signs that usually read something like, "Coming Soon," and there's usually a picture displayed that reflects what the finished product will look like. Behind or somewhere near the picture might simply be a vacant lot or a partial structure that has no resemblance to what it will be when it is completed.

The image that is shown in the picture at the construction site began in someone's mind, and others were brought in who could take that vision and run with it.

Those individuals are tasked with doing the necessary work in order to make the vision (the picture) manifest in the material realm. It had to be pulled from just a thought or vision in someone's mind to an actual structure that others could not only see but use and benefit from in some way. This is how vision works. It is given so that we can take that image or impression that has come from God and give it back to Him (through prayer) so that He can, in turn, give us the wisdom, direction, and resources to make it manifest.

When you and I ask the Lord for vision, we must understand that He will begin to reveal places, things, and people that we may have never considered as being part of His plan for our lives. I often hear people quote 1 Corinthians 2:9: "But as it is written: Eye has not seen, nor ear heard, nor have entered into the heart of man, the things which God has prepared for those who love Him."

I observe that most people become very excited when they get to the part that says "eye hath not seen nor ear heard," but what they fail to grasp is that the scripture goes farther to state **"but God."** This is cause to pause because it gives a clear indication that something is coming that builds upon or gives another perspective to what has been stated. The scripture says to us that it's true that the natural eye hasn't seen, nor has the natural ear heard, nor can the heart of a man perceive these things, *but God hath revealed them to us.* Us who? Those who are born of His Spirit, those who can receive from Him through His Spirit. God has revealed to His children those things that are otherwise hidden from the natural man. How? By His Spirit! We see, we hear, and we perceive! The child of God sees, hears, and perceives those things that are spiritually discerned and that can't be perceived by the natural man or by our natural senses. So then vision far exceeds sight, for it allows us to see in the spirit far beyond what our natural eyes could ever behold or envision. Isaiah 64:4 reads, "For since the beginning of the world, men have not heard nor perceived by the ear, nor has the eye seen any God besides You, Who acts for the one who waits for Him."

As God imparts vision, we must be prepared for others around us to scoff at what we see, simply because it will often be hidden from them. Be careful not to fault those who can't see what you see. This is to be expected on some level, as we walk out our own story and God's will for our lives. Do you recall what happened to Joseph in Genesis chapter 37 when he shared his dream with his brothers and evidently anticipated that they would be excited and accepting of what God had shown him? Of course, we know that excitement and acceptance were far from the responses Joseph received from them.

As we pull from the written pages of God's word, it's important to understand that what God showed to Joseph already existed but had not been manifested in time. Fast-forward to the part of the story when Joseph's brothers came to him in Genesis chapter 52 when God was about to allow him to reveal himself to them. The Lord was working forgiveness in Joseph's heart when he allowed Joseph to say to them, "You meant it for evil but

God meant it for good". Wait a minute. Did you catch that? God meant it for good? God already knew the end of this story? God already knew the horrible things that Joseph's brothers would do to him because of their jealousy, envy, and hatred of him? Yes! Nothing caught God by surprise. When Joseph stepped into the time that had been set aside for this encounter, God was already there, provision had been made, and most importantly, the vision manifested! What God has shown to you already exists because it is a part of your story. You only lay hold of it and see it manifest if you dare to grasp it by faith and hold on to the vision in spite of how others around you, even those closest to you, feel about it or how they'll treat you because of it. Remember that the vision didn't originate with you. It was shared with you, and through obedience and knowing that it belongs to God, you will see it manifest at the appointed time.

Refusing to obey is to disobey, and procrastinating with regard to the things of God and His direction can cause us to miss our season. Remember that walking by faith requires that we have an assurance of what God has spoken or shown to us and a determination to hold on to that assurance in the face of contrary circumstances and opposing situations. Doubt and fear will always come to oppose our faith, but the Lord has supplied everything that we need to carry out His will. You've been chosen and equipped for such a time as this!

After we've grasped and accepted the vision, another important step is to put into writing all that the Lord has revealed. Do you recall the scripture in Habakkuk 2:2 where God spoke to Habakkuk and told him, "Write the vision and make it plain on tablets"? This book of Habakkuk has only three chapters, and what people remember most are the words that God spoke to the prophet during troubling times in the land. God shared a vision that was contrary to what the circumstances looked like, so in order for this vision to be impressed upon the prophet in a profound way, God instructed him to write it and to make it plain on tablets. Something else that God said, which is interesting, is that part of the reason for writing was not only for the prophet to remember but so that others could read and run with the vision that was written. In other words, the vision wasn't only for the prophet. Sometimes and most of the time, what the Lord has given to us is not just for us. That's why it's so important to be clear about what the Lord has said, to pray over and meditate on His instructions, because many other lives will be affected.

We're encouraged through scripture to wait on God and to know that He hears, sees, and will surely intervene and provide an answer to our situations. By chapter three of Habakkuk, the prophet had grasped faith and was praising God for what was spoken rather than being overcome by the strife, contention, and evil that presented itself all around him. When we come to verses 18 and 19 in the third chapter, the prophet declares, "Yet I will rejoice in the Lord, I will joy in the God of my salvation. The Lord God is my strength and He will make my feet like hinds' feet, and He will make me to walk upon mine high places."

Why would God tell the prophet to write the vision? Well, we all know that there is something to be said about pulling visions, thoughts, and dreams from the conceptual state in the mind and placing them on paper or in some written context, because then we are forced to handle the words that are written; we can touch them and see them. This is powerful and has been used in many secular settings for prospering in business and everyday life. Time after time, people are instructed to write their goals, whether short- or long-term, because somehow after doing so, the will is ignited to put feet to that which exists on paper and make it translate to reality. Bosses of successful organizations often have their employees write their goals, not just think about them, and revisit them throughout a designated time frame leading up to the time for completion. We now make things such as vision boards and even host vision board gatherings so that people can keep before themselves a tangible representation of what they see as part of their lives that is yet to manifest.

I said all of that to say that God did the same in the case of Habakkuk. He instructed him to "write the vision" and went on to assure him, "For the vision is yet for an appointed time, but at the end, it shall speak and not lie: though it tarry, wait for it; because it will surely come, it will not tarry" (Hab. 2:2–3). This is not something that smart businessmen have come up with, but God in His wisdom knew that once the vision was written, it would bring clarity and focus to the prophet and it would set faith in motion in the natural realm, causing what God had already ordained in the spirit realm to manifest. The prophet was told to write and to make the vision plain so that those who would read it would be able to take it and run with it. Can you see that the Lord's plan included individuals who were appointed to be a part of the manifestation? At the appointed time, those who were to read and run would, no doubt, gravitate toward the prophet and begin to move according to the will of God. At the right time and under the right circumstances, the vision **had to come to pass.** It was for an appointed time!

It works the same for you and me. Remember that any vision that the Lord gives is for a set time, an appointed time, and though it may seem to tarry, it will come to pass. If we hold within our minds what the Lord has placed within our spirits, we run the risk of it getting no further than that—just thoughts that we ponder and revisit in our minds. So after receiving the vision, we must write it down in order to maintain clarity and focus on what has been spoken, as this is the first step to pulling it out of the intangible to the tangible, out of the spirit realm into manifestation. Next, trust that the Lord has appointed others who will grasp the vision, take hold of it, and help you to run with it. God-given vision is never solely for us, but it's always connected to the advancement of the Kingdom of God. So write it, make it plain, pray over it, and watch the Lord bring it to pass. What we must constantly call to mind is that the vision doesn't begin with us;

it begins with God, and it is already accomplished in the spirit realm before the Lord shares it with us. It is done!

I certainly encourage you to take the time to read the entire book of Habakkuk. I have deliberately avoided getting entrenched in the circumstances that Habakkuk faced since our focus is on gleaning and learning from how God chose to deal with him. What you will notice is that along with the vision came instructions or direction. He was to write, to make plain, and all for a specific reason: so that others might read and run with it. Receiving a vision from God is only the beginning. After getting the vision, we must obtain direction from the Lord so that we will know what to do with what He has shared with us.

Let's take some time now to briefly delve into the importance of receiving and following the direction that comes from the Lord after He imparts a vision or dream to us. We'll leave talking about Habakkuk for now and relate this to our lives today. Let's pull this off the page and apply it to our own situations.

Pause now and write down what comes to mind when you're being asked to write the vision that you believe God has placed within your heart. Next, pray over it and ask the Lord to give you clarity and direction as you desire to see His will fulfilled in your life (Prov. 3:6).

Inspiration Break

Everything that God has spoken over your life has a set time, and it will come to pass.

Your profession of faith must be that you refuse to stop believing the Lord in spite of what natural circumstances may present to you. (Say that out of your own mouth.)

Declare that you hear the Lord's voice and that a stranger's voice will never be accepted, nor will you follow it.

The Lord will not only share visions and strategies with you, but along with that, He will give instructions and opportunities for you to obey.

Declare that you will be quick to obey the voice of the Lord.

You have various gifts and talents that the Lord has entrusted to you, and His desire is to open doors for you to use them in order to bring glory to Him and to edify His people.

I encourage you to anticipate and wait with expectation for the opportunities that the Lord will make for you.

In all things, the Lord's will and desire is that we would operate in His wisdom. He has made it available to you simply for the asking.

Daily ask God to fill your very being with His wisdom. This is wisdom that does not come from reading books or adding years to our lives. It is God-given.

Remember to exhibit an attitude of gratitude. This must come from the heart. Think now upon all of the wonderful things that the Lord has permitted in your life, the exceptional people who have been a part of your experience, and the blessed opportunity that you have to know Him and to commune with Him as your Lord and Savior.

You are truly blessed!

Trust and Move!

Have you ever started out on a trip and made a wrong turn only to find yourself going around and around and around as you stayed off-course? Well, with all of our technology and navigation systems in place, some may consider that thought to be absurd. Many of us only use navigation systems for long road trips; others, such as one of my sisters, have no idea how to use them; and then others may choose not to use them because they typically do not travel to destinations that they are not familiar with.

Some of us who have relied on these systems have encountered situations where we've been dumped in the middle of nowhere after a journey of ins, outs, twists, and turns. I can recall a time when a friend of mine and I were traveling and we were looking for a specific place to eat, so we plugged the desired destination into the navigation system and began to "proceed to the route" as the friendly voice advised us. As we followed the instructions to "Turn right" and "Turn left," we soon found ourselves sitting in the middle of a parking lot and heard the voice say, "Arrived." What? We looked at each other in disbelief. What had just happened? Maybe the restaurant used to be there, or maybe it was the specific navigation system we used, as it was known for getting people lost. We had all kinds of racing thoughts as we dealt with the frustration of the time put into this detour only to end up disappointed and still hungry at the end of it. Some of you may be sitting in a spot right now that doesn't look anything like the destination you thought you were headed to or that you envisioned.

In most cases there are many ways to get to the same destination, but why travel three hundred miles out of the way when your destination is thirty miles down the highway? As I've stated before, the Lord has promised that He will direct our paths. In other words, He will give His children direction so that we're not left to wander aimlessly around as we walk out our God-given purposes. Maybe you're moving in the right direction, but it doesn't hurt to consider that there's a possibility you're not. Why don't you pause right where you are and ask the Lord to direct your path?

In order to ensure that we're traveling the path that is illuminated by the light of Christ, we must always acknowledge Him in our decision-making, not trusting our own inclinations as though we already know the way. Proverbs 14:12 says, "There is a way that seems right to a man, but its end is the way of death." Also consider Proverbs 3:6, which reads, "In all thy ways acknowledge Him and He shall direct thy paths." There's no need for us to beg or plead for the Lord to lead us or to be anxious in our times of decision-making because His word simply tells us to "acknowledge" Him. This means to consider Him. We are to consider His desire, will, and plan for our lives as we try to navigate the paths of life. Seeking and waiting for direction from the Lord is the best way to have an assurance that we're moving forward in the right direction toward our purpose.

As you move forward, there will be times when circumstances may cause you to become anxious because the way may seem obscured or not totally clear. Refuse to panic. Don't fret. Faith is not just a shot in the dark with a hope that we will hit something. No, it's quite the contrary. The man or woman of faith realizes that the Kingdom of God, that which is spirit and unseen, is more real than what we can see. Our circumstances will not necessarily line up with what the Lord has spoken regarding our lives or the next move that we must make. But faith is our compass from the inside, within our spirit man (which is that part of us that communicates with the Lord), and it often causes us to move in a way that goes against logic.

Faith is not blind, nor is it simply wishful thinking. However, faith allows the believer to see, grasp, and hold on to what the Lord has revealed as though it is so, even before it manifests in the natural realm. Faith gives substance to all that we hope for. Read Romans 8:24, which says, "For we were saved in this hope, but hope that is seen is not hope; for why does one still hope for what he sees?" Think about that. Why do we hope for what we see?

Here the scripture is speaking of seeing with our natural eyes. In reality, we don't hope for the things that we see, because there's no need to. There is no need for hope, no need for faith, if we can see what it is that we desire of the Lord. When we can see it, touch it, handle it, then we're not operating in faith. Faith gives substance to what we hope for because it causes us to trust God to be faithful in what He has spoken or shown to us before we ever see or experience the manifestation of it. We serve a God who not only *will not lie* to us but *cannot lie*. There's a difference in trusting someone who says they won't lie to us and trusting our God, who *cannot* lie because it is not in His character to do so. He is truth. In Him is no darkness at all. So although it may sometimes seem difficult, we can reflect on the character of God and know that He can be trusted to direct and orchestrate our lives.

There have been many occasions when I've been a part of Bible studies or have taught in settings where we talked about walking by faith or hearing the voice of God. I strongly believe that the devil keeps so many of us from obtaining what God has for us because he cripples us with the vicious cycle of questioning, "Is this me?" "Is this the devil?" or "Is this really God?" We can hang out in this cycle for days, months, and even years with no progress in our faith walk. Faith demands action. Faith without works is dead. I can speak about this because I've done the same thing, but what I've found is that as I commit to prayer and sincerely ask the Lord for His will regarding a matter, generally I experience strong inclinations regarding next moves, and those strong inclinations or tugs just will not go away. The reality is that I may ignore them or talk myself out of responding to them, but they are with me nonetheless. Other times, I've had experiences where the Lord sends someone my way to share a word, which is confirmation to me, and they have no clue about the fact that I've prayed about something that they have spoken to me about.

I can recall a time after our family had relocated to the DC area after being stationed on the island of Guam. I worked at a job in Washington, DC, for about four years. I was becoming a bit restless on the job and really had a desire to stop working for a while. One day while I was walking from the ladies' room, I overheard two coworkers talking in the hallway about buyouts for employees, and they were discussing the necessary qualifications that one would need in order to be eligible for the program. Employees had to have been with the agency for a minimum of ten years in order to qualify.

I went back to my desk somewhat disheartened because the buyout sounded really good but it seemed that I didn't qualify. Let me add that leaving the job was a desire of my heart but not something that I had prayed about, fasted about, or even mentioned to anyone. My next move was to ask around for something in writing about the buyout so that I could read some of the details (I just felt the urge to do this). Within the reading material, I found out that military service years counted as years on the job. I had been in the air force for six years! Are you hearing me right now? My time on the job, along with those six years, gave me ten years, and that meant that I could submit my paperwork for the buyout! This happened for me without any foreknowledge on my part regarding what was being set up by the Lord.

Which came first? Was there a desire in my heart that the Lord heard without me even praying, and then He fulfilled that desire, or did the Lord place the desire in my heart to come off the job and then make the way for it to happen by setting up the circumstances? I don't know the answer to those questions, but what I do know is that my steps are ordered by the Lord, and He allowed me to hear a conversation that was occurring at the exact moment that I walked by on my way from the ladies' room, and since there are no coincidences for Christians, I now know that it was a divine setup. Hallelujah!

Follow the leading of the Spirit of God. He will never lead you wrong. The Lord is faithful and He has every one of our tomorrows in His hands, but we have to be willing to trust Him and move!

Declare that you know the Lord's voice and the voice of a stranger you will not follow (see John 10:4,5). Remember that your steps are ordered. What other scripturally based declarations can you make regarding your Christian walk and your ability to hear the voice of God?

Wisdom in Action

There will be many instances when the next move that the Spirit of God is leading us to take will not make sense to our natural minds but our walk of faith must be strongly supported by our trust in the wisdom and counsel of God. Consider what the scripture says in 1 Corinthians 3:19: "For the wisdom of this world is foolishness to God." The English Standard Version reads, "He traps the wise in the snare of their own cleverness." The Lord's ways are past finding out (Rom. 11:33), but we can have the calm assurance that our God knows the end of all things from the beginning and His Spirit will always lead us according to His will. So let us be careful not to be wise in our own conceits but to realize that we have great need of the wisdom of God. The Lord has not called us to walk blindly but to walk in confidence as we adhere to the wisdom of God when the dictates of the world and all that is around us fail to line up with the revelation that He has given concerning us or our situation.

Isn't it wonderful to know that as His children, we have access to the wisdom of God simply by asking? Once we admit that we lack wisdom and we're willing to humble ourselves and ask from the only source who can provide it, it will be given to us without reservation. The scripture implies that in order to receive the wisdom that comes from God, we must first recognize our lack, for it reads, "If any man lacks wisdom, let him ask of God" (James 1:5). The truth is that all men lack the wisdom of God, but to obtain what is offered in this passage of scripture—the wisdom of God without measure—one must first recognize his or her need and humbly ask God for what He alone can supply. So "if any man lacks wisdom, let him ask of God."

While life experiences can certainly cause us to become *seasoned* or knowledgeable in certain areas of life, Godly wisdom, on the other hand, needs no life experience to support its existence. There's simply no way for the child of God to have experience in every situation that we will face or that we will be called upon to help someone else go through. I'm sure that you've heard people say, "You can't tell me anything if you haven't gone through what I'm going through." Perhaps you've even made such a statement. It's really rather ridiculous for any of us to have such an expectation, because the reality is that none of us can experience *every* situation that could possibly be presented as a challenge in the course of a lifetime. In addition to that, although two individuals may have similar circumstances, those circumstances remain unique to the individuals. Each won't experience it in the same way as the other. Yet the believer can speak truth, life, and deliverance in times of need for those who are in desperate situations, although we may not have confronted the same obstacles or trials per se. I don't have to experience the same type of sickness that you're confronting in order for me to declare that the Lord is a healer and that He can heal your body. The word of God declares that He is our healer and we are simply to agree with the word of God by faith. Whether or not He chooses to heal is His prerogative. It's not necessary for me to turn my back on God in order to minister to someone who has turned from the faith. God's word declares that those who are strong should restore those taken in a fault considering themselves lest they find themselves in the same predicament (Gal. 6:1). Whether or not we've experienced the same challenges, temptations, or setbacks, all believers can be armed with the word of God that will *never* lose its power.

It is wisdom in action when we refuse to be overtaken by fear in spite of what our circumstances look like. Instead we realize that we can simply pause and ask God to help us to make the right decision in our time of trouble. The **fear** of the LORD is the **beginning** of knowledge, but fools despise wisdom and discipline (Prov. 1:7). The **fear** of the LORD is the **beginning** of wisdom; all who follow his precepts have good understanding (Ps. 111:10). This is not the type of fear that causes us to run from and resist our God. Quite the contrary. When we have respect and reverence for our Lord and Savior to the extent that we look to Him and seek Him in all areas of our lives, then we are moving and operating in wisdom. This is a healthy fear and reverence for His Majesty, His awesome power, His unsearchable wisdom and glory. Those who have no regard for or fear of the Lord are walking apart from the wisdom of God. One of the major missing links in our world and in society today is man's lack of fear and reverence for God. So many people, places, and things have been placed ahead of God in the lives of mankind.

Take hold of wisdom and understand that anything that God's word declares, the child of God can preach it, teach it, pray it, and share it in times of crisis or trouble. Above all, have confidence to stand on it. Agreeing with the word of God means that we agree with what we read and hear from the word. That in and of itself is wisdom. Let's take a brief moment and consider some of the ways that we can begin to see the wisdom that comes from God and from His word as it begins to manifest in our lives:

- ➢ We can meditate on passages of scripture during our quiet times,
- ➢ memorize passages of scripture during times of study and devotion,
- ➢ speak passages from the word of God during our times of prayer, and
- ➢ pause and ask the Lord/the Holy Spirit to guide us before making decisions.

All of this will help to solidify our faith, as it gives assurance that we're seeking to live and to pray according to what the Bible has declared, which is God's will. Then we can be assured that we are not just living or praying based on our own desires or our selfish inclinations. There have been many occasions when I have picked up the Bible and read from the Psalms as though it was coming from my own heart, as though the situation was mine and not David's or whomever the writer might have been. Have you ever tried that?

As we get more of the word of God down on the inside of us, we will think, talk, and act differently because the word will change us in every aspect of our lives. In this way, we are experiencing the reality of being transformed as our minds are renewed. The word of God says that as believers, we have the mind of Christ. How do you suppose that happens? It's not just one of those things where we get saved today and tomorrow we think like God and walk in His wisdom with understanding. No, our minds must be constantly renewed and our lives transformed by taking in the living word until it becomes a part of us and we come to the realization that we have become one with Christ as the scripture has said. (See 1 Corinthians 6:17: "But he who is joined to the Lord is one spirit with Him.")

Let's face it: During times of great disappointment or discouragement, we may not feel like praying and we certainly may not feel like or think that we are one with Christ. But in those difficult and trying seasons, we can turn to the word of God, the Bible, and find passages of scripture that speak to the deep feelings that we are experiencing. Not everyone has developed a prayer life, and some may feel quite awkward when speaking words aloud in an attempt to pray in a manner that sounds like others who we may have heard praying in group settings. Please allow me to submit to you that we can express ourselves using the written word of God, which often goes much deeper than what we would typically find ourselves expressing in our personal times of prayer.

Take this simple challenge to step out of your comfort zone: Open the Bible and boldly declare some of the areas of scripture that resonate in your heart and that express those things that you truly want to say to the Lord. It's okay to use the words that are written there in the text and to gradually add your own words according to what comes to your heart and mind as you pray. This can be a very practical way of building your prayer life on a daily basis. Read the word, pray the word, and pull it from the written pages by practicing what it says. This is in no way about being "super deep," although I'm not one to apologize for desiring a close relationship with the Lord.

It's probably safe to say that you want more in your spiritual life. If you're ready to believe for more, what is it that keeps you from experiencing the power and anointing that we read about in the Bible? I am convinced that God wants to pull the scales from our spiritual eyes and give us vision. Part of Paul's prayer for the church at Ephesus in Ephesians 1:18,19 was, "And I pray that the eyes of your understanding being enlightened; that you may know what is the hope of His calling, what are the riches of the glory of His inheritance in the saints, and what is the exceeding greatness of His power toward us who believe, according to the working of His mighty power." Trust that God is going to begin to reveal His plan and purpose to you.

Paul's earnest prayer was that the eyes of the believer's, the saint's understanding would be enlightened. We can pray for spiritual enlightenment and understanding knowing that it's within the will of God to do so. The key to being able to operate in areas where we have no prior knowledge or experience is simply being able to trust our God, who is all-knowing, all-wise, and who is privy to all things obvious and hidden. He is privy to things that man has not even imagined or thought of doing yet. That means that in any given situation, He knows what our thoughts and actions, as well as the thoughts and actions of those around us, will be far ahead of the time when we think or execute them. There's no need to be concerned or to worry about what lies ahead, because He's already there. He's already in our tomorrows.

Therefore, we find that when we read accounts of believers who agreed to move forward with the instructions God had given, He would first give them the directive to "fear not." Why? The child of God, whether young, middle-aged, or older must be totally convinced that when the Lord is sharing His thoughts and perspectives with us, we can trust Him totally. We are to have a reverent fear and respect for our Lord rather than to walk in fear of our circumstances or what man might propose to do to us. God has given the Holy Spirit to the believer to serve as a Guide, Counselor, and Friend throughout the course of our lives on earth. He will never leave or forsake us. Never! The Lord instructs us to resist the spirit of fear because it must be put under subjection in order for us to move ahead in faith.

God told young Jeremiah, "Say not, I am a child: for thou shalt go to all that I shall send thee, and whatsoever I command thee thou shalt speak. Be not afraid of their faces: for I am with thee to deliver thee, saith the Lord" (Jer. 1:7,8). God said to Jeremiah that He knew him before he was formed in the belly, or in other words, conceived in his mother's womb. Throughout the book of Jeremiah, God's message to Jeremiah is "Fear not!" Jeremiah had to know that whatever was given to him to accomplish, it would be accomplished through the direction, might, and wisdom of the true and living God. His age had nothing to do with his victory, but his trust and obedience, on the other hand, had everything to do with the outcome of victory not only for himself but for those around him whom God had chosen for him to lead.

You might say, "Well, God hasn't called me to lead anyone." Just know that the path that the Lord has chosen for your life is not an isolated one. It will surely intersect with others, and the decisions that you make regarding the plan and purpose of God for your life will affect those around you, sometimes directly and other times indirectly. Just as the Lord made choice of Jeremiah, He has made choice of us, and He stands ready to give us the strength and power to stand against our fears as we trust His infinite wisdom. Dare to look beyond what the enemy presents to you in an attempt to deter you from your desire to move and operate in faith. Fear not! The Lord has gone before you, and the way has been carved out for your destiny. It's your faith that will allow you to see and experience in the spirit those things that are not visible in the natural.

Prayer for Wisdom: Lord, I thank You because You have made choice of me even before the foundation of the world. In obedience to Your word, I ask for wisdom and boldness to walk in the paths that You have prepared for me on the journey of fulfilling destiny in my life. Thank You for those whom You have ordained to intersect with my life and to become faith partners with me. I pray for them now, although many of them I do not know and I believe You to speak to their hearts, to order their steps, and to rebuke the spirit of fear that would come to hinder and to war against Your plan for our lives. Let Your will be done in us! In Jesus's name, Amen!

Inspiration Break

2 Corinthians 10:4 (KJV): "For the weapons of our warfare are not carnal, but mighty through God to the pulling down of strongholds."

2 Corinthians 10: 4 (AMP): "The weapons of our warfare are not physical [weapons of flesh and blood]. Our weapons are divinely powerful for the destruction of fortresses."

Revisit the preceding scripture and others that will be given here as you use this inspiration break to meditate on the word of God and listen to what the Lord wants to share with you at this time.

Focus on the fact that our weapons are mighty—mighty through God. They are not the weapons of the world, but they have divine power to demolish strongholds.

The weapons that the Lord has given to us are spiritual, and every work of the devil that comes against us has to fall and become subject to the weapons that He has given to us.

Prayer, praise, worship, and your shouts unto God are all part of your spiritual weaponry.

We are free. Jesus has made us free. John 8: 36 (NKJV) says, "Therefore if the Son makes you free, you shall be free indeed." You can rejoice in that. This scripture declares that there is nothing holding you; there is nothing constricting you unless you desire to be in bondage.

The word of God admonishes us not to allow ourselves to be entangled again with any yoke of bondage (Gal. 5:1). This indicates that we have some power over this bondage that would come to take hold in our lives.

Isaiah 54:17 (AMP): "'No weapon that is formed against you will succeed; And every tongue that rises against you in judgment you will condemn. This [peace, righteousness, security, and triumph over opposition] is the heritage of the servants of the LORD, And *this is* their vindication from Me,' says the LORD."

This is the heritage of the servants of the Lord. This isn't saying that weapons won't be formed against you or that lies won't be told about you, but neither will prosper.

Satan has no weapon that can really prosper against you, but he doesn't want you to know that. He doesn't want you to believe that, and he certainly doesn't want you to walk in that.

Meditate on the Lord, quiet yourself in His presence, and think on Him.

God Orchestrates the Dream

Have you ever felt like the Lord has spoken something to your spirit, and you became so excited about it? Then you started right away trying to make it work and became frustrated when it didn't manifest in the way that you thought it would. I won't go into great detail here, but in my first book, *Essentials for Frontline Living*, I share the story about Joseph in a chapter titled "It's Not Your Dream." His story is a prime example of getting a word, a vision from the Lord, and becoming so excited about it that it becomes hard to contain. So, not unlike us, Joseph felt compelled to share his dream with others, more specifically his brothers.

When we get exciting or intriguing news, typically we may share it with others who may not be appreciative of it or who may actually reject it. This is what happened in Joseph's life after his life-changing dream. He just wanted to share it. That's natural because it seemed so very real to him. We all have probably had those moments when we just knew that the Spirit of God had shown us something and we immediately wanted to run it by someone else whom we trusted only to come away feeling rejected and anything but supported. Even in those situations when others may support our dreams, we may still find ourselves in a place of wondering and asking, "Now, how is this going to work out? Where do I even begin?"

The fulfillment of the dream that God had given to Joseph was not contingent upon his family's acceptance of what was shown to him. Whether they liked it or not, agreed with it or not, since it was of God and not something that Joseph had conjured up, nothing was able to stop it. Oh, yes, others put stumbling blocks in the way; they sought to hinder God's plan, but ultimately the plan of God prevailed and Joseph's family members and countrymen were blessed and sustained because of it. As I stated previously, what God has designed to do through each of us is never solely about us. Joseph's dream was not just about God exalting him to a place of prominence and wealth, but God positioned him to be able to save not only his family but an entire nation during a time of great distress.

The major takeaway for me as I looked over Joseph's life story was not so much how the Lord blessed him with wealth and took him to a place of prominence. Note that in Genesis 41:37–57, Pharaoh declared that there was no one in the land as discerning and wise as Joseph, and consequently he gave Joseph charge over the palace and all of the people in the land. Pharaoh declared that only with respect to the throne would he be greater than Joseph;

otherwise Joseph was to be in charge over the whole land of Egypt.

All of this was due to the wisdom of God that operated in Joseph's life and had become evident to those around him, namely Pharaoh. The entire account of what happened in Joseph's life from the time that he experienced the dream until he made provision for his people had more to do with how he operated in Kingdom authority and wisdom than it had to do with the riches and material gain that he was afforded. He came through excitement, rejection, betrayal, and abandonment, to name a few. It's easy to grab hold of the glory of his story and to want to identify with that, but we have to accept the reality of what turned out to be very bitter pills that Joseph had to swallow in order to get to the place of prominence, although he was who God said he was all along. He was who God called him to be even when he was in the pit.

Joseph's position of prominence and wealth gave him every opportunity to repay evil for evil and to make sure that retribution was carried out to the fullest. But the wisdom of God, not his own wisdom, allowed him to see and caused him to profess to his brothers, "But as for you, you meant evil against me; *but* God meant it for good, in order to bring it about as *it is* this day, to save many people alive" (Gen. 50:20). That was wisdom speaking, not Joseph. He had to be hurting very deeply because of how he was treated by his brothers—those who he thought would support him when others would not, but they had plotted to get rid of him.

None of us knows what we'll be faced with on the road to fulfilling the plan of God for our lives. As a female in ministry, I have faced so many obstacles and repercussions from others' beliefs, male and female, regarding women in ministry. Some of the worst enemies for women in ministry can be other women. As women we just seem to have this thing about other females doing something positive and being rewarded or esteemed highly because of it. Couple that with being anointed by God, something that we have nothing to do with, and you have a recipe for harsh treatment and sometimes outright rejection. Some men still wrestle, either covertly or overtly, with God's ability or will to use women at all, as absurd as this is, considering that the Lord mightily used women throughout scripture. I've experienced times when I've had to serve with men who did not believe in women taking part in the gospel ministry. Sometimes they wouldn't speak it outright, but the Lord would reveal it to me. The truth is that through every trying circumstance, the Lord has been faithful and has shown me that what opposing forces or people meant for evil, He would turn for my good. Those circumstances have helped me to grow and to seek to get closer to the Lord.

For some of us, there will be opposition from family or close friends after the Lord places a call upon your life. Just let go of the notion right now that everyone will be happy about what the Lord has planned and ordained for your life. There is going to come a point in your Christian walk when you must determine that whatever the Lord has given you to do, you will do it in spite of the opposition and regardless to where or through whom the opposition comes. Until this is resolved in your spirit, you will always struggle and halt between opinions when it comes to fulfilling the plan of God in your life. There will always be those who think they have a better plan for your life than the Lord does, and they will sometimes shun you when you refuse to do things their way. Remember that Jesus was confronted with this same mindset or spirit. Others thought that they knew God and the plan of God better than He did, not knowing that He proceeded directly from the Father and lived to do His Father's will. He was God incarnate.

One of the strongest hurdles that most of us will ever face is that of getting over ourselves and dealing with the voices and thoughts that come from within. Become acquainted with the person that the Lord has called you to be and ask the Lord to help you to accept your gifts and callings. We don't earn gifts or positions within the Kingdom of God. All of this is God-given, preordained, and sometimes may not seem fair to us or to others. Refuse to compete but seek rather to bring glory to God with all that He has entrusted to you. Remember that all that we have belongs to Him and we have simply been given stewardship over His belongings.

You and I may never be put in a position to save a nation as Joseph was, but trust that we will have an impact on our families and those around us when we are in a position to hear God and when we are determined to heed His instructions. Our obedience will always have far-reaching, supernatural results as we allow the Lord to orchestrate the dreams that He has placed inside of us.

The Lord is already in our tomorrows and can give us the wisdom to make decisions today that will literally save our lives when we reach the trials and tests of our tomorrows. It is the wisdom of God that will afford us the ability to respond in faith to what God has spoken to us and over us without being deterred or thrown off track by the plots and schemes of those who doubt that we've heard from Him and furthermore doubt what He has said.

We read in 1 Corinthians 10:13 that "there is no temptation that has taken you but such as is common to man." This says to us that those whom we read about in the Bible were not the only ones to contend with struggle, disappointment, discouragement, and times of triumph, but we will have our fair share as well. Therefore, we can go to the word of God and find those areas of scripture that speak to our circumstance and decide to cry out to God from that place. We can use those portions of scripture to supplement our praise to God and help us to move into a place of spontaneous praise and worship. Laying hold on the truth of the word of God and the documented experiences of those who trusted and placed their faith in Him can serve somewhat as a springboard for us, launching us into that deeper place that is ours alone as we commune with our personal Lord and Savior with whom we share a relationship. We can pull from the written pages of scripture, which is God-breathed, and allow the Spirit of God to help us apply that living word to our everyday lives.

What is the most challenging thing that you're dealing with right now? Is there something that the Lord has shown to you that He wants to fulfill in your life, but you've turned away from it because of the opinions or doubts of others? Maybe the strongest opposition is coming from within. It can be that way sometimes. Keep a forward momentum and trust God to show you where you are in your story. Ask Him to allow His will to unfold in your life, then determine to move ahead with all that is within you. Don't allow yourself to align with those who doubt the vision of God that has been spoken over you or shown to you. Wherever you find yourself, move on to the next sentence, the next paragraph, the next chapter, or the next book that makes up the story of your life—just move!

Prayer: Father, in the name of Jesus, I ask now for the vision, direction, and wisdom that you have promised to me and to all of Your children through Your word. I believe that You have spoken a good plan over my life; I believe that You are orchestrating Your plan, and I receive it now by faith. Amen.

The Necessity of Transformation

Romans 12:1,2

We are all familiar with Romans 12:1,2 (NKJV), which reads, "I beseech you therefore, brethren, by the mercies of God, that you present your bodies a living sacrifice, holy, acceptable to God, *which is* your reasonable service. And do not be conformed to this world, but be transformed by the renewing of your mind, that you may prove what *is* that good and acceptable and perfect will of God." Let's deal with some of the words found in this passage of scripture from a natural standpoint before we move forward to talk about why it's so necessary for us to be transformed as children of God.

To conform means to behave according to socially acceptable conventions or standards (pressure to conform in order to be accepted). If we're honest, we've all dealt with this on some level from childhood into adulthood. There's always pressure to conform on some level in different areas of our lives. From the first time that we step outside of the nucleus of our family setting, there is a strong pull to conform to the norms of the world in order to fit in and to survive. The world system will push us to keep everything that pertains to God as secondary and to remain silent regarding any relationship with Him when in the presence of others who might become *offended* because we are said to be infringing upon their rights.

We must be mindful of subtle yet obvious ways that conformity is pushed by the world in which we live, because it is easy to fall into patterns of behavior that may grieve the Spirit of God all for the sake of fitting in. Small children are taunted and bullied at school for simply bowing their heads to pray over their lunch as they've been taught to do in their homes. Sometimes the bullies aren't other children but adults who have taken a position of shutting down any and everything that reflects belief in or a relationship with the Lord. In most high schools, there can't be a moment of silence before or during ceremonies such as graduation. For most adults on their jobs, they are pressured to keep their beliefs hidden in order to blend in with everyone else who is a part of the workforce. All of these are examples of a push toward conformity to a world system that hits at various levels and facets of our lives. It affects all of us from the youngest to the oldest.

You see, although we may be able to blend in and mesh with the crowd by keeping our faith hidden and on the back burner, so to speak, a truly converted life can only remain hidden but for so long. We have to be keenly aware of the fact that we are in this world but not of this world.

Our lives are to be a testimony whether or not we're able to speak a word regarding our faith. There are some things that we simply will not do, say, or take part in as children of God. This is not because we can't but because the Bible states that "everything is permissible for me, but not everything is beneficial" (1 Cor. 10:23). If the intended outcome for any action that we take part in is not to build up, to encourage, or to improve a given situation, then it does not coincide with our purpose.

The fact remains that there are conformists who are angry with God for varying reasons; some are running from a call that the Lord has placed on their lives and others have a total misconception about God and are unable to perceive of the great love that He has for them. They want nothing to do with anything that resembles organized religion or a saved life, and that includes people who reflect either. That means that it could boil down to you or me being the target of their anger and inward rage toward God, His teachings, and His ways. You may be the target, but you're not the reason. Make sure that your children understand this as well, because sometimes they're subjected to the evil tactics of other children or adults who actually have a vendetta against the move of God. A vendetta is a series of retaliatory or vengeful acts, such as a blood feud, that are carried out over a period of time against those who stand in opposition to those who hold the grudge. Sound familiar? This feud has been going on since the beginning of time, but you must remember that the kingdom of darkness no longer has a grip on you after you come to Christ.

In Romans 12:1,2 Paul makes it very plain that we are not to conform to this world or to try to blend in with it. He gives an option for us, which is the only option, in fact, if we're going to be successful as we navigate within this world and its systems without becoming entrenched in it. We may find ourselves doing okay in one area while conforming or going along to get along in another. So Paul tells us that there is an alternate path to take in order to avoid the slippery slope of conformity, and that is to be transformed instead. This condition of transformation requires intentional, committed effort on our part. It's not a matter of just sitting back and waiting for the Lord to transform us.

When we look at the definition of *transform*, it means to change in form, appearance, or structure; metamorphose. Another definition puts it this way: "To change (something) completely and usually in a good way; to change in condition, nature, or character; convert." After accepting Christ into our lives, we don't change in form, nor do we change in our physical appearance or structure, but I'm drawn to the part of the definition that speaks of a change in condition, nature, or character.

I want to briefly share a personal story about the change in condition, nature, and character after an encounter with the Lord. Remember that our journey together through this book is all about finding ways to pull from the written pages of the Bible in order to have real and lasting experiences with this God whom we read about.

My journey toward a changed life began after a year of study at Western Kentucky University in Bowling Green and a summer spent with my aunt and uncle, Maceo and Helen Bishop, in Cleveland, Ohio. I was a theater major, which I enjoyed, and I was crowned second runner-up for Ms. Black Western, but somehow I had no desire to return to school after my summer break. I began talking to my uncle about joining the military, and he took me to see a recruiter. The rest is history. Traveling has always been in my blood, and I signed the dotted line to become a part of the United States Air Force.

Before I knew it, all of my good-byes had been shared with family and I was headed to Lackland AFB in Texas for basic training. After completing basic training, I was assigned to Sheppard AFB in Witchita Falls, Texas, for my tech school in order to learn to become a General Accounting Specialist in the air force. My desire was to serve outside of the United States and to do all of my assignments on foreign soil, so I signed up for consecutive overseas duty.

My first duty assignment was to Osan Air Base in Korea. As a young teen, I had been exposed to drugs (marijuana, mescaline, and windowpane acid). I know that I'm dating myself with these terms, but I am just being candid. We're still moving toward the transforming power of God, so don't think that I've lost track of where we are. To show you how the enemy works, while on the flight to Korea, a young man began talking to me and told me that he had friends who were already stationed there and that they would be able to "hook us up." How did he know anything about what I was into? Don't you think for a minute that the enemy is not out to set you up for a long path of destruction. That's his job. The Bible tells us that "the enemy does not come except to steal, and to kill and to destroy" (John 10:10). If he's coming, he's only coming for those reasons. However, the Lord has a plan and purpose for our lives as well. Never lose sight of that!

Two days after arriving at Osan Air Base, I met a group of young men who invited me to a baseball game, and afterward they invited me to join them for a choir rehearsal at the chapel on base. I have always loved to sing, so I thought, *Why not?* Well, I was supposed to go outside the base that night and into the village to make some connections with the young man whom I had met on the plane, so I invited him along to the rehearsal and told him that we'd go off base afterward. Long story short, after the rehearsal, they asked us to stay for a Bible study and we stayed.

There was a life-changing word that night. I had never heard anything about being born again, but the message came through loud and clear, and I knew that this was something that I wanted. I went forward to accept the Lord as my Savior, and to my surprise, the young man who had come with me went up as well. After the service and all of our conversations with others who had attended, I walked out of that chapel knowing that my life had been changed. There's no way that I could explain it, but I knew that something had happened within me.

As soon as we stepped outside of the chapel door, the young man with me asked me, "So do you want to go get high?" I couldn't believe it! I thought that we had just had the same experience, but evidently we hadn't. The desire for getting high was so far from my mind. That simply speaks to the fact that we can be in the same place physically but have an entirely different spiritual experience or encounter. This happens Sunday after Sunday in numerous cities and denominations across the nation and around the world. I didn't look down on him or think negatively about him but asked whether or not he felt different at all after our encounter. He admitted that he had walked forward because he was following what I had done.

The truth is that whether he felt differently or not, if he had asked the Lord to save him, things had actually changed for him in that chapel just as they had for me, but we can't give someone else's testimony. Each of us has to know for ourselves that we have had an encounter with the Lord, because it's intentional. We are to believe with our hearts and confess with our own mouths that Jesus is Lord. That's not something that anyone else can do for us. Well on this journey to transformation, we're right back to "all things have become new," as I've shared several times now in other chapters as well. What we need to grasp here is that *all* things have become new whether we feel like it or not. Somebody needs to let that sink in right now. The Spirit of the Lord is speaking to you because this is an area where the enemy continues to trip you up, but you've become a new creation in Christ after accepting Him. It's something that takes place in the spirit realm, and the proof of this change is not determined by what we see in the mirror. All things had become new for me and for my new friend, if he had accepted Christ, but we're all required to move forward by faith because we have a part to play in walking out our salvation. I felt different, I felt so clean, but I realize that's not everyone's experience. I also know that this walk is by faith and not by how we feel. Of course, I know this now, but at the time, I knew literally nothing about being a new babe in Christ.

We accept the Lord by faith, and anything else that becomes a part of that experience simply becomes a wonderful part of our testimony of being born again. Certainly I have no idea what the Lord saved me from in the natural sense that night. My entire military career could have ended if we had been caught with substances, or I could have found myself in a horrible set of circumstances with people whom I didn't even really know, as my plan was to hang out with this person whom I had just met two days prior. Thank God that nothing even remotely close to those possibilities happened. My life was completely changed just two days after setting foot on Osan Air Base, and without even knowing it, I was on my way to transformation by way of a renewed mind.

We can look at transformation from both a natural and a spiritual perspective. Transformation is something that begins on the inside and is not a natural process. We have a part to play in it, but we don't perform it or bring it to pass in our lives. It is supernatural! How does this change take place? As believers, we're all being transformed. It's an ongoing process. Let's take something that is studied by scientists and in the classrooms of many elementary schools on a regular basis. We're all familiar with the caterpillar, which is known to undergo or experience what would be called a total transformation or metamorphosis. The explanation for what happens to the caterpillar usually begins with a very hungry caterpillar hatching from an egg with the sole purpose of eating. It gorges itself until one day, when the time is right, it spins a silk wrapping around itself that we know as a cocoon. This period of the caterpillar's life is a time of great vulnerability, for it is now hanging under what it once fed on, usually a leaf of some sort, and has no way of defending itself against whatever might prey on it. What once fed and gave nourishment to the caterpillar now becomes its shelter and covering while something miraculous takes place in the place of obscurity.

The caterpillar digests itself, getting rid of its initial state, and becomes an oozing, soupy substance that, if the cocoon is disturbed, will ooze out, preventing the completion of a process that is necessary to get the caterpillar to its next state. It is morphing or transforming across all levels. It is dying as what it once was. When it emerges from that cocoon, it looks different, it functions differently, and the truth is that it cannot operate in the manner that it did in its former state. We see it in its glory and beauty and seldom think of its beginning. But the reality is that it started as a caterpillar—to some loathsome and ugly. The butterfly can never be a caterpillar again. It must now fly!

Potential was always in the caterpillar, but the process had to take place. We are created in the image of God, and our potential must be developed in order to push us to the place where we live and dwell in the realm of the supernatural and bring the will of God to earth through the means of our transformation. Note what the scripture tells us: Paul says; "I beseech you, I urge you by the mercies of God." With what you know about God's mercy, you know that you can trust Him with your whole self. Paul then urges us, the readers of the word and those who would choose to believe and apply the written word, to present our bodies.

Romans 12:1,2 (NKJV) reads, "I beseech you therefore, brethren, by the mercies of God, that you present your bodies a living sacrifice, holy, acceptable to God, *which is* your reasonable service." Presenting our bodies speaks of the whole self. To *present* indicates an action on our part. This means that no one brings us, but it is a conscious decision on our part to present our lives and to stay on the altar, the place of sacrifice before God. The reality is that a living sacrifice has the power and can choose to move away from that sacrificial place, that vulnerable place. We present ourselves by faith and with faith. We must resist our selfish, ungodly desires and agendas daily if we are sincere about seeking the will and plan of God for our lives. To present our whole selves to God is "our *reasonable act of worship*" as one translation or version says (italics mine).

To decide to give ourselves to God is an act of worship because we are essentially saying, "I am willing to give my life for the cause of Christ, for Kingdom purposes, and I surrender all that I am to you, Lord." You see, it's one thing to read and memorize these scriptures, as most of us have at one time or another, but it's an entirely different thing to make the decision to allow them to become a reality in our lives. That's exactly what this book is about and what will be referred to over and over again simply because the body of Christ cannot reflect the glory and power of God solely by educating us with the word. It must become a part of us. This is what so many of us are longing for, and there are no shortcuts to experiencing the power and anointing of God. Too many have been content to stay in a place of potential. Remember that every caterpillar has the potential to become a butterfly; however, that can never happen without it having to go through a very vulnerable process on its way to unbelievable transformation. In its transformed state, there is no resemblance of what it used to be. It doesn't look anything like what it has come through to get to its present glory.

Be not conformed to this world but be ye transformed. How is this to take place? By the renewing of our minds. Note that we're not dealing with intellect here—not that intellect isn't important, but it isn't key when we speak of transformation or excelling in the things of God. The word *transformed* speaks of change across all domains, as *trans* means "across"—*transport, translate*, etc. To be transformed includes how we think and feel (responses to both) and how we act—essentially what we do. All of these are seated in the mind. Proverbs 23:7 states, "As a man thinketh in his heart, so is he." The mind and thought processes affect who we are and how we respond to the world around us. We can think of a man or woman's character as the sum of all his or her thoughts as those thoughts pertain to him- or herself.

Many of the messages that we receive daily, whether internally or externally, are erroneous. Erroneous information filtered through a mind that has not been renewed or regenerated is a recipe for disaster. Reels from the past that relate to our old selves, our former nature—where we've been and what we've done—seek to play out in our minds and to hold us captive. The mind that has not been transformed constantly reminds us of our low state, our first state, our state of becoming, our state of potential. So much potential lies within each one of us, but we were not created to live in a constant state of potential. We were created to become—to become like Him, to become the salt and light in this world, to become heirs and joint heirs with Christ. That is the place or status to which we are called to transition.

Our true identity is found in the word of God, and we must train our hearts and minds to agree with what the word of God has said. People can appear to be free and walk openly around us while being chained, constricted, and held hostage within their minds. Somehow when we feast on the word and make it our delight, when we meditate on it day and night, our character changes.

It's an inward working. The sin nature can no longer have dominion over us unless we yield to it (Rom. 6:14). Before Christ, we were slaves to sin, and somehow—even after we're born again—the enemy will use opportunities to creep in and try to convince us that the word of God is not enough. He tries to convince the transformed believer that the word of God won't work, but the truth is that the word has not lost its power. The word of God still has the power to transform our low estate, our **character**, and our **sin-sick nature to a place of coming under subjection and obedience to Christ.** We must declare what the word says until we truly believe it and can see it manifested in our lives.

This is very much a part of living a faith-filled life. This is why we are admonished in scripture to meditate on, think on, concentrate on the word of God day and night because we are responsible for making it a part of our very being. Where are the seekers, where are the hungry? They are the ones who shall find; they shall be filled. As we feed on the word of God and resist the delicacies that the world has to offer, our character will change and our nature will reflect the nature of our Lord more and more. Yes, there will sometimes be battles just as Paul shared in Romans 7, where he talked about having a desire to do one thing but constantly finding himself doing contrary to those desires.

But thank God for Romans 8:1 (NKJV), which boldly declares: "There is therefore now no condemnation to those who are in Christ Jesus, who do not walk according to the flesh, but according to the Spirit." There is no way that we can feed on the word of God on a regular basis with a sincere desire for intimacy with the Lord and yet remain the same. We must have a desire for Him. We can eat and grow fat with knowledge yet refuse to allow the word to change us. We have to present ourselves—our whole selves—to God, withholding nothing. Every single person reading this book can commit more time to reading God's word, more time to prayer (not just listening to prayers, but praying), and more time to making a concerted effort to apply the word of God in some aspect to a greater degree on a daily basis. All of us are continually growing in our walk with Christ.

We simply can't think differently, act differently, talk differently, or be different until our minds are renewed. The daily temptation is to present ourselves to God but then to slowly climb off the altar of sacrifice and walk away determining to once again do it our own way and make excuses like God knows my heart. The bible says that when we love our sins, the world and things that displease God more than we love Him, then we cannot be His disciples. We all make mistakes and fall short but to live a continuous lifestyle of sin is not the life of a believer. The Bible encourages us to present our bodies as living sacrifices and we must encourage one another daily as our prior lifestyles, habits and other distractions will compete for our attention and affections.

That's what presenting ourselves as living sacrifices is all about. There is a constant letting go of things that have held us hostage and kept us from the fullness of our life in Christ. We invite the Lord to burn all of that away so that the only thing that remains is a changed heart that desires more of Him. This is the way of the Kingdom. This is why we must know Kingdom principles, because they don't look like what we've been taught from the perspective of the world system. The world says to "look out for No. 1 and get all that you can get." On the other hand, the Kingdom is still about seeking God and His righteousness first and trusting that everything that we need will be added to our lives (Matt. 6:33).

This sounds ridiculous when we're not operating by Kingdom principles, but this is exactly where we will find the desires of our hearts. It's not by chasing what the world offers to us, which in reality will only cause us to be exhausted after the lifelong chase, but it is a promise that things will be added to us when we keep our priorities straight. Kingdom first. I encourage you to pour out your heart to the Lord and tell Him that you need Him to take those addictions, longings, strongholds in your life that you just can't rid yourself of. Pour out! Cry out! He will answer and change will come.

We started by defining *transformation* by bringing emphasis to the change that it brings with regard to our nature or character and function. It's important that we give some attention to our condition before we move on to our function. The condition for many of you may be that you're in the place of obscurity right now. You're hidden, you're like the caterpillar in the cocoon, but there's a process taking place that must have its complete work. If you have fed on the word, you will find that the same word that fed you and nourished you will now cover and shield you. Remember the caterpillar hanging from the underside of the leaf? You're now in a vulnerable place, a place where, if disturbed, your process will be incomplete. You're in the dark room where the best work of transformation takes place. You see, some love the finished work, but they don't want the process. As has been stated, this is a supernatural process. You can't do it on your own, but you have to trust and yield to God in order for this process to be perfected. Take full advantage of this time in your life that can cause you to feel like you're being overlooked and under-appreciated. The Lord knows exactly where you are. Draw close to Him. Read your Bible more; shut down some of your devices and pray more. Get quiet and practice listening, and don't worry if sometimes in the stillness, you seem to hear absolutely nothing. You're morphing, you're changing, and when you come forth, you must embrace your new function. Remember that a butterfly can never be a caterpillar again.

Did you note that I said that when you come forth you will have a new function? Let that sit with you for a moment. Too many of us are trying to operate in the same manner that we may have operated one, two, or three years ago, and the Lord is trying to move us to something else. Our function has changed. Our function has shifted. Everything that we do is for the building up and edification of the body of Christ. We serve a living and creative God who is not stagnant.

Be flexible, pliable, and willing to embrace your new function as the Lord carries you from level to level and glory to glory. Your function has changed if you have been transformed. You are not who you used to be and you simply cannot operate in the way that you've been accustomed to operating or functioning before your transformation. This is where a lot of people want to get off. The enemy says, "That's not you!" But the reality is that The Lord always does **exceeding abundantly above what we could ever ask or think**, so in reality most of the time, we're just as much in awe at what the Lord has done and is doing in our lives as those around us. He is the One who has done exceedingly abundantly above, and what He has done in our lives is absolutely amazing.

Get ready for the opposing voices, the naysayers. The opposing voices will scream, "You can't fly," "Nobody that you know flies," "That's not the way that we do it." Jesus had to deal with this type of opposition, and even worse, because His function, His purpose, was to present the Kingdom of God on earth. So many were waiting for their Messiah to come with pomp and splendor as one who would overthrow the Roman government and deliver them naturally. That wasn't His mission, and because He didn't look or operate the way they thought He should, they rejected Him. Many still do. We are joint heirs with Christ. We are the righteousness of God in Christ Jesus and we have the mind of Christ. The word of God declares it! We can't be afraid of the word. We can't be afraid to confess it and to stand on it. As we're transformed on the inside, the outward manifestation will come. Go ahead and allow the Lord to amaze you! He wants to do great things in and through the lives of His people.

As we move with purpose toward our destiny, we will find that our perspectives about many things may become different. We may find that some of the things that we were taught about the Lord or scriptures were in error while other things that we have previously rejected, we find that we may now embrace as our relationship with Him is strengthened. Take note that the Bible states (I'll paraphrase) in Ephesians 2:6 that "we're seated in heavenly places in Christ Jesus now." Not that we *will be*, but according to the scripture, we're seated there *now*. We hear from the throne room *now* because our position is above and not beneath. We have been given direct access to the throne room of God, as the scripture in Hebrews 4:16 tells us to "come boldly to the throne of grace, where we may obtain mercy and find grace to help us in the time of need." This scripture is so empowering because it lets us know that as children of the King, we don't need to have anyone else go to Him on our behalf. We can enter into His presence and speak to Him without fear, and He is ready to give us mercy and help in our times of need. For this we glorify His name!

What does it mean to "glorify the Lord" or to "give God glory"? We hear these expressions often within Christian circles. I checked for an explanation at https://www.seedbed.com/mean-glorify-god-free-lesson, an article by Chasity Opphile from December 16, 2015, and in short came away with two different aspects of the word. First, to glorify means to shine, to demonstrate, and to manifest the divine. In other words, glory represents the Lord's presence. The second aspect of the word *glory* means to reflect, to show forth, to demonstrate, and to express the image of an object or person so that it may be seen by all.

We pray that as born-again believers, we will become more sensitive to the Lord's presence and that we will recognize the glory. Many around Jesus didn't recognize Him or receive Him, and our given definition tells us that glory represents the Lord's presence. John 1:11 (NKJV) reads: "He came to His own, and His own did not receive Him." A popular song by J.J. Hairston and Youthful Praise makes the assertion that "there will be glory after this," but my question to you is, "Can you recognize the glory *in* this?" Before God turns your situation around and before He brings you out, can you recognize His glory as you go through your trials and difficult circumstances? Whatever it is that you're going through, whatever you're faced with, the question remains: "Can you recognize the glory in this?" The enemy sees the glory upon us and that's why he fights us so hard, but the tragedy is that we don't recognize the glory until we're completely out of our trying circumstances. The Lord is with us in it! Yes, right in the middle of the struggle, the Lord is there!

There's glory in the midst of the storm, for the Lord is there. That's why we don't wait until everything is over to shout the victory. We're transformed from glory to glory. According to 2 Corinthians 3:18, "**But we all, with** unveiled face, beholding as in a mirror the glory of the Lord, are being transformed into the same image from glory to glory, just as by the Spirit of the Lord." We walk in the wisdom that the Lord gives and not the wisdom of this world, which is foolishness to Him. What are you hearing? Come up to your God-given vantage point so that you may hear from Him. We always want the Lord to come down, "reach way down," but He's saying, "I've called you up out of the dark place, the dry place, the mediocre place, the defeated place, the painful place, and the empty place!" Come up and partake of that which has been prepared for you even before the foundation of the world.

Prayer: Father, in the Name of Jesus, I thank You now for Your transforming work in my life. I declare according to 2 Corinthians 5:17 that I am in Christ and therefore I am a new creation. Old things have passed away and all things pertaining to me have become new. I am being transformed and changed into the image of Christ day by day as my mind is being renewed by the word of God, which strengthens me as I live a committed and surrendered life in this present world. Amen.

Inspiration Break

Trust that by faith the Lord is shifting some things in your life as He transitions you and allows transformation to take place in your life.

The new territory that will be revealed to you may look nothing like what you expected. Remember that you've been prepared for the new place whether you feel like it or not.

You may be living in the same house, driving the same car, living in the same city, or even working at the same job, but I declare that you have entered into a new place in your life and your walk with the Lord.

As the Lord transitions you, you will not operate in the same manner that you have before. Allow Him to do new things in your life. Allow Him to place a greater demand on the gifts that He has entrusted to you so that you can be empowered to operate from an anointing that you have not experienced up to this point in your walk with Him.

I declare that the Lord has enhanced, empowered, and expanded your gifts to reflect the reality of what He has called you to do and to be. Receive it!

Refuse to rely on your feelings. Sometimes our feelings cause us to hold on to things that have been given to us while at the same time, preventing us from embracing and moving forward to the new place that the Lord wants to reveal in our lives.

Thy Kingdom Come

Colossians 1:16,17: **For by Him all things were created that are in heaven and that are on earth, visible, and invisible, whether thrones or dominions or principalities or powers. All things were created through Him and for Him. And He is before all things, and in Him all things consist.**

Do you recall the prayer that the Lord taught His disciples in Matthew 6:9–13 and Luke 11:2–4? Many call this the Lord's Prayer, though Jesus would not have to pray a prayer regarding being forgiven of sins or trespasses because He was free from all sin, although He was tempted in all points as we are. He shared these words for the sake of His followers in order for us to pray in a manner that was in agreement with the Kingdom of heaven. Part of the prayer specifically states, "Thy Kingdom come, Thy will be done in earth as it is in heaven." That's the part that we will explore a little here.

We know that our triune God alone reigns in heaven. The Kingdom of God is manifested and reflected on earth through His people. When we consider the word *reign*, it connotes authority, dominion, or lordship. As has been stated in other chapters, you and I live in the midst of two kingdoms that coexist. Once we've been born again of the Spirit of God, we're 1) birthed into the Kingdom of God, 2) authorized to operated from that place or vantage point, 3) given the authority and permission to use the name of Christ, and 4) thus we bring His Kingdom and will into the earth realm as we operate in these privileges.

There is a reason and purpose for our existence and an eternal Source from which all things flow. God's word has made it very clear to us that we're not owners, but we have access to the One to whom everything belongs, and He has entrusted it all to us. Everything that we see here on the earth was created by God and for Him, including you and me. Our faith grows by filling ourselves with the word of God and subsequently allowing that word to freely manifest in and through our lives. Now, all of that is nothing more than empty words on a page until we can learn to trust the Lord through our life experiences and watch Him fulfill his promises to us.

In the West, we've had things so good for so long until most of us never speak of what it means to even need faith the size of a grain mustard seed. Men and women seem to prosper, are exalted, are given status, recognition, and fame because of the money that they possess or the things that money can buy. All of this can serve to bind us to a world system that seeks to cloud our vision of God since all of us want to prosper and do well as we traverse through this life. The message of the church can very easily become one that is rooted in ways to prosper financially, ways to obtain material things, and all while using the same context that our God owns everything and therefore we should have access to all of this world's riches without limits. Let's take a look at how we have been abundantly blessed as we operate from a Kingdom perspective, position, and mindset.

Access to the Kingdom gives us authority— Kingdom Authority.

The word *King* relates to *dominion*, which speaks of the King's authority and power, while the word *Lord* relates to *domain*, which speaks of territory, property, geographical area over which his authority extends. Our God is King of Kings and Lord of Lords. Our authority has been delegated by God.

Scripture tells us that the thief (the enemy, Satan) cometh not but for to steal, to kill, and to destroy. His task is to blind you to your authority, make you doubt your authority, or strip you of your authority. Why would he do this? Plain and simple: you won't seek to use what you don't think or know that you have.

We tend to sum up our worth and ability based on what we know of ourselves from the world system that we've operated in for the majority of our lives, and that summation is a fallacy. We are operating within an earthly system while seeking to fulfill Kingdom

business, and those earthly or worldly customs and mannerisms that have become second nature to us must now be placed under subjection to Kingdom Authority that reigns in our lives.

As we pray for God's Kingdom to come and His will to be done on this earth, God is calling His people out of systems and methodologies that do not line up with the Kingdom of God. The existence of systems and religious structures is nothing new. When Jesus came on the scene, He was thrust into opposition from an existing religious *system*. He was constantly dealing with the religious figures of that time who were keen on telling Him what could and could not be done according to the system that was in place. He was and is the One who is the answer to all that men have ever searched for, all that men have longed for, waited for, and yet there He was right before them and they were rejecting Him. Why? Simply because He wasn't doing things according to the system, the world system. Jesus came and basically told them that everything that the system had spoken of and had attempted to lead them to and to help them to acquire could only be found in Him. He taught that everything that this world offers, although pleasurable on many levels, is only temporary and will endure but for a season. They wanted Him to overpower their natural enemies and to cause them to triumph over fleshly oppressors in order to prove that He was the long-awaited Messiah. Christ, on the other hand, consistently taught about a Kingdom that brings victory over powers and principalities that seek to destroy the lives of men and women now and for all of eternity. He promised abundant and eternal life. This was indeed different from everything that the system of the world could provide.

The same is true today. All that we desire and aspire to achieve for our lives and the good of this world is found in none other than the Lord Jesus Christ. Herein lies the distinction between the operation and focus of systems and the direction, power, and movement of the Holy Spirit on the earth. He gave to every believer the ministry and message of reconciliation. This is why Jesus taught His disciples, including us, to pray, "Thy Kingdom come, Thy will be done on earth as it is in heaven." How is it to be done? Through the child of God who lives and walks in the earth realm with the resident power of the true and living God on the inside of him or her.

We have authority to preach and teach the word of God. We have authority in prayer to agree with heaven and to intercede on behalf of others. As children of God, we have the authority to lay hands on the sick and to believe that they will recover. We have the authority to say no to the urges and desires that satisfy our flesh. Agreement with Christ's completed work by faith gives us the authority to operate from the position of the Kingdom. As we are submitted under Kingdom Authority, we have the power to live above our circumstances rather than beneath them and to resist condemnation from the life of bondage from which we have been delivered. This is greater than your role on your job as a supervisor, unit manager, director, president of the company, or president of the nation, although that is earthly authority and we respect all authority, for it is from God. What we speak specifically of is Kingdom Authority!

Don't be deceived by what it looks like in the media or in prominent social circles. This world is in trouble, and the real stabilizing force is the much-forgotten and pushed-aside voice of the intercessors who cry out to the Lord day and night around this world for the needs of the nations, our leaders, communities, churches, and families. Never underestimate the power of prayer! Through prayer we take authority over the works of the enemy and make way for the Kingdom of God to manifest in the earth. Prayer gives access to heaven.

Resist systems or organizations that present as the church but place little to no emphasis on prayer, the need for much prayer, and the power of prayer to change lives and circumstances. God is moving and orchestrating the next move of His church, and He wants to be at liberty to do whatever He chooses in and through His people. The word of God is very clear in John 15 that He is the Vine and we are the branches. Without Him, we can do nothing! That literally means that we can do *no thing*.

When we talk about bringing the Kingdom of heaven into the earth realm, we must understand that God is calling us out of our comfort zone and into places that cause us to rely on the power of God to do what we are unable to do on our own. Now is the time to recognize the need for Kingdom work and Kingdom Authority.

When Jesus walked the earth, He told those who would give ear to Him that the Kingdom of God was now among them. Access to the Kingdom of God gives us access to the authority that Jesus walked in. Access to the Kingdom of God brings order, for there is order in God's Kingdom. The Kingdom of God is not a democracy; it is a theocracy. The order of things for those called by the Name of the Lord is that we seek first the Kingdom of God and His righteousness ... first things first. The question is, why are we not seeing this more in the everyday lives of believers? There are so many who desire a closer walk and more intimate relationship with the King.

I will submit that there is disorder in many of our lives because we have failed to seek the Kingdom first and have decided to do what looked best to us regarding areas in our lives, not just spiritual areas but natural areas as well.

We've purchased homes, bought cars, taken jobs, entered into relationships oftentimes without seeking the counsel of God. You might say, "Why is that important?" The steps of a good man are ordered by the Lord. The order is God first, not my will first, after which I then carry my will to God in order for Him to fulfill it or to bless it. That's out of order! God has an agenda and a plan. This is why we are to seek Him. Following His plan will always set things in order in our lives. Kingdom order recognizes that He must speak first. He must give direction first. He must approve first—not me, not you, not this worldly system. His word brings order that overrides systems, religious practices, and false teachings that cause us to walk in a way that is apart from the move of God and totally out of order and out of sync with the rhythm of the Kingdom. We have the authority to come against our own inclinations to become presumptuous and to take matters into our own hands concerning our lives, concerning the ministries that we've been entrusted with, and concerning the church.

How dare we become entrenched in a system that would divert us from the course of fulfilling God's good plan for our lives and for the lives of those to whom we are connected! No, the stakes are too high! It's time for the true church to stand up and take its place in the midst of the kingdom of this world, this world system, and begin to operate as those who have Kingdom authority over the powers, principalities, and forces that are at work all around us.

It's not ours to decide. We don't get to decide how, when, or where we will be used. We have no control over how the Lord will manifest His plan through us as we move to bring the Kingdom here on the earth.

So I ask, whose agenda are you carrying out? When Jesus came, He shared with others that His Father had an agenda. He said, "My will is to do the will of Him who sent me" (John 6:38). In other words, "I'm not here on my own agenda, but somebody sent me and I'm here to carry out His agenda." In John 4:34 Jesus said, "My meat is to do the will of Him who sent me," and that same verse in the New Living Translation says, "My nourishment is to do the will of Him who sent me." Can you imagine what your life and my life would be like if we thought about the will of God in this way? If we thought about the will of God as our meat and our nourishment, nothing would ever be able to come close to distracting or deterring us from doing His will. That's how it was for Jesus. He was the Kingdom personified. He let the disciples know that the Kingdom would be in them after His return to the Father. He let them know that He was with them for a season but the time would come when He would be in them through the Holy Ghost.

Kingdom access brings blessing and favor. When the Kingdom has priority, we don't chase things, things chase us, so the blessings of God overtake us. The last part of the scripture that says "Seek ye first the Kingdom of God" ends by stating, "and all these things will be added unto you" (Matt. 6:33). That's powerful! The world system teaches us to chase things, to be identified by things and possessions by becoming captive to the currency that controls the world—money. The currency that controls the Kingdom is faith, and faith will give us access to what money can never buy. We can't buy audience and time in the presence of the Creator of the universe; we can't buy this opportunity that we have to partner with the Spirit of God in ministry so that His power can be revealed in and through us. Eternal life can't be purchased, but it can only be obtained through faith. Faith has opened many doors of blessing and deliverance that no man can shut. This list could go on and on. Faith moves heaven, and without faith, it doesn't matter how much money we have—it's impossible to please God. Our faith brings heaven to earth and causes the hand of God to move in our situations. Our faith carries us into the presence of God, where we find that communion with Him brings order and peace. This is a peace not as the world gives but an ability to live and walk in the peace of the Savior even in the midst of adversity and storms. We must know why we're here. We can never afford to lose sight of the fact that it is the resident power of God in His people that is sustaining this world and preventing total destruction.

Jesus knew why He came, and nothing could distract Him or deter Him from accomplishing the will of the Father that He was sent to do on the earth. The coming of the Kingdom is delayed because the people of God are so distracted. We must pray and agree with heaven for the return of our King soon. We must pray for His will and His work to manifest in this earth as it is done in heaven.

Jesus's life reflected order.

- ➢ **He didn't step into ministry before His time,**
- ➢ **He didn't reveal who He was before the right time,**
- ➢ **He died on time,**
- ➢ **He was resurrected on time, and**
- ➢ **He's returning on time and just in time.**

So likewise for the church, we are to carry out the plan and purpose of our Lord and our King as our first priority.

He has a set time for the things that He is accomplishing in our lives. We are ambassadors, and we must follow His Kingdom agenda.

Let His Kingdom come, let His will be done on earth as it is in heaven, and let it start with us.

Prayer: Our Father, who art in heaven, hallowed be thy name; Thy kingdom come; Thy will be done on earth as it is in heaven. Give us this day our daily bread; and forgive us our trespasses as we forgive those who trespass against us; and lead us not into temptation, but deliver us from evil. For Thine is the Kingdom and the power and the glory forever. Amen. (Matt. 6:9–13)

Chosen and Sent

Do you realize that God chose us before the world was even formed? That's what Ephesians 1:4 tells us. He chose us first. Thank God that we can have confidence in the fact that He has chosen us and it is He who has sent us forth into this world. Jesus was sent from God the Father and willingly came so that we, through him, could enjoy an abundant life here and eternal life to come.

The Apostle Paul made it quite clear in the letters that he wrote to various churches that his calling and appointment had come from God and not by the choice or will of man. In practically each of his letters from the book of Romans to Philemon, Paul typically starts his letters by clearly stating that his authority and calling are not of himself, nor are they of man. He uses such statements as: "Paul, a servant of Jesus Christ, called to be an apostle, separated unto the Gospel of God; Paul, called to be an apostle of Jesus Christ through the will of God; Paul, an apostle, (not of men, neither by man, but by Jesus Christ, and God the Father, who raised him from the dead); Paul, an apostle of Jesus Christ by the commandment of God our Saviour, and the Lord Jesus Christ, which is our hope; Paul an apostle of Jesus Christ by the will of God, according to the promise of life which is in Christ Jesus; Paul, a servant of God, and an apostle of Jesus Christ, according to the faith of God's elect, and acknowledging of the truth which is after godliness; and Paul a prisoner of Jesus Christ."

He knew that many did not accept him or his ministry because of the fact that he had persecuted the church prior to his conversion. He actually thought that he was doing the will of God and that those who were a part of "the Way" (the name initially given to those who followed Christ) were the ones outside of God's will. The reality was that God had chosen him for great works before the world was formed, and it was only a matter of time before Paul would have a life-changing experience with the true and living God on the Damascus road. It may seem that Paul, in his writings, was reminding others of his appointment from and by God, but on some level, I'm inclined to believe that his salutations also served as a reminder to himself. The constant reminder, no doubt, fueled his faith and gave him the boldness that he needed in order to address the needs of the brethren and churches for which he was responsible.

Paul suffered many things, yet his life is a powerful testament to the fact that our past doesn't dictate our future. We may have done horrible things, shameful things that people have a hard time forgetting or that we sometimes find hard to move past, but we must constantly remind ourselves that it is the Lord who has chosen us. Furthermore, it is He who has sent us to do a work for Him on the earth.

Acceptance by the masses is not the test as to whether or not the Lord has sent us. We can't rely on the reactions of people as a measure of our appointment from God, for we are reminded of John 1:11, which states, "He came unto His own and His own received Him not," yet He was sent. So the litmus test for us is not acceptance. Jesus was certainly rejected, but because He was sent, He had to remain focused on the work that He was sent to do. Although we are being sent forth as sheep among wolves, God is with us, and more than that, He is for us. We are not to fear.

What do we need to understand as those who have been chosen and sent? We've already established that, as believers, we have been chosen by God just as every disciple who we read about in the Bible was chosen. It is the call of God that draws and brings men and women to Him, not just a thought or decision that we make at any given point in time. The decision that individuals make regarding the surrender of their lives to the Lord is really a response to the love that He has extended and shown toward us. He loved us first and He calls us to respond to His purpose for our lives. We have a choice.

As Christians we all have a life that we lived before coming to Christ, no matter how young or old we were when we accepted Him as our Savior. None of us was born saved. None of us have been Christians for our entire lives as I've heard some say, and maybe you've heard that too. You may have heard someone say, "I was born a Christian." This is simply not true because just as Jesus told Nicodemus in St. John chapter 3, all of us have to be born again, meaning born from above, born of God. Nicodemus was a Pharisee, and Jesus's response to him was terminology that had deep meaning for him since the teaching of the Pharisees was natural generation or acceptance by God through Abraham. Jesus, on the other hand, taught that there had to be spiritual generation from God regardless of our natural lineage or connections. We all come to this life through natural birth, "born of water," but then we must be born again, born of the Spirit of God (John 3:5,6), in order to claim salvation through Christ and to live pleasing lives unto God.

Jesus came to mankind and lived as a man so that we could all have direct access to God. Jesus's disciples are now sent forth into the world, all over the world, in order to carry out His work through the power of the Holy Spirit, who is our Guide. What's sometimes challenging is that our history, or our past, always seeks to hold us hostage. The enemy will always try to use our past to obscure our future. This can be one of the greatest hindrances to those who desire a close and effective walk with the Lord. There are accounts in the Bible, and many of us have our own testimonies today, of how the enemy continues to taunt us with the things that we've done, the horrible errors that we've made while in our sinful state before we accepted Christ.

That's one side of the coin, but the other side is those who think that they've lived a good life and have basically done nothing that would be considered terribly wrong. They see themselves as morally good people. This mindset is just as bad because it's prideful and arrogant, lending to confidence in self rather than confidence in God. No matter what our past may look like, the good news is that our past does not disqualify us from our future! If anything, our past is a testament to the grace and power of God at work in us. The Lord uses these marred and flawed vessels (our bodies) to exhibit His glory so that there can be no question that the "power is of God and not of us" (2 Cor. 4:7).

We have been made heirs and joint heirs with Christ, and we have to take on that identity and walk in it if we truly desire to experience the anointing and power of God. Otherwise we will always be held captive by our past, and that is not the plan of God for any of His children. So how do we pull this off the written pages of the Bible and begin to live in a way that reflects our freedom, victory, and newness in Him?

Well, we know that our minds definitely have to be renewed. That's the only way that we can begin to understand our worth and purpose as children of God. If we refuse to go through the process of transformation and renewal, we will continue to live far beneath our privileges as children of God.

I can recall how different it was for me when I joined the military. There were certain things that were required of us as new troops in the Air Force, and we were no longer able to govern our daily lives the way that we may have been accustomed to doing before taking the military oath. It didn't matter where any of us had come from before we arrived at Lackland Air Force Base for basic training, how much money we had, what our parents' last name was, or if our civilian wardrobe consisted of only designer clothes. When we arrived at Lackland and were assigned to our squadron, everyone was issued the same type of clothing and we were told what time we would be getting up, when we would eat, and when we would go to bed. Like it or not, that was the deal. This was our new lifestyle. I actually enjoyed the disciplined, regimented lifestyle that came with being in the air force. Little did I realize that I was being transformed from being governed by a civilian mentality to having the mindset of a soldier and all that comes with it.

Now you may be asking what this has to do with having a renewed mind or living a Christian life. Everything that a new enlistee learns during military basic training is about learning the new life that they've now become a part of. Being military means learning what the expectations are and gaining knowledge of the military way of life after having lived as a civilian for so many years. The soldier has to become trained and skilled in tactics and weaponry that he or she may have no prior knowledge of in order to survive the constant threat of being confronted or attacked by enemy forces that one may not have even known existed.

As new recruits, we were all flooded with so much new information over the course of six weeks, and it was a total eye-opener. Although many others had been enlisted and may have shared their stories with me before I made the decision, I soon found out that every experience is unique, although we all made a choice to become subject to the demands of the armed forces. Each of us as recruits had to understand that for all intents and purposes, our lives were no longer our own. During basic training, we soon learned what it meant to function as a unit, and above all, we had to quickly come to the realization that our private/personal agendas had no place among our ranks, because above all, mission comes first. The military member must have the mission at the top of his or her agenda. We had to recognize that we represented the military at all times whether in or out of uniform. Our lives were governed by the Uniform Code of Military Justice (UCMJ).

Needless to say, many didn't make it through the rigorous training—the long, tiring days of marching in formation, shining shoes, preparing our uniforms for inspection, and scrubbing down the latrines (bathrooms). Some just could not or would not endure the necessary transition from the civilian world to that of the military. It's a totally different mindset that leads to an entirely different perspective and way of life. Although it may be easy to lose sight of the depth of one's commitment during times of peace, the military member must be willing to put him- or herself in harm's way in order to protect this country and those civilians who would remain behind when or if there was a deployment for war.

I used the military as an example because within the ranks there are those who are there simply to have a steady job, income, and the assurance of a decent place for their family to live. Some joined due to a promise to "see the world," and others joined to obtain an education and training for better opportunities outside of the military after completion of their tenure. Within all of the foregoing reasons for enlistment lie various levels of commitment to country and service. All of this and more is represented within the ranks, and they all work together to fulfill the mission.

I certainly don't mean to make light of the transition to a new life in Christ by using my experience with the military as an example. The journey that leads us to Christ is so personal and looks so different for each of us, yet the ultimate outcome of surrender to Him is new birth into a totally different Kingdom, the Kingdom of God. We must learn to operate within that Kingdom, and although all of the physical characteristics and things around us are the same after we commit our lives to Christ, spiritually all things have become new (2 Cor. 5:17).

You will find that this scripture in 2 Corinthians 5:17 is cited in several chapters simply because I believe that it's such a foundational truth if we are ever to walk in the liberty of Christ. It bears repeating numerous times in order to get it settled in our hearts, minds, and spirits. The scripture is very clear that *all* things have become new when we're in Christ, and that has nothing whatsoever to do with how we might feel or look.

In my first book, *Essentials for Frontline Living*, I wrote about two kingdoms that coexist and how each of us who comes to Christ must learn to operate within the

Kingdom of God just as we had to learn how to operate in this natural world into which each of us was born. Being born of the Spirit brings transformation and the wonderful process of obtaining a "renewed" mind, which is only possible by the power and help of the Holy Spirit. It's not just a changed mind, something that we do of our own volition or "willpower," but we must be fed, taught, and guided as we grow in the knowledge of Christ through His word, the Bible.

Many people accept the Lord as their Savior but never allow Him to be Lord of their lives. Another chapter within *Essentials for Frontline Living*, is a chapter titled "His Name Shall Be Called." That chapter speaks about the different aspects of knowing Christ. He can be the Savior, yet He wants to be so much more to each of us. We can build on our relationship as we get to know Him as Healer, Provider, Protector, Friend, Confidant, Counselor, Our Peace, and much, much more. This simply speaks to the fact that the Lord wants us to get to know Him, to commune with Him, and to depend on Him. Each of us can enjoy an intimate relationship with Him, but not unlike any other relationship, we must do our part to build it, to sustain it, and to protect it.

The comparison of the life of the Christian as a soldier or one in warfare is also very real. Our spiritual enemy, Satan (the devil), is not a myth or a fictional character made up to scare people into doing good. The Bible speaks clearly of him, and the reality is that he is consistently waging war against us on all fronts while he enlists men and women to join forces with him against the cause of Christ in the earth. I can recall someone making a statement in one of my graduate classes that the devil is not real and that he isn't mentioned in the Bible. I knew immediately that this person was not familiar with scripture, because the Bible clearly states in 1 Peter 5:8 (NKJV): "Be sober, be vigilant; because your adversary the devil walks about as a roaring lion, seeking whom he may devour." In other passages, he is referred to as our enemy. The only way that we can resist him is by remaining steadfast in the faith.

Many are used and manipulated by the enemy unknowingly, but others join his forces willfully. In her book *He Came to Set the Captives Free* , Dr. Rebecca Brown shares how she "served her master, Satan, with total commitment" before devoting her life to the Lord Jesus Christ. Hers is a powerful account of the saving and delivering power of God. The spirit realm is real, and the enemy fights hard to keep us blinded to the fact that there is just as much or more activity within the spirit realm that we don't see as there is in the natural realm where we consciously operate. The Lord wants us to be keenly aware of the devices of the enemy, as we can be exposed to the occult and spirits of darkness unknowingly.

One summer during my teens years, I went to visit an aunt and uncle in Ohio. One day they took me to another relative's home, where guests were gathering, laughing, talking, and eating, which is usually what families do when they gather. At some point during the gathering, a young lady who was older than me (she was maybe in her late twenties or early thirties and I was around fifteen or sixteen years old) invited me to come with her to a room that was like a loft in the house so that she could show me something.

We made our way upstairs, and when we got there, a gentleman was already there and seated on the floor. We all sat on the floor with our legs crossed in crisscross style. I soon noticed that one of the man's hands was very small. After introductions were made, I was asked if I had any idea why one of his hands was smaller than the other. I stated that I didn't. Before proceeding to tell me the reason, they began to tell me that they could see a man in the town where I was from and that this man walked through the streets with a horse and that he seemed to have mental health issues. I immediately knew who this person was and was now intrigued by what I was hearing, because I had never been exposed to such. No doubt, they could tell that I was now interested and open to hear more. I wasn't saved and certainly had no understanding of the operations in the spirit realm. They proceeded to tell me that the man's hand was small due to something that he had done involving theft in his past life. The conversation went on with the use of cards and explanations regarding past lives and having to experience "do-overs" as a result of our past experiences.

Little did I know that this was an open door to the spirit realm that would have to be closed with much prayer and the help of seasoned believers later in life. I made no connection at all. There had also been innocent play with Ouija boards and deep connections with horoscopes, which is nothing more than worship of stars and constellations and trusting in their alignments, etc. As I look back, the loft experience was one of many experiences when I interacted with the opposing spirit realm in total ignorance, and this happens to many every day.

The word of God explicitly states that if Christians hide or veil the gospel, it is hidden to those who are lost. When we are lost, we are at a total disadvantage because the god of this world, Satan, also called the god of this age, has blinded the minds of those who don't believe. He does that in an attempt to keep us from gaining the knowledge of the saving power of Jesus Christ. He does that so that the glorious light of Christ will not have entry into our hearts (2 Cor. 4:3,4). In Ephesians 1:18, Paul states his desire that the eyes of our understanding would be enlightened. Paul's earnest desire and prayer was that the Father of glory would give us the spirit of wisdom and revelation in our knowledge of Him. He could identify with the necessity of having the eyes of our understanding enlightened as he called to remembrance with each letter that he penned that it was God Himself who had called him, set him apart, and anointed and equipped him for the calling that had been placed upon his life in spite of himself or the opinions of others.

Before we come to Christ, we walk in darkness and are not aware of the spiritual warfare that goes on around us on a daily basis. We war with carnal weapons of hatred, malice, racism, grudges, knives, guns, and on and on. We may find ourselves acting out whatever evil our fleshly minds can bring up to give us the satisfaction of retaliating and getting revenge on others as we settle scores that come against our egos. Although many of us may feel like this doesn't describe us at all, the reality is that the root of all of this, which is sin, lies within each of us, and we are all susceptible to doing things that displease God and that hurt one another. If we never *did* anything at all, the fact remains that each of us was born in sin and shaped in iniquity, and therefore we have no access to God on our own.

But thanks be to God, who gives us the victory through our Lord Jesus Christ (1 Cor. 15:57). As children of God, we walk in victory, and God has equipped us with spiritual armor for the warfare that we must face. Scripture reminds us that the weapons of our warfare are not carnal (not fleshly) but *mighty through God* to the pulling down of strongholds (2 Cor. 10:4). It is needful that we are reminded of this because the issues that we face on a daily basis are not unlike those that countless others have to confront. There are concerns, hardships, injustices, and personal battles that cause us to sometimes want to retaliate from a place of hurt and disappointment with the world around us and the systems that govern it. That is not to say that we simply stand back and take the position of praying and doing nothing except waiting for God to change things. No! We definitely pray in all circumstances, and then we allow the Holy Spirit to lead us regarding strategies and actions to take that will bring about change in our personal lives, our communities of worship, our cities, our government, and beyond.

The children of God are change agents on the earth. When Jesus taught His disciples to pray "Thy Kingdom come, Thy will be done on earth," that was for a reason. The Kingdom of God can only be revealed in the earth realm through His people, His chosen people who have decided to agree with heaven and to operate at His command. We must come to grips with the fact that we have been chosen and sent for a purpose. It is imperative that we align closely with churches, fellowships, and Christians who believe the Bible without reservation. This may seem like it doesn't even need to be said, but there are so many who have dissected the word of God to the extent that they hardly believe anything that is written; therefore they are powerless and far removed from being doers of the word. How can we be doers of a word that we don't even believe? Do we believe in the God who still saves, delivers, heals, changes lives, fills, and empowers by His Spirit? This is the God of the Bible. He does not change.

Yes, my brother, my sister, we are now under totally new leadership and authority. The Bible speaks of those who live apart from Christ or who resist His plan and purpose for their lives as "children of disobedience." We all governed ourselves that way before coming to Christ. If we're honest, the fact that we know that we've been chosen, set apart, and sent doesn't keep us from still trying to live according to our own rules, plans, and agendas. Unlike when our parents or the military called the shots in and for our lives, we must now submit and bring our stubborn wills under subjection to a much higher authority.

The Kingdom of God is not a democracy but a theocracy where God alone reigns and Jesus is Lord whether or not we choose to allow Him to be Lord over our lives. In order to fulfill His plan and purpose, we must trust Him and know that every thought and plan He has for us is always good and never evil. His plan is always designed to bring us to an expected end.

We all serve Him within the Kingdom in different capacities, but none of us is any less important than the other in His eyes. God's word lets us know that each of us is precious and so necessary to His plan. Resist the temptation to compare yourself to others, as this will impede your growth and your progress toward the unique purpose that has been carved out for you. Remember that no one is without challenges. I'm sure that we've heard many times from many sources that the need is for us to see challenges from a positive perspective. Challenges help to strengthen us because with the challenge comes some form of resistance, and when we deal with the resistance and don't back away or avoid it, it will build us and it becomes less of a challenge than it seemed to be at the outset. We've sometimes counted ourselves out because of our age, our race, our level of education, our handicaps (real or imagined), our past mistakes, our marital status, our gender ... Do I need to go on? I think that you get the picture. The problem is that none of this matters to God. He called us in spite of all or any of these things that we may contend with as challenges. He has chosen us in spite of ourselves, and His word calls us more than conquerors! It's so important that we remember that *it's through Christ* that we can do all things, *it's through Him* that we find strength to persevere, *it's through Him* that we pull down strongholds that the enemy sends against us! Our weapons are supernatural, not carnal, and they are mighty *through God* to the pulling down of strongholds. Any challenge that we face is designed to make us, not to break us. That sounds cliché, but it's true. The Lord is glorified when we decide to live our best lives in spite of the challenges that present themselves along the way.

Since the Lord has chosen us and has sent us forth on the earth to effect change, let's agree with His word; let's say what the word says about our God, about our Savior, about us, and about the power that we've been given to exemplify His Kingdom here on earth for this appointed time. In order to pull from the written pages, you and I may have to do exactly what Paul did before taking on any task that is set before us. Before he addressed people who were connected to the ministries where he was sent, he put everyone on notice that someone greater than himself had placed him on the path that he was on. He did what he did not by the will of man but because of the will and power of God. It's no different for us. Remind yourself of this fact daily if you have to. This is how the word will become a reality in your life. You did not call yourself, but the Lord Himself called you, set you apart, and has sent you to this world. Dare to make a positive difference while you're here! We're now soldiers in the army of the Lord, and the command is always to move forward and never to retreat.

Prayer: Lord, thank you for choosing me even before the foundation of the world. What a privilege to be sent forth into this world as Your ambassador, carrying Your Name, Your will, and sharing Your message wherever I go. Forgive me for the times that I have placed my agenda before Yours. I am determined to follow Kingdom agenda as You lead me by Your Spirit so that you are reflected in all that I do and say. Help me to be keenly aware of the tactics of the enemy and to walk in keen discernment regarding the voice of Your Spirit with a quickness and readiness to always obey. In Jesus's Name I pray. Amen.

God Always Had/Has You in Mind

Stop what you're doing and take time to consider this thought. God has always had you in mind, and not a day goes by that He isn't concerned about you, thinking of you, and planning ways to bless and enrich your life. Think of that. Let that sink in for a moment. I know that someone reading this may say, "Well, it certainly doesn't seem like God is concerned about me as I consider all that I'm dealing with in my life right now." But in spite of what we may deal with on a day-to-day basis, we're able to handle it and go through it and withstand it because we know that He is causing everything to work for our good. His thoughts toward us are always good and never evil. The passage of scripture in Jeremiah 29:11 was not just for Jeremiah but for each one of God's children. He thinks good thoughts toward us and is constantly leading us and pulling us toward an expected end.

Let's take a fresh look at Jeremiah 29:11. The Amplified Version reads, "For I know the plans *and* thoughts that I have for you,' says the LORD, 'plans for peace *and* well-being and not for disaster, to give you a future and a hope."' The New King James Version reads, "'For I know the thoughts that I think toward you,' says the LORD, 'thoughts of peace and not of evil, to give you a future and a hope.'" And the New International Version reads, "'For I know the **plans** I have for you,' declares the Lord, '**plans** to prosper you and not to harm you, **plans** to give you hope and a future.'" All of these versions of the same scripture speak of thoughts and plans, and as we note in the NIV version, *plans* is repeated three times. Just the fact that it is repeated is something that warrants our attention, but the other thing that we must note is that the word is plural. God doesn't just have *a plan* for us, He didn't just have *a plan* for Jeremiah, but He had and has **plans!**

God is always working a plan, a good plan for our lives, and we're in His **thoughts**, innumerable thoughts daily. That is simply mind-blowing! Every single plan, every single thought, is good and not evil with the intent to bring us to an expected end. God has declared that His purpose, plans, and thoughts are all about peace, ensuring that we have hope and a future. How many people give up on life because they just lose hope? That could look so different if people only knew that there is a Creator who has always had us in mind and His will for our lives is that we have hope and a future.

Think about people who lose hope. They have no joy, no reason to get up in the morning, no song in their heart, no ability to dream and see beyond the moment. They are miserable. They're miserable because that's not the way that God intended for us to live. He wants us to find joy in the truth of His word that no matter what we're facing, our circumstances have to work for our good when we love the Lord and are called according to His purpose (Rom. 8:28). Yes, there are times when bad things happen to good people, but it's during those times that the word of God allows those who know Him to rise above their bad circumstances with a lifeline called hope and to continue to look toward better outcomes. They have the understanding that no matter how dark it may seem, things won't always be like this. Things don't always remain the same. Without hope it's almost impossible to see or understand this perspective. Hope gives us the will to live and to survive in the midst of the most difficult times!

Many of us can attest to times in our lives when everything seemed so rotten, so horrible, but just when we would have thrown in the towel and walked away, somehow our circumstances began to change. We could see a glimmer of light at the end of the tunnel. That's what hope does for us. It causes us to hold on, keep pushing, keep believing that things can get better and that they can change for us. Hope for a better day is what causes us to get up when our desire is to pull the covers over our heads and not face the dawning of another day with the expectations of others that we will somehow participate and be a part of this thing called life.

My friend, we need hope. It is fueled by our faith. Faith is what gives substance to those things that we hope for but can't yet see, touch, or experience in this physical realm. "Now faith is the substance of things hoped for, the evidence of things not seen" (Heb. 11:1, NKJV). The NIV states it like this:, "Now faith is being sure of what we hope for and certain of what we do not see." We have to pull this truth off the pages of God's word and begin to live it, applying it to our lives when times get tough and our outlook is bleak. Refuse to lose hope. Hope in God with all of your heart and let faith arise within you until you can begin to see beyond what your natural eyes can see. It's then that you'll find yourself getting to the point where you can almost reach out and touch what you hope for before it manifests in the physical realm. This is faith at work! This is faith giving substance to what we hope for and evidence to what we have believed and trusted in based solely on what God has said because His word is sure and He cannot lie.

What is important to understand and grasp here is that the word of God becomes a reality, or comes alive, in our personal lives not when we walk around quoting scriptures all the time but when those circumstances, situations, tests, and trials of life come our way and the Lord steps in to prove that He will show up for us just as He did for those whom we read about in the Bible. We'll all be faced with situations and circumstances in this life that we just don't understand, that make no earthly sense. In those times, we're being pressed and our faith is being tested in order to stretch us to a place in our relationship where we will simply trust and dare to respond to others and life's situations in ways that reflect the strength and power of the word of God, not our own. The Lord wants to manifest Himself in our lives in such a way that we and those around us can attest to the fact that the power that is at work in our lives is of God and not of us.

2 Corinthians 4:7 reads, "But we have this treasure in earthen vessels, that the excellence of the power may be of God and not of us." That treasure (the precious Holy Spirit) within these vessels of clay (our bodies) reveals the power of God in our everyday lives. Perhaps you're able to profess along with me that there's no way that I could have withstood that struggle that I went through with my health, in my marriage, with my children, on my job … but for God! He revealed Himself in and through me, and now I know, and those around me must surely know, that the power is of God and not of me.

You see, it doesn't require much faith to live a "religious" life; however, when we choose to live a Spirit-led life that is guided by the Spirit of God, this will place a demand on our faith and on a strength that goes beyond our natural capacity. If we are not walking after the Spirit and seeking a more intimate relationship with the Lord, we will gravitate toward the works of the flesh and find ourselves carrying out the dictates of our minds and our own will.

God had you in mind when He set you apart before you were born. He had you in mind when you were a child, a youth, a young adult, and found yourself in situations that were extremely dangerous or could have proven deadly. You were in His thoughts, and nothing about you is a mistake. He has you in mind now as His hand rests upon your life in order to favor you and to do what only He can do in and through your life. He's just looking for someone to trust Him. In these turbulent times when it seems that justice in the land is nowhere to be found, God is calling for His church to reflect His presence and character in the earth. You and I can operate in our gifts and callings with confidence that the Spirit of God will empower us to accomplish everything that God has given us to do.

I'm writing this book during a pandemic known as COVID-19, and what we have known as "normal" in our lives and in the world before this time just doesn't exist anymore. Those who are living through this time when we are affected on all fronts by COVID-19 can attest to the fact that God has called His people outside of the four walls of the physical church. That has been a comfort zone for the people of God. Of course, we know that the true church has no walls, for it exists in God's people.

The effects of this pandemic have reached so many facets of my life, and some days I'm really left without words as I feel helpless to do anything of significance in order to bring an end to the senseless tragedies that play out before our eyes day after day. Many of us have been ill, have had loved ones who have become ill with COVID, and some have transitioned from this life. It has been a most trying time for everyone. I can personally say that my prayer life has become more focused during all of the calamity in our nation during COVID-19, the killing in our streets, the blatant attacks on men of color, and the divisive spirits among leaders.

In speaking with others, it has proven to be the same for many of them as well. For many of us, our focus has shifted. We're more in tune with what the Lord is saying and doing. We are aware that as the enemy becomes bolder in his acts of hatred and deception, the Spirit of the Living God is raising up an army of disciples who will say and do what the Spirit of the Lord is leading them to say and do in this critical hour. There is such a pull in the Spirit to seek the mind of God, His thoughts, and His plans because so much in our circumstances reflects division and hatred from the leaders of our nation as well as leaders within our communities whom we once thought we knew.

Someone candidly asked me, "Where are the leaders of the church in all of this? Why are they not speaking up?" I must admit that there were many days when I became very angry while watching the news come across my computer (this is where I basically read news and get headlines, as I don't watch much television). Like this person and others who asked me about the absence of the church, I too had become resentful of those who held positions within the community where their voices could be heard on a much broader scale, but they seemed to be content to remain silent. In order to release some of the pent-up anger, resentment, and hurt, I began to use my social media outlets to share thoughts of hope and the realness of pain with those who cared to listen. I found that many were feeling the same way. We maintained our faith, yet we grew desperate to see the hand of God sweep through our communities, our nation, and the world, which seemed to be growing more and more bold in displays of evil by the day.

The enemy's job is to make us lose sight of the fact that God is still in control and that He has never left us, nor will He ever leave us. He has us in mind! We're in His plan. There have been times when I've felt so frustrated and small. With all that is playing out around us within our communities, our society, and our world that is blatantly wrong and outright evil, sometimes we can feel helpless because we have no idea where to start or what to do in order to bring about change. Seize every opportunity to speak for right, for justice, and never be afraid to rebuke evil even when it comes from the highest natural power in the land. God is still greater! We must never allow the enemy to take our voice.

Use the platform that you've been given, wherever that might be and no matter how insignificant it may seem to you at the time. Continue to stand for what you know is right even in the midst of opposition and the atrocious acts of those who resist constitutionality. Coupled with all of this, my word to you is, *do not stop praying*! Prayer still works. We may not see the results right away, but whenever we pray, heaven is moving and God responds. He responds to our cry, your cry! I believe that if more Christians believed that, we would spend more time in prayer. The heart of the king is still in God's hand. That will *not* change!

Prayer: Lord, as many are focused on the invisible enemy of COVID-19 and the very visible enemies of systemic racism and hatred, we are keenly aware that You are still in control. By the power of Your Holy Spirit and faith in the Name of the Lord Jesus, we declare that Your plan will be carried out in the earth as it is in heaven. Let it begin in me. We rebuke, resist, and oppose every foul and contrary spirit that comes against the move of Your Spirit in the earth realm. We choose to walk by faith and not by sight, and we declare peace and deliverance over our nation and leaders in the Name of Jesus. Amen.

Inspiration Break

In 1 Samuel 8 we find the children of Israel going to Samuel after he had grown old, and they asked him to appoint a king over them to lead them, just as all of the other nations had. Their reasoning was that Samuel's sons were not following his ways and that they were following after dishonest gain, accepting bribes and perverted justice.

Samuel wasn't pleased with their request, so he prayed to the Lord. The Lord responded that Samuel should give the people what they were asking for because what they were doing in trying to be like other nations that had earthly kings was rejecting the Lord as their King. They were going to reap heavily because of this choice that they made.

There is murmuring and rhetoric among people today regarding the need to have a god who looks like us. The rhetoric says, "All other people have a god who looks like them, and we need a god who looks like us."

Who has seen God at any time? Jesus has revealed Him. The word of God declares that God is a Spirit and they who worship Him must worship Him in spirit and in truth.

The Lord is saying to His people that it's time to come back to Him in the spirit as man's dilemma is our need to look more like our God rather than to make Him look more like us. We are spirit beings having an earthly experience.

We see His image daily since mankind was created in the image of God. Do we esteem that image? Do we celebrate and appreciate that image and divine expression of our God that we can see, touch, and hold on any given day as we behold others who live among us?

I declare that from this day forward, you will begin to look like and reflect the image of your Spiritual Father and will operate more like the spiritual self that you were created to be. The Spirit of God will awaken a greater appreciation within you for those who reflect God's image around you. This doesn't always mean that they will present as lovable.

The Lord speaks to our spirits that we seek to make gods who look like us when we rebel against His requirement that we look like Him. This is the beginning of the decline of any people.

I declare that you are being conformed to the image of Christ daily in accordance with Romans 8: 29 (NKJV): "For whom He foreknew, He also predestined *to be* conformed to the image of His Son, that He might be the firstborn among many brethren."

A Life of Faith/Nothing Less

On this day as I begin to write, it's early evening and I'm thinking of a session that I took part in during the morning with a great man of faith, Apostle I.V. Hilliard. My senior pastor and bishop, Dr. Chad Carlton, had Apostle Hilliard to speak to leaders virtually during what we know as an ImPWR (pronounced "empower") session. Apostle Hilliard was called by God at the tender age of nine years and began to preach at the age of ten. Because of his faith walk, he is now able to pour into others and to share what it means to live by faith. He defined faith as believing, obeying, trusting, and glorifying God.

One thing that was pointed out in that session (and I don't intend to write this entire chapter about that session but about faith) was that each one of us already has what we need in order to see the miracle of God's plan manifested in our lives. We have it! Many times as I've shared the word of God, this passage of scripture in Psalm 119:105 will come up: "Thy word is a lamp unto my feet and a light unto my path." The Lord spoke to me years ago that "paths are designed to be walked upon." The path of our lives is illuminated as we go, as we move forward and trust God. We do not need a path to be illuminated that we refuse to walk upon because of our doubts, fears, or unbelief. By faith we must trust that the word of God will show us the way as we go. It will become a lamp unto our feet when we make the decision to go.

We are called to live a life of faith. It's a must. There is simply no other way that we can survive and live victoriously in this world apart from faith. Most of us don't even consider the fact that we use faith on a daily basis although it may not be directed toward God. At the end of one day, we may make plans for the next day because we have faith that we'll wake up the following morning. It's not guaranteed, yet we have faith that it is so, and I would venture to say that most of us don't lie down worrying about whether or not we'll wake up. We get into our cars or head to the bus station or train station with the expectation that at the end of a set amount of commute time, we will arrive at our jobs. It's not a guarantee, yet we have faith that we will get to our destinations as planned.

I could go on and on, but I'm sure that you get the understanding that all of these are simple acts of faith on our part. We have faith that something will happen, and we take action toward that. We make preparation for the next day, get up with our minds on what we believe lies ahead, check our wardrobe for clothes to wear, and determine the time to depart, and at the appointed time, off we go. For some, there may have been thoughts of God or a prayer spoken to Him during all of this routine, but whether that happened or not, there were acts of faith taking place from the time that we lay down to rest and throughout our waking hours. We exercise faith, but many times that faith isn't directed toward God. We have faith in a system of employment and trust people whom we may not even know to ensure that at the end of every week or two weeks, we will be paid as compensation for time that we have given to a job or service.

The word of God says that "the just (those who know God) shall live by faith." Furthermore, we know that without faith, it is impossible to please God. Here we're talking about an intentional and directed faith toward the Lord. We go through all of the same routines as others, yet our routines must include an acknowledgment of the Lord and an understanding that although I may have gone through this routine a thousand times, I can take nothing for granted. My faith in God causes me to thank Him at the close of the day because I know that today could have been my last. Upon waking, praise is in my mouth because I'm aware that this day was not promised and the alarm clock certainly could not be credited with waking me.

When we live by faith, we are still compelled to plan and to take necessary actions in order to be successful and fruitful throughout each day but always with the Lord at the center as the One who guides us and directs our paths. The Lord Himself has placed within His children that deep-seated desire to please Him and to do His will. Philippians 2:13 (NKJV) says: "For it is God who works in you both to will and to do for His good pleasure." He gives us both the desire and the ability to carry out His will for His good pleasure. Faith is the life of the believer because much of what we must grasp pertaining to the life that we now live for Christ is not revealed to our natural senses. Yet a faith walk is not something eerie or weird but a lifestyle that requires us to live with an expectation above and beyond what this world can offer.

You and I must always be mindful that we are not alone. We don't walk this walk alone. Jesus is still Emmanuel— God with us! One thing that I am sure of is that there is a remnant of God's people who believe in His supernatural power and who yearn for Him to be manifested in and through their lives. They want to be used and empowered for His glory and that alone. If you're one of them, then this chapter is for you!

Jesus did not leave us alone, but everywhere that we go, every step that we take, the Spirit of God, the Holy Spirit, is with us. God's plan is for us to be empowered by His Spirit, Whom He promised and gave to us as a Companion, Counselor, Guide, and One who would lead us into all truth after Jesus ascended back to heaven. Jesus did not leave us comfortless. We have Someone who has come to take up residence within us, is part of our daily affairs, and shares with us what He hears from the very throne room of God. What a blessing! The Holy Ghost/ Holy Spirit helps us as we seek to build our relationship with God our Father and with the Lord Jesus Christ. He will give us the desire and unction to pray while also leading us regarding what and whom to pray for according to the will of God.

By faith we trust the gentle nudging of the Spirit of God and we learn how He speaks to us and guides us. Each of us has a personal relationship with the Lord, and it's not the same as anyone else's relationship. You can listen to and read about the relationship that others have with the Lord and how they conduct their reading and study times, but be willing to develop what works for you in these areas. For instance, I've always set aside time to pray and spend time with the Lord, but that time of pulling away has certainly increased during the COVID-19 pandemic for many reasons.

Like many others, I pray for the sick, those in nursing homes, those who have lost loved ones, those who are living alone and can't have the company of friends as usual, etc. Well, just to share an example of how the Spirit of the Lord gives us promptings or unction, one afternoon when I went to my room to pray, I felt led to take out my cell phone and to pull up my list of Facebook friends. I said to the Lord, "I'm going to call out every name that I come across during this prayer time, and I ask that you would meet every need that they or their families might have." As I called out names, sometimes the Lord would have me pause and pray for their children, their spouses, their jobs, habits, their finances, and sometimes I would be able to simply call out the name and say, "Lord, please meet their needs." I didn't get through the entire friend list, of course, but that's just an example of ways that the Lord will lead us to be creative in our prayer time with Him. That situation is not an everyday occurrence but an example of how the Lord will lead us to move in ways that seem "out of the box" as we seek to have intimacy with Him.

Our church has 6:00 AM prayer via Facebook Live, and during the prayer segment, those joining the prayer often post prayer requests or needs. So typically after the prayer or later that evening, I will go back over the comments section and call out the prayer requests before the Lord along with the names of every person who came to the prayer line whether they placed a request there or not.

The reason that I'm sharing these instances with you is because I want you to consider that there are so many creative ways for us to build our life of faith and our relationship with the Lord on the road to becoming more sensitive to His Spirit. Think about things that you see or hear about in the news, whether they're relevant to our nation, world leaders, family violence, sex trafficking, or any number of things. Use those things to build your prayer time or study time. Make prayer time not only about talking and sharing what's in your heart to say, but make a practice of silence and anticipation for the Spirit of the Lord to share with you during your time of quiet and focused meditation. If your mind begins to wander, speak a word out loud or think of a word or words that will help you to regain focus, i.e., *deliverance, healing, Comforter*. Then pray as the Holy Spirit brings things/people/situations to your mind to pray for. This is how we pull those acts of faith from the written word and begin to see them become an active part of our own lives.

There is simply no way that we can walk a faith walk or attempt to live a faith-filled life without the Holy Spirit. We need Him! Otherwise the Lord would not have promised Him. He said in John 16:7, "Nevertheless I tell you the truth, it is to your advantage that I go away; for if I do not go away, the Helper (the Holy Spirit) will not come to you; but if I depart, I will send Him to you." The Holy Spirit is God in us. We are faced with spiritual warfare daily, and as spiritual forces come against us in our daily lives, we must be able to take hold of the word of God that reminds us that the weapons of our warfare are not carnal but they are mighty through God to the pulling down of strongholds. The only way that we pull down spiritual strongholds is through the Spirit. The scripture is not speaking of a natural or fleshly fight, and we're no match for our enemy without the mighty power of God that is at work in our lives. All of us face so many situations each day that could really lead to our destruction, but because of the fact that the Lord has placed His ministering angels around us and because His Holy Spirit guides us around pitfalls of the enemy, we're often not even aware of the dangers that are so close as we go about the normal course of our day.

You see, the Holy Spirit doesn't only bring power, but He *is* the power of our Christian walk. There's no way that a Christian can live a victorious life in Christ without the indwelling power of the Holy Ghost. That's the plan of Almighty God. Jesus told His disciples that He would no longer be with them but that He would be in them. Glory to God! Thank God for the Spirit of God who lives within the believer. That was God's plan for us from the very beginning.

The Lord is still moved by prayer and He is constantly looking for faith in the earth. The second part of Luke 18:8 says: "Nevertheless, when the Son of Man comes, will He really find faith on the earth?" The scripture doesn't say that he's coming back looking for those who are religious, those who can preach the best, or even those who have great names, titles, or positions. He is looking for faith because it's only faith that allows us to please Him, and it's only faith that causes His hand to move on the earth to change the circumstances of this world in which we live. It has always been praying men and women who have caused the Lord to bend low to the earth and to intervene in the affairs of man. The life of prayer and faith reflects relationship.

I once listened to an online lesson shared by Lion of Judah ministries regarding our ability to train our spirits to become more in tune with God. Just as we can train our bodies, we can train our minds and our spirits. My take-away from that lesson was that the real issue for most of us boils down to a lack of discipline rather than lack of time, which we often blame for our failure to complete many tasks or accomplishments. We train our spirits to recognize the voice of God through time by reading His word, prayer, and meditation on the scriptures. When we speak of voice in this sense, it's not so much an audible sound that we're speaking of (although the Lord could certainly speak to us that way) but the ability to discern what has proceeded from the mouth of God because we are well acquainted with His character and what He has declared in His word. False spirits can be tested by the word of God because God will never operate in opposition to His word. He watches over His word to perform it and when He has spoken a thing, He will make it good. This is why we must have a working knowledge of the word of God. That doesn't mean that we quote scriptures from cover to cover but rather that we can attest that we know Him.

Paul expressed in Philippians 3: 10 that he wanted to know Christ. He wrote, "That I may know Him and the power of His resurrection, and the fellowship of His sufferings, being conformed to His death." To know Him! That word *know* in this context is such an intimate word, as it speaks of a deep, personal communion and being like him. The apostle is not speaking of a theoretical knowing or something that is gained by simply hearsay. There's something about an intimate relationship with another. When we have that type of closeness, we won't readily accept what others may have to say about the individual and we know almost immediately when what is being spoken is true or not. Why? Because we know them and we know what their character represents. As it pertains to God, the word says, "My sheep know my voice and a stranger that will not follow." We simply must, and we can train our spirit man to have dominance over our flesh by spending quality time in the presence of the Lord, saying no to the distractions that seek to take that quality time from us and being quick to obey when we're prompted by the Holy Spirit in any area of our lives.

The Lord speaks to us through our spirit man and not our flesh or feelings because the flesh is at enmity with, or opposes, the things of God. Take the simple things, for example. Have you ever felt led to go on a fast (this is a means of putting flesh under subjection to the spirit) but as soon as you decide, someone bakes your favorite dessert for you or there's a special luncheon at the office? I'm sure that all of us have encountered these types of situations, and they happen in order to cause us to be distracted from the fasting and subsequent victory that comes with it if we're able to follow through. Consider the example of listening to the audio Bible to fall asleep. Now, there's nothing wrong with listening to the audio Bible; in fact, that could be considered a great *supplement* to any of our regular study time. However, when the Bible is used to fall asleep and we've had little to no waking hours of study, this will not have a major impact on our spiritual growth. To be a disciple requires that we discipline ourselves to spend time in the presence of the Lord and to hide His word in our hearts. We desperately need time with the Lord when we're awake, alert, and attentive. There is simply no other way around it.

Whenever I read books by individuals who devoted much time to prayer and study, such as E.M. Bounds, who wrote such books as *The Reality of Prayer*, *The Power of Prayer*, *The Weapon of Prayer*, *The Necessity of Prayer*, and so many others, I always come away feeling that there's so much more that I should be doing in order to draw closer to the Lord through the art and discipline of prayer. I've read how shameful it is for the Christian to allow the non-Christian to wake and start his day before the man or woman of God gets up to commune with God and to seek His face for the activities and plans for the day that lies ahead. Every day should start early with a conversation with our Savior and an opportunity to inquire of Him before making any plans or commitments for the hours that lie ahead. We are not only to look to Him in times of trouble, distress, and hardship but at all times. We are to acknowledge Him in all of our ways, and prayer is an act of acknowledgement and humble submission.

Jesus has always desired and spoken of a relationship with His followers. If you notice throughout scripture, He said things such as, "Faith without works is dead," "Why call Me Lord, Lord, and do not the things that I say do?" and "Your faith must exceed that of the scribes and Pharisees." Why do you think He would say things such as these or inspire writers in the word of God to make such statements if He didn't have a genuine concern regarding the relationship that His followers share with Him? Some have a desire for a personal relationship with the Lord, yet they have not entered into that relationship. It's as simple as confessing that you are a sinner and asking the Lord to come into your life and to have His way in your life. After that initial step toward Him, we don't continue with our lives as usual; instead we begin to read God's word and talk with Him daily as we would a friend. Every single person has a life of worth and purpose in the eyes of the Lord. He simply invites us to accept Him and come into relationship with Him. This is the relationship that makes us complete and whole. It's a relationship that we can find in no one else, and it changes the course of our lives now and for all of eternity.

Turn your faith loose! Dare to draw closer to God. Let's seek Him above all else and all others. The Bible promises that if we draw close to Him, He'll draw close to us. What do you say about it? The Lord requires a life of faith, nothing less. The just shall live by his faith (Habakkuk 2:4).

Prayer: Lord, thank You so much for Your plan and provision for a life of faith for each and every believer. I choose not only to read about the faith of others but to live a life of faith by the power of Your Spirit. We know that without faith it is impossible to please You, so You've given to each of us the measure of faith that is needed for whatever purpose You have assigned to our lives. My desire is to draw closer to You today, and I lay hold of the promise in James 4:8 that if I draw close to You, You'll draw close to me. I receive that promise and declare that I will live by faith and the power of Your Spirit. In Jesus's Name. Amen.

God Has Crowned You with Favor

Esther 3:8: "Haman told the king about a *certain people* scattered and dispersed among the people whose laws were diverse from all people so much so that they did not even keep the king's laws. Haman was given authority to do with these people as it seemed good to him."

This chapter is taken from a message that I shared at a women's conference in South Carolina with the theme "The Call of the Crown—Godly Women in Alignment for the Kingdom Assignment." We note in the scripture text that is given that there were "certain people" whom Haman told the king about. These people were standouts, nonconformists who followed and adhered to laws that were different from all other people. They were so different and distinct that Haman pointed out that they did not even keep the king's laws. Haman was given permission by the king to do whatever he pleased to such people who would dare to stand in such stark noncompliance. Little did he know that these people were set apart by the King of kings, and it was His laws and commands that they adhered to.

There's hardly a woman of God who is not familiar with the story of Queen Esther on some level. By reflecting on her story, I want us to consider the importance of being in alignment with our Kingdom assignment for such a time as the time that we live in right now. Whenever you are privileged to read the book of Esther in the Bible, just know that Esther made a tremendous impact on the history of the Jewish people, and now there is a span of time when the Lord has allowed you and I to live and to make an impact on the earth. She was a part of those whom Haman referred to as a "certain people."

The book of Esther is different and was almost excluded from canonized scripture because nowhere does it reference God by name or make reference to Him directly. However, it is evident that the hand of God was at work in the lives of His people and in the life of Esther specifically.

It becomes very clear throughout the book of Esther that the God of Israel is indeed a God of covenant and He watches over His people. He exercises His power to ensure that His will is carried out in their lives in spite of difficult circumstances. Let's explore some takeaways from the portion of Esther's life that is shared with us throughout this book that is called by the same name.

The first thing that we need to make note of is that the favor of God will open doors for us that would otherwise not be opened. It is undeniably the Sovereign God who controls and directs all the seemingly insignificant *coincidences* that we read about in this intriguing story. He exercises His control over His covenant people. Certain things are inherent when we're in alignment with our Kingdom assignment and God's purpose for our lives. Alignment is about the position of agreement or alliance. It is about being in correct or appropriate relative position.

Who was Esther before she went to the palace? She was a Jewess living among her people, who were in captivity. She was under the care of her cousin Mordecai, who took her in as his own daughter and raised her because her parents were deceased. The scriptures let us know that her given name was Hadassah and that she was fair and beautiful. King Ahasuerus put away his wife, Vashti, whose name means "beautiful woman" after she failed to come to him so that he could put her on display before his drunken guests. He wanted to parade her beauty in front of his guests because, according to scripture, she was "fair to look upon or beautiful to behold."

Vashti refused to be placed on display for the pleasure of the drunken guests, although she had been summoned by the king. Needless to say, the king was terribly angry and quite embarrassed. The consequences for her were grave: the king decided to put her away after those around him gave him counsel regarding the impact that her failure to adhere to the king's request would have on other women in the land. The king was convinced that this act of blatant disobedience could not be tolerated or overlooked but that it must be dealt with swiftly and harshly.

In Esther chapter 2, we find that after the king had put away Queen Vashti and his anger was appeased, his servants who ministered to him came up with an idea that fair young virgins should be sought for the king to take Vashti's place. So the king allowed officers to go into all of the provinces of his kingdom to seek out young virgins and bring them back to the house of women at Shushan, the palace. There the young virgins would be placed in the custody of Hegai, who was a eunuch (meaning a castrated man who could be placed in charge of a harem), and he was keeper of the women. Esther found favor with him, so he did all that he could to ensure that she had everything that she needed. Esther had not revealed the fact that she was a Jewess out of obedience to Mordecai, yet neither of them knew that the sovereign God had a great plan not only for the two of them but for all of His people.

Like all of the young virgins, Esther had to go through twelve months of purification before she would be permitted to go before the king. There were six months of being prepared with oil of myrrh and six months of sweet odors and with other things for the purifying of the women. The favor of God rested upon her, and the scriptures reveal that Esther found favor in the sight of all who looked upon her. When she was taken unto the king, he looked upon her and loved her above all the women, and he set the royal crown upon her head, making her queen instead of Vashti. The reality is that there was a crown that Esther wore before she was crowned by the king. It was the crown of God's favor.

The favor of God was upon Esther before she reached the palace. It was actually His favor that escorted her there. For those women of God who may be reading this, as daughters of the King, you are royalty and you are highly favored. Let's talk about that for a moment. We all live and move between two kingdoms. We're part of this earthly realm that we see, touch, and experience on a daily basis, and we're also very much a part of a spiritual realm that has a tremendous impact on our lives. We are being influenced by both. There is much going on in the spirit realm wherever you may find yourself right now. These two kingdoms coexist, and we can respond based upon the influence of either at any given time. We determine which of these we will submit to and allow to have authority over our lives.

Esther's people ran into opposition because they refused to adhere to the customs of serving other gods even to the extent of following commands given by the king that did not coincide with their faith. The opposition that so many face today is a direct attack of spirits who are assigned to bring thoughts of rejection and the lie that we are not favored. The intent is to cause us to miss the divine appointments that have been set up for us before the beginning of time. Yes, there are divine appointments and intersections in our lives. We'll refer to these as "defining moments" in a later chapter. Royalty has status in the natural realm, and those who are children of God have status in His Kingdom or the spirit realm. The Bible has called God's people a royal priesthood, a holy nation.

When we've answered the call of God on our lives, our status has changed within the spirit realm, although we may not see it reflected naturally. That change in status is a transition from the kingdom of darkness to the Kingdom of God. The only way to pull this from the written pages of scripture and make it applicable in our lives is to get a grasp on what the scripture has said. The word of God is our anchor. Take a look at Colossians 1:13,14 and read it daily until it penetrates and resonates within you. It reads, "He has rescued us from the dominion of darkness and brought us into the Kingdom of His beloved Son, in whom we have redemption through His blood, the forgiveness of sins." We have been rescued not just from the kingdom of darkness but from its dominion over us. The enemy knows who you are although those around you may have counted you out and you see no apparent difference in your life. Do you remember the account in Acts 19:13–15 when the opposing spirits spoke up after the seven sons of a Jewish high priest named Sceva tried to call them out by using or invoking the name of the Lord Jesus although they didn't really know Jesus? The spirit spoke up and said to them, "Jesus I know and Paul I know, but who are you?" The enemy knows who you are if you are aligned with Christ, meaning that He is your Savior. The spirit realm responds to you and wars against you because it stands in opposition to your King. It's not really about you!

Blood-washed, born-again Christians represent the authority of the Kingdom that is greater than the one that we live and operate in here on a natural level. Many things that we face in our lives are setting us up for elevation in the spirit realm. Do you recall that I just mentioned a little while ago that we are operating in two kingdoms that coexist? It's true. Sometimes our elevation in the natural realm is not solely about what we can see or comprehend with our natural minds. Understand that elevation may come as doors are opened, but we must have freedom from the entrapment of elevations. I once heard a preacher who is highly esteemed say that we shouldn't make a difference between people by referring to some as born-again believers, children of God, etc. I find this to be very dangerous because the Bible is very clear about the difference in our lives before we come to Christ and our lives after we are born again. This difference is reflected in the scripture that I shared with you from Colossians (and there are many more) that speaks of our lives as being under the dominion of the god of this world (Satan) as opposed to being under the authority of the true and living God. It reads, "The god of this age (Satan) has blinded the minds of unbelievers so they cannot see the light of the gospel of the glory of Christ, Who is the image of God" (2 Cor. 4:4). There is a distinct difference that's noted here after we are no longer under the dominion of the god of this age who has for so long blinded our minds.

Acceptance of Christ as our Lord and Savior is necessary in order to walk in relationship with Him and to be empowered by His Spirit. Only then do we have all of the benefits of salvation. One of the major issues for many

Christians is the trap of trying to fit in. We can never fit in with the world because we've been called out, set apart, and the favor or anointing of God upon our lives makes us distinct—not "better than" but distinct. There is no getting around this. So as we embrace elevation on natural levels, we must always with a grateful heart seek God and ask what He is doing in the spirit realm that we may need to be aware of.

Bishop T.D. Jakes preached a time-transcending message titled "Nothing Just Happens," and the child of God would do well to always keep this in mind. We're not arbitrarily going through this life. Grasp that, because the reality is that life didn't just begin to happen to us or for us after we said yes to Christ. "Nothing Just Happens" is not just directed at believers. God is in control, and His will is that none—not one person—would perish but that all would come to repentance. Life's journey is designed to help us to see the hand of God at work in our individual stories. Some will but some will never acknowledge His sovereignty or His plan. If we take the time to look back over our lives, we will see that the hand of God was there in our circumstances all the time. We may not have acknowledged Him or invited Him into our situations, but He was there while we made the decision to do things our own way and to reject His plan and purpose. Some of us actually denied and rejected His very existence. As we continue with the account of Hadassah, we find that God was very much involved, although He was never mentioned in the chapters of the book. What a plan He had for Hadassah! What a plan He has for each one of us!

Just as we find in reading Esther's/Hadassah's story, the glory, the power, is usually not totally revealed in our times of natural elevation. Just as Mordecai wouldn't allow her to simply stop and rejoice in the fact that she had made it to the palace and to the place of honor as the queen, nor can we stop there as we read and learn from her story. Yes, her journey from obscurity to the palace was wonderful—quite glorious, in fact—but there was a greater story behind what was happening to her at that time. I know that this story has been told numerous times, but each time that we read it or share it, we can allow it to minister to us in a new way. Her elevation carried responsibility. It was not simply about living a good life in the palace with the king. She had a higher calling that came from the King of kings, the Deliverer who was in covenant with her people. Remember: To whom much is given, much is required.

We can become enamored with status and lose sight of purpose. Note Esther's words in chapter 4:10–11 that she sent to Mordecai after she was informed of Haman's plot to totally destroy the Jews with the king's consent. In verse 11, we find the message that she sent to Mordecai: "All the king's servants and the people of the king's provinces know that any man or woman who goes into the inner court to the king, who has not been called, *he has* but one law: put *all* to death, except the one to whom the king holds out the golden scepter, that he may live. Yet I myself have not been called to go in to the king these thirty days." The natural crown gave her earthly status, but there was a crown that she wore that was not seen with the natural eye, and yet it superseded all power inherent in the one that the king had given to her to wear on her head. The time had come that she had to be made aware of the power behind the crown of favor that she had been afforded the opportunity to wear by her heavenly King. It was time to lose herself and risk everything in order to see God move on behalf of His people.

I need to say to you that your elevation has taken you into an area where sacrifice is necessary. We must lose ourselves! To be in alignment with the Kingdom is to be in agreement with the Kingdom and not working our own agenda! We must be keenly aware of purpose and keep that before us. You're ushered into the large place, the expanded place, for a reason. It's not necessary for us to understand everything that the Lord is doing in order for Him to use us to carry out His strategic plan. All He needs from us is a willingness to be used. We don't get to choose when or how He will use us.

Mordecai let Esther know that it was time for her to reveal who she was in order for her purpose to be fulfilled. His response to her message regarding not being allowed into the king's presence unless she was called was: "Think not with thyself that thou shalt escape in the king's house, more than all the Jews" (Esther 4:13). In other words, "Don't you think for a moment that just because you now live in the palace with the king and have all of the perks that such a life brings, that somehow you will escape when all of the other Jews, your people, are killed."

God will never leave Himself without a voice in the earth. He's speaking right now. There was a voice that found Esther. It made its way to her. We all need a Mordecai in our lives, someone to keep us grounded and focused on purpose especially when we might otherwise be susceptible to forgetting what time it is and for what purpose we have been connected to a specific point in time. "For such a time as this"—think about what that means. You and I won't get this time back again. We must be ready to seize the moment because we have been prepared for it and it has been prepared with our name on it. What God has for you is for you. The king's heart was prepared for Esther!

There comes a point in time when we must come out from hiding in the shadows. There is something down on the inside of us that is designed to bring glory to our God and to benefit the body of Christ, His people. After God through His faithfulness has prospered us, we cannot remain comfortable looking good, wearing finery while those around us are dying for lack of being touched and edified by our God-given gifts, not our elegance or our beauty but our spiritual gifts.

We must pray while others play. We must be willing to ask, seek, and knock for others while they are oblivious to the dangers that are around them! So many want the anointing of God but often fail to realize that there is a cost. I'm not speaking in the sense of something that we must pay for but the cost of allowing our desires to become second or third place to whatever the Lord has deemed best for us.

As we reflect on the story of Hadassah, there were so many things at her disposal while she was there in the palace. She could have been content to carry on with her assumed name, her elevated status, and protection from the reminders of the life that was hers outside of the world that she had now become acquainted with. She was beautiful Queen Esther, yet she was also Hadassah. She was the one whom God favored, the one who came out of the lowly place and was ushered up to the large place. The time came for a decision to be made. She could choose to hold on to the joy and prestige of the placement that had been afforded to her by the natural crown or she could choose to operate in and through the power behind the crown that was hers by God's design and purpose through His favor. Some may say that, in reality, she had no real choice at all because destiny called to her and she had to answer.

This is Esther's story, yet it becomes the story of so many who are willing to allow the power of God to usher us to new levels beyond what we could have ever dreamed of or prepared for ourselves. It is then that we are positioned to be used for a purpose that goes far beyond that which is only for our benefit. You see, the life of the believer is never about our own selfish gain at the expense of others, but there is always a reminder that someone else is tied to our next move in God, our next elevation, our next moment of deliverance. All things are possible with God. When the Lord has crowned us with His favor, the greatest obstacle in our way is often ourselves. There's so much power behind the crown that you've been graced to wear! We all need the Mordecais in our lives who will cause us to adjust our crowns and to walk in a way that brings dignity and honor to the place where we have been called, remaining mindful of the people to whom we are attached.

We don't get to choose when or how we'll walk in our anointing when we've aligned ourselves with the Kingdom. We don't get to decide how the Lord will serve us to the world. Kingdom agenda always takes priority, so we must align with the Kingdom and seek the Kingdom first (Matt. 6:33). Certain things are inherent when we're in alignment with our Kingdom assignment and God's purpose for our lives. Just as there was a plot against the Jews of Esther's day because they chose to serve their God and to reject the standards of the world, there is a plot and scheme to destroy all those like you, if you are a child of God. This is a divisive hour that we're living in, and we must recognize that. The enemy seeks to destroy those who name the Name of Christ. There are rumblings, and we must be discerning of the voice that alerts us to the plots and schemes of the enemy. Some of us are around too much noise. The Lord is setting us apart so that we can get into His face, hear His voice, focus, and get realigned. Sometimes we need a realignment! Like Esther, many of you have been hidden, but God has positioned a Mordecai in your life, one who is unyielding to the opposing forces of the world and is sensitive to the move of God.

Hadassah had been given an awesome opportunity that only the favor of God could have afforded to her, and yet she was faced with another opportunity that was so much greater. She was faced with an opportunity to change the course of her people, a nation. The natural crown that she wore gave her power, but there was a higher calling in her life, a power behind that crown. We're not to be distracted by finery because all that this world boasts of belongs to God. I often say that God's promise to us in Matthew 6:33 is to add "things" to us as we seek first His Kingdom and His righteousness. The reality is that when people are impressed with us and the things that we may possess, they are simply impressed with what has been "added" to us. We owe it all to God. He adds and multiplies in our lives.

The natural crown yells "See me, serve me!" and the authority of that crown is focused on people, positions, and a worldly power structure. The crown that God gives causes the wearer to proclaim, "My power and strength are not my own, my life is not my own, and I submit to an unseen power that is much greater than any visible crown that I may wear." This unseen crown gives authority over principalities, powers, the rulers of the darkness of this world, and over spiritual wickedness in high places. We have dominion; we destroy yokes and set captives free. That's who we are; it's not just what we do!

So Mordecai had to remind Esther that the space in time where she was walking and experiencing was so much greater than her marriage to the king. It was about her relationship with the King, and she was about to learn a life-changing lesson about the covenant-keeping God who is always present and working to fulfill His plan in our lives. Not only was her life changed, but the lives of all to whom she was connected, the Jews, were spared. Mordecai's life was changed and he was elevated by her one act of obedience. It was not an easy choice on her part, because the reality is that she could have lost her life in the process. Yet her obedience brought liberty to so many. Mordecai wasn't in search of a position or elevation. He was simply a wise man who was used by God (whether he was aware of that or not) as a mouthpiece to bring direction to Esther at the crucial point in the history of the Jewish nation.

The world is no match for the woman or man of God who will war in the Spirit through the weapon of prayer. We cannot end this chapter without taking a look at what Esther decides to do, knowing that it could mean death for her if she showed up before the king without being summoned. In chapter 4:15–16 Esther sends word to Mordecai and says, "Have everyone to fast for 3 days, don't eat or drink. I'm going to do the same. My handmaids and I will fast likewise and so will I go in to the king. If I perish, let me perish!" I believe that somehow she recognized the power behind the crown, the power to not only save herself but an entire nation of people. Say *favor*! Say *surrender*!

The favor of God rests upon our lives, although sometimes we are not aware of it. Favor is not based on how we feel or what may be going on in our lives. Thank God for His unmerited favor that is at work in your life right now. Make a determination to keep walking in that favor as you pull from the example that has been given to us by the lives of Esther and Mordecai.

Remember that someone else is tied to your next move in God. You've been strategically placed, and your life can affect so many others from right where you are.

Prayer: Father, in the Name of Jesus, I thank You for the favor that rests upon my life and affords opportunities to me that I may not otherwise experience in this life. May Your divine will always be done in and through my life. I realize that my life is not my own, I have been bought with a price (the precious blood of Jesus Christ) and I surrender my life and will to You. Be glorified in my life. Amen!

Inspiration Break

If you ask most people, they will say that they want a miracle. Whether or not they are living in expectancy of a miracle is another story.

The famous gospel recording artists, the Clark Sisters, sang a song titled "I'm Looking for a Miracle." The lyrics went on to say, "I expect the impossible, I feel the intangible, and I see the invisible." That song, like most all of their recordings, was a huge success.

What is a miracle? It is defined as "a surprising and welcome event that is not explicable by natural or scientific laws and is therefore considered to be the work of a divine agency" or "a highly improbable or extraordinary event, development, or accomplishment that brings very welcome consequences."

What will you do with your miracle? You're a walking, breathing miracle, an ambassador for Christ with dual citizenship, present physically on the earth yet interacting with the spirit and supernatural world on a daily basis.

Heaven listens to you when you speak, takes note of you when you shed even one tear, and admonishes you to be aware that what you bind on earth will be bound in heaven and what you loose on earth will be loosed in heaven.

You can come boldly to the throne of grace (Heb. 4:16), and there you will obtain mercy and find grace to help you in a time of need. Where is that? Where is the throne of grace? It's in the very presence of our true and living God.

You have access at any time of the day or night to go into the presence of the living God, the creator of the universe, and no man or opposing spirit can stop you. The problem is that most of us overlook this miracle.

You have the mind of Christ according to 1 Corinthians 2:16. What does that mean exactly? You're constantly becoming more like Jesus, learning to abide in Him and to think His thoughts. That's a work of the Spirit.

The person whom you see in the mirror may look the same, but he or she is forever changed. Behold, all things have become new. That is nothing short of a miracle!

No longer will you nurse who you were, but you can agree with heaven and embrace the miracle of who you are.

The Power of Image in Christian Leadership

This chapter is taken from a teaching session that I shared at a leadership conference. It is significant to me because when I went to the conference, I was not on the schedule to teach a session but was there solely to glean from others. However, one evening as I was on my way to retire and relax in my room for the night, my lead pastor and bishop, Dr. Chad Carlton, approached me and told me to prepare to take his place in a session that he was to teach the following morning. Many of you reading this may be surprised that such a request would be made, but those who know our bishop know that this is par for the course, and since it was a leadership conference, I needed to step up and deliver some leadership skills. Needless to say, I didn't do much sleeping that night. The title of the scheduled session was "The Power of Image in Christian Leadership." Given the time constraints, the slide presentation that I prepared had to be basic, and what follows is a portion of what the Lord gave to me to share in that morning session along with additional information that is being integrated for this chapter.

The word *image* is defined as a representation or general impression. What comes to your mind when you think of *image* in Christian leadership? (What are some of the images of Christian leaders in today's world?) Remember that we noted the definition of *image* as a representation or general impression. Everything is about image now. We talk a lot about social media because it's huge in terms of displaying images that the user may want to convey to a group of "followers" or "friends."

How many of you identify yourselves as leaders? Remember that holding or carrying a title is not what makes you a leader. People can be drawn or driven by the image that we present as leaders. Many of us have had experiences whether on a job or in the context of the religious setting where we've encountered some who were very poor leaders and who had a way of making us feel small or inferior. Then there were others who had a way of making us think that we could do anything, succeed at it, and be appreciated for our contributions. People are initially drawn to what leadership represents externally, which could equate to power, prestige, notoriety, or financial security. A quote by well-known author John C. Maxwell states it this way: "A leader is one who knows the way, goes the way and shows the way." I want us to consider this in the context of Christian leadership, although that is not specifically the angle that Mr. Maxwell was taking. However, he defined a "leader" in terms that certainly can be applied to those who operate within the realm of Christian leadership.

First, the leader must "know the way." In the only letter from Jesus's brother, Jude, we find a stern warning against false teachers who were invading and beguiling the church. To beguile is defined as "to charm or enchant (someone), sometimes in a deceptive way." How might someone do that? By presenting an image that people want to see and to be identified with. Images are powerful, and the power of an image to draw or repel is real. Many in Christian circles are drawn to roles of leadership because of what they see in the leaders around them or, on the other hand, what they see or experience may cause them to want no part of leadership, although the Lord may have every intention of using them in a leadership role.

Let's think about the power of image in Christian leadership for a moment. If the image that we portray, the word that we preach and teach, is not based in the reality of the word of God, then what happens? In short, those around us will be delusional and we, as leaders, will be held accountable to God. We will attract what we portray with our image, and *we* must provide for anything that our image has caused to manifest apart from the character of Christ.

The Lord gives vision and direction to His leaders. As those leaders connect with the plan of God, He will ensure that what He has spoken or ordained will come to pass. So does that mean that the leader can never come up with ideas of his or her own as we traverse this life of ministry? Not at all! However, what makes the life of those called to leadership in Christian circles distinct from all others is that we must realize the importance of constantly checking in with the One who has the master plan for all dreams, visions, and ideas. That One is the Lord. He gives dreams, unfolds visions, and imparts ideas. To avoid His leadership and direction is synonymous with walking in pride and is really a disqualifier for successful Christian leadership. Christian leaders are called to serve the people, and this is done best when the leader walks in submission to the Lord and not according to his or her desires. God still requires that those who are called by His Name would humble themselves, pray, and seek His face in order to have confidence in the promise that He will hear from heaven and allow us to experience results in the earth as He heals the land. Our land needs healing. Our nation is in desperate need of healing, and it must begin with sincere and earnest prayer on the part of those who know Christ and who are willing to lead men, women, boys, and girls back to the place of power that is at the feet of our Lord. We must be willing to humble ourselves (2 Chron. 7:14).

When the Lord places vision within a man or woman of God, then births that vision through him or her, trust me, He'll take care of it. The reality is that only He can. Vision that comes from God through the leader is always so much bigger and broader than what the leader could ever conceptualize or accomplish on his or her own. Many are romancing the image of what they perceive or understand Christianity to be, and it may not line up with the reality of the word of God at all. It's easy to become enamored with what some portray positions of leadership to be—all about finery, glamour, power, influence, and all those things that you can name as well. It boils down to a false image that charms and entices. Jesus dealt with the same thing. Although He wasn't one who was rich in earthly goods or one who walked around in finery, He certainly attracted all types of people. They took note of what He did, how He spoke with authority, the miracles that He performed, the crowds that He fed, and they flocked around Him but often did not remain. Why do you suppose that they left?

In John 6:26 Jesus speaks of those who followed or pursued Him not because of the miracles that He performed, which were intended to teach spiritual lessons, but because they became full on the natural food that they were given to eat. They were excited by the miracles but wanted no part of the spiritual teaching that went along with it. It equates to those who are drawn by excitement in the church—the music and all of the programs—but when it comes to teaching foundational truths, they don't have time or interest. It is the foundational truths that will sustain us. How can we claim to be followers of Christ when we're not comfortable with sharing with others how to come to Him and how to develop a relationship with Him? This is foundational! The hype and excitement won't always be there to keep the crowd engaged, but that's when the necessity of a personal relationship and spiritual guidance and understanding take center stage in our lives. This is what Jesus set out to teach and to preach. All of the excitement around the miracles was merely a setup to teach about Kingdom and the power for living that only comes through Kingdom connection. Jesus didn't need for anyone to school him on what was in man because He made man (John 2:25). One version says, "No one needed to tell Him about human nature, because He knew what was in each person's heart." He knew that many were only following Him for the loaves, the fish, and the next miracle, but they had no interest in learning about life in the Spirit. It is important for us to tie this in with the role of those who may be in leadership.

Despite what some may think and what others may attempt to portray, those who are gifted and anointed by God aren't always ready to shout, dance, and speak in tongues. Leaders are human, they're vulnerable, they hurt, they are challenged with burnout, they deal with failure, and oftentimes they just simply fall short of the expectations of those around them. Many of them wrestle with the fact that they have fallen short of the expectations that they may have had for themselves. We don't like to hear that, do we? I believe that's why we and others in leadership must guard against portraying false images that neither we nor anyone else looking on can realistically live up to. So many have been hurt due to poor leadership, and leadership is often poor because there is such a shortage of "good" leaders who will take the time to pour into the lives of those who are coming behind them or those who are serving alongside them.

The church is in dire need of leaders who dare to show their scars as they lead the way. What is your story? Does anyone serving with you know that story? Certainly those whom you lead should know where the Lord has brought you from and how He has delivered you. Who were you before you walked behind that title that you now wear? What are some of your struggles, the painful losses or betrayals that you have endured? The word of God assures us regarding Jesus, "For we have not an High Priest which cannot be touched with the feeling of our infirmities; but was in all points tempted like as we are, yet without sin" (KJV). The New King James Version reads "who cannot sympathize with our weaknesses" in the place of "which cannot be touched with the feeling of our infirmities." This should give us comfort and boldness in going to Jesus with whatever we're dealing with in life. Those around us need to be able to look to leaders with whom they serve and have some sense of the ability to overcome adversity, obstacles, and hardship. Why? Because my leader(s) did it! He or she may have been addicted to crack cocaine at one time, but they persevered and obtained a degree, which lets me know that what I have a desire in my heart to accomplish can be done. He or she may have been at death's door, but they're standing today because the Lord healed them. Maybe they suffered the tragic loss of a loved one even after praying that their loved one wouldn't transition, yet they have found the will and fortitude to persevere through that heartache and pain.

I say all of this because I'm convinced that the Lord is gathering in a remnant from the world who are not impressed with positions or titles, nor do they care to compete for them. After they have been converted, they will be unstoppable and uncompromising. They will be real about where they have come from, the mistakes that they have made, and the battle scars that they now wear due to the pain and suffering that they have endured. I believe that the Lord will use them to call out the false ways and the false images that many in the church have embraced for so long because they're coming in search of change, truth, and power. Organized "religion" just cannot produce this. The church needs a move of God's Spirit! There are leaders among the ranks of God's people who are yearning for a fresh anointing and move of God!

Having a degree is fine, but we must watch the false image that has crept in among us to portray that those with higher education are God's elect, His preferred ones. No! This is not what qualifies us. We must go back to the foot of the cross, back to the feet of Jesus, and cry out, "Lord, it's You that I need, and only You!" Because that, my friend, is the truth of the matter, and in that cry from your heart lies your success in this Christian walk, in leadership, in marriage, in family life, and in anything else that you may set your mind and heart to accomplish. Education is fine, but that is not what grants intimacy with God. We all have access through the precious shed blood of Jesus

Christ, and to the dismay of some, the Lord will continue to use those who in the eyes of many are unlearned and unworthy. The requirement to be used mightily in the Kingdom is a heart that seeks after God and a desire to be used for His glory. You can't get that from a textbook. What a tragedy that men have now come along and sought to keep others out of the service of the Lord because they don't have degrees or higher education. This is grievous to the Spirit of the Lord. The Lord has the prerogative to use those with the highest degrees as well as those who have no formal education at all.

Leaders, we must understand that our gifts cannot compensate for an organized, disciplined life where there is time for study, reading, and prayer because we make time for them. No matter how charismatic we are or how much the people love us, the power of any gift and ability that we've been graced to carry in this life is the Holy Spirit of God. He is the giver of the gifts, the unction, and the anointing. We must spend time getting to know Him, understanding how He speaks to us and leads us, and becoming aware of our spiritual gifts that are given as a means to build up and edify the body of Christ. Every spiritual gift must operate from a foundation of love or it is useless (1 Cor. 13).

It's imperative that we take time to read material that will help us to enhance our abilities to affect others in a positive way. We need to be able to place a demand on integrity, honesty, and stewardship starting with our own lives before having any expectation of others. We can absolutely determine to be on a continual journey of learning, growth, and personal and spiritual development.

There has been a long-standing debate regarding whether leaders are born or made. Even if you believe that some are born with the propensity to lead, they must have opportunities for education, growth, and development of the skills that will enhance their God-given abilities. If leaders are made, then that takes us back to those who walk in leadership and are in tune with the voice of God so that they can discern the qualities and gifts in those who serve with them in order to help equip them to become successful leaders.

Although many assume positions of leadership, being an impactful leader is not something that just happens. In his book *Rediscovering Our Spiritual Gifts*, Charles V. Bryant identifies "Leadership" as a gift. This book was one of several identified by our bishop as essential reading for lay pastors. We may not necessarily agree that leadership is a gift, but Mr. Bryant likens those with this gift as "ones who lead, guide or direct other members of the body of Christ to fulfill the church's commission." He asserts that the leader "has an extraordinary ability to envision God's will and purpose for the church and to demonstrate persuasive skills to capture the imaginations, energies, skills, and spiritual gifts of others to pursue and accomplish God's will."

For years people have tried to become leaders by simply watching others. However, we've learned that we must be taught, skilled, and we must embrace the truth that an active prayer life is what fuels successful ministry and leadership. Jesus is our first example of this. He spent time with His disciples, He taught them, He identified and called forth the gifts that were within them. Jesus modeled prayer before them while sharing an expectation that prayer would be the driving force in their lives and in ministry. The scriptures give various accounts of Jesus pulling away alone to seek the Father in prayer, sometimes for extended periods of time.

The Charismata or gifts of God have a drawing effect. People may think that they're drawn to the leader when the reality is that they're drawn to the *treasure* within the person. We have a *treasure* (the Holy Spirit) inside of these earthen vessels (2 Cor. 4:7). The Lord desires to do powerful things through His people, so that it is evident that the power is of God and not of us. You certainly don't have to be in a position of leadership in order for the Lord to use you and to use you mightily. We just happen to be talking about Christian leaders at this time. A good leader will teach others how to yield to the Holy Spirit so that the gifts of God can be manifested throughout the body of Christ and the entire body can be enriched and edified. A good leader knows the way. He or she knows how to show by example that every member of the body matters and that no one is insignificant. This is a major truth that leaders must constantly share and live in order to avoid the deceptive spirit of division that often creeps in due to competition and feelings of inferiority within the body of Christ.

Discerning leaders will be challenged to confront hard things. I can't begin to tell you the many times that I've ministered to women in the church and women in ministry who are victims of intimate partner violence (IPV) or what some know as domestic violence. I must also state here that men can also be victims of IPV as well, but they report it less due to the stigma toward males that is associated with this type of abuse. According to national statistics, women are more often victimized. This type of abuse crosses all socioeconomic lines, races, ethnicities, and age ranges. IPV is on the rise among dating teens, and those within the senior community are victims as well. This is a horrible offense, yet when it is allowed to go on within the church among the ranks of those in leadership as well as within the congregation, there is no doubt that it grieves the Spirit of God. Wives and children of those in leadership are forced to live a lie as they watch their loved one move forward in ministry as a totally different person than the one whom they experience within the confines of their home. This simply must be addressed.

I can recall ministering in a conference that I hosted, and the Lord led me to pray for those who were victims of abuse. The crying and wailing was unbelievable! I knew that the Lord had led us in that direction. One woman at the back of the room cried so loudly, and after I was led to go and minister to her separately, she soon found strength and courage to share with the rest of the group how her spouse, who was a pastor, had been abusing her physically for years. She stated that when she finally found the strength to share this with those in leadership whom she thought would help them, she was ostracized by the congregation and was put out of the church. Hers is only one story. This is not about shedding a negative light on those in authority or leadership but simply a call for all of us to do better. We cannot afford to continue to look the other way and act as if nothing is happening within our ranks while families are hurting. Abuse comes in all forms and knows no barriers due to race, socioeconomic level, titles, or positions that we may hold within the secular or religious setting. It may be physical, emotional, sexual, financial, or otherwise. The point is that all leaders, all who name the Name of Christ, should always be striving to be and to become our best selves.

People are hurting among us, and we must take the time to attend to their hurt, their shame, and to help them to heal. Many have the testimony of going to leaders only to be told to go back home and try to work things out. Some have lost their lives and others have been injured physically and certainly emotionally. We simply must do better. Families are God's choice for revealing Himself in the earth. That has always been His plan, and not to address this dilemma appropriately is a great disservice to the plan of God for the body of Christ. This is very much needed if we declare that we know the way. We are all flawed individuals who are in great need of the Lord, and that becomes the greatest part of our testimony as the surrendered lives of the flawed ones become forces to be reckoned with within the Kingdom of God, against the enemy, and not against one another.

If you'll search scripture, what you'll find is that the Lord has always used vulnerable and ordinary people to fulfill the tasks pertaining to Kingdom building. It's not the whole ones or those who seemingly have it all together who are found to be the ones whom He typically calls or sends. He's more apt to call the shady tax collector, the one who stutters, the hot-tempered one, or the one who feels as though he or she is the least of the least among the chosen ones. What's amazing, though, is that after these individuals say yes to the call of the Lord and He places them in His service, the power of the Spirit of God transforms them. This is why many in leadership have testimonies that others sometimes find hard to believe. It is simply because when we surrender our lives to Christ, He makes all things new. The leader in the body of Christ must "know the way" and, because of his or her lived experience with the Savior, be able to point others to a new and living way. Leaders must help others to embark upon the journey of change and restoration because it is available to everyone who desires to be a part of the Kingdom of God.

What makes leadership within the Kingdom of God so very intriguing is that God chooses ordinary people and performs extraordinary exploits through them. He has done this over and over again throughout the ages. It's His prerogative to do so, and although many times there will be those in the midst of leaders who think that they can handle the tasks of the leader in a better way, the man or woman of God is covered and equipped by God to fulfill what has been put in his or her hands to do. When anyone fights against or seeks to make the way difficult for those who have been called and anointed by God, that person may find themselves fighting against God Himself. Therefore, it is a must that the life of the leader is marked by humility and that he or she is very careful to let people know that those called by the Lord have a treasure and what others see and aspire to attain is not about the leader at all. It's really about Christ. There must be no mistaking that the power is of God and not of us (2 Cor. 4:7). The reality simply remains that God has made a choice of us, and we have to be so very careful to point men and women to Him rather than allowing them to lift us or to exalt our roles, titles, and positions. All of this is about knowing the way.

So next we must "go the way." What do we mean by this? Jesus said in John 14:4, "And where I go you know, and the way you know." Now we know that He is the Way, but the path is not always crystal-clear, so that is why we pray and seek Him for direction. The image that we some-times portray is that we have it all together. Oftentimes we won't pause or stop to seek direction. Our Christian walk is designed for us to inquire of the Lord on a regular basis. We're to speak with Him daily and inquire of His plan for our lives. When we as leaders portray an image that we have it all together, that is a false image, and the tragedy is that we reproduce after our kind. So if you're a leader and you don't have time to pray and others never see you pray or hear you speak of the importance of prayer, then those who are connected to you will likely have that same mindset. "Why stop and pray when we can figure it out on our own? We won't bother the Lord with the small, petty stuff." Have you ever heard that? There should be no question that a vital, consistent prayer life is necessary in order to live a life of faith. How will we know God's plan, the direction that we should take, or the decisions that we should make if we're not consistent with setting aside time to hear from Him? It's just not possible. Don't wait for a crisis before taking the posture of prayer.

Do you believe that God has a plan for you? There's a road map for each of us. If we're going to "go the way," then we must have a *nevertheless* attitude. When Jesus prayed to the Father in the garden of Gethsemane, "olive press," or "Mount of Olives" as it is referred to in Luke 22:39–46, the scripture tells us that He was in anguish and His sweat fell as great drops of blood to the ground. He laid His heart out to the Father and prayed that if it were possible, He would prefer that the forthcoming cup of pain and sacrifice would pass from Him. He knew that what was before Him was a way that led to ultimate victory by way of much suffering and shame, even death on a cross. He was fully God and fully man. He felt the anguish of what was before Him. One of the most degrading, reprehensible types of death awaited Him. Death on a cross was an emblem of shame.

We find that at the end of the prayer Jesus prayed in the garden, He closes with *nevertheless* ("Never will I settle for less"—my interpretation), not my will but Your will be done. Why? Because the will of the Father is always higher, it's always better, it's always for the greater good! In this instance, Jesus's death opened a door that the enemy can never shut. It opened the door to the way of salvation for *all of mankind,* for *all time.* Now, all who will place their faith and trust in Jesus as Lord have the privilege of becoming children of the King and living in this world with access to His heavenly Kingdom. Period! Thank You, Jesus, for Your sacrifice and shed blood that still saves, delivers, and sets free!

Just as Jesus was tempted in the garden to circumvent the Father's plan, the enemy wants all of us, whether we consider ourselves to be leaders or not, to reject God's good plan, to abort, and to fall short. One of the major issues with "going the way" is that it may not look like you thought it would—trust me on that. The enemy wants us to keep glimpsing what or who we used to be or who we thought we were, but *that's not you anymore*! Nothing remains the same! As we traverse this life, with its innumerable twists and turns, ups and downs, we must be pliable in the Lord's hands because He is constantly molding us for the next tasks that lie ahead. Don't get too comfortable where you are. With God, there's always more! He's a God of increase and multiplication. We have to begin to see ourselves being it, doing it, walking in it long before it happens. Whatever *it* is. If we're going to "go the way," then what others see or think doesn't matter nearly as much as what we see as we walk this walk of faith. We have to dare to see it God's way. No more running from it. If He called you to it, He has qualified, justified, and equipped you to handle it.

It is so important that we settle within our hearts and minds that we're not called to positions or titles. Every one of us is first called to relationship with the Lord. The mistake that is easy for leaders to make is to begin seeing titles or positions as the calling while losing sight of the relationship as the core of our calling. We're called to a relationship first. Note in John 21:15–17 that the Lord asked Peter the same question three times and the question had everything to do with a relationship. He didn't ask Peter if he felt that he was anointed or if he felt that he was equipped or even how confident he was about tasks that might lie before him. His question was, "Peter, do you love me?" ("Peter, lovest thou me?")

Why? Because a relationship with, and our love for, our King, our Lord, will always dictate the strength of any title that we carry or position that we may be afforded to operate in. No matter how dynamic our spiritual gifts may be, if we do not operate from a place of love for the Lord first, then there is no way that we can or will exhibit care for His sheep. The strength of any position is our relationship with God and our ability to hear from Him. The question remains the same: "Lovest thou the Savior?" Do you love Him? If not, there is no way to serve the people of God, because true leadership is about servanthood, and that speaks directly to our submission first and foremost to our King, the Lord Jesus Christ. If the leader is not in a strong relationship and communion with his or her Lord, they will cast the sheep aside for their own selfish gain. It is the Lord who has qualified you, called you, equipped you for His service. If you are in leadership, He has entrusted much to your hands for safekeeping. He will open the right doors for you to walk through in order to accomplish His will as it has been ordained for you to do before the foundation of the world.

If we truly believed that there is a place for us, much of the competition among leaders would be eliminated. There would absolutely be no need for it. Just as children are taught to take their turn and not to bully others, there's no place for the bully in the operation of the things of God. The reality is that, sadly enough, we see and experience the bullying spirit among believers. The image that is sometimes portrayed is that you have to be a bulldozer and plow over people if you want to get to the top, even in the ranks of the church. What happens is that the same tactics and mindset of the world are carried over into the church, and rather than operating in an atmosphere of faith, it can get to be dog-eat-dog just like what we've encountered before our introduction to leadership within Christian circles. We've all seen individuals placed in positions and given titles because of the relationships that they have with people of authority within the church. I'm not going to act like that doesn't happen, and anyone who denies that it does is not walking in reality. The reality is that there are some in the pews who have the spiritual gifts for the positions that others have been placed in by man. Those individuals who are trying to operate outside of their gift and anointing are actually miserable and often make the lives of those around them miserable as well. This is where wise, discerning overseers for leadership are so vital in pouring into the lives of those leaders who truly want to "go the way." The task of the overseer is very much a part of this next area that we will touch on briefly.

The last area taken from the quote by John Maxwell concerning a leader is one who "shows the way." So, let's talk about that. *Show the way!* We can't show the way with a false image. The closer one gets to those operating in leadership within the Kingdom of God, they should see the image or reflection of Christ—someone who can be strong yet vulnerable, able to weep, hurt, and feel pain. Jesus wept and He had a way of feeling *with* the people, being *with* the people. True leaders, those who are called to leadership by God, have an understanding that they are sent to serve rather than to be served. The body of Christ is hurting for lack of "servant leaders." The mark of a good leader in *showing the way* must also involve knowing when to take the separate or higher road even when others won't understand it, and teaching others to do the same. Integrity, honor, dignity, and honesty are all characteristics that should align with leaders whether they are functioning within religious or what would be deemed as secular settings.

The Apostle Paul, someone who gave us the majority of the New Testament writings, was a leader who never tried to exalt himself but rather allowed himself to be vulnerable through his writings by sharing his struggles with those who would read and be able to identify with him. He shares a discourse in Romans chapter 7, being transparent about having the desire to do what is right but finding himself doing the exact opposite at times. Who can't identify with that? He was very clear that the overcoming power that he desired did not lie within himself but that he was reliant upon the strength and power of the true and living God. This is leadership! Leaders who dare to show people their scars make it possible for people to see their Savior much more clearly. He is the One who causes you to rise, to triumph, and to live above condemnation.

Leaders must be able to show the way. Image is so powerful, but we don't have to walk in a false one when we know who we are in Christ. The enemy knows who you are! He wants you to keep relying on your knowledge, your skill set, and your expertise. That's an image that may draw others to you for sure. But if we don't show the way and point men and women to Christ after the image that we portray has brought people our way, we will produce after our own kind, resulting in a body full of intellectuals with lots of skills but no power. It's a very weak message when we can point people no farther than ourselves, because each of us is vulnerable and reliant upon the Lord.

Leaders must show the way by insisting that those who serve with them attend to self-care to include not only the physical body but also our mental health. Too many leaders have ended their lives by suicide as a result of becoming overwhelmed with the very real challenges of life and tragically coming to the conclusion that there is no one who they can reach out to or confide in. As we read about those hurtful situations, often their closest family members had no idea that they were living in such a dark space as they continued to preach, teach, sing, or do whatever else that their ministries depended upon them to do. We simply must as Christians pull down the strongholds that keep people bound by the false narrative that says that we lack faith if we admit or confess that we're hurting, that we're struggling with seasons of depression, mania, or any other form of mental challenge. We must stand against the stigma surrounding the need for self-care around our mental well-being because being Christian does not cancel that out. Too many have been made to feel ashamed or to feel as though they must somehow be out of touch with God or lacking in faith because of the challenges that they face. Every contrary wind or challenge in our lives doesn't point to demon possession, nor is it of the devil! As the body of Christ, we simply must begin to do a better job of caring for, supporting, and nurturing one another. This is really the way that others are to know that we are Christ's disciples—when we love one another and love is definitely an action word, not simply a spoken word.

Take a look at Psalm 42:5 (NKJV) and ask yourself why the psalmist would write such a statement if those who love God are exempt from times of disquiet and somberness. He writes, "Why are you cast down, O my soul? And why are you disquieted within me?" Next, I want you to note that he speaks to himself regarding a remedy that is all too often neglected or overlooked during our times of challenge and despair. The second part of that same verse reads, "Hope in God, for I shall yet praise Him for the help of His countenance." That same verse in the Amplified Bible reads, "Why are you in despair, O my soul? And why have you become restless and disturbed within me? Hope in God and wait expectantly for Him, for I shall again praise Him for the help of His presence." Typically those who linger in a place of despair find themselves in a state of hopelessness, which can be very detrimental because we must seek to maintain a mindset of *waiting expectantly* for the Lord even in our times of struggle. When we lose hope, our loss of expectation is usually not far behind, so we must speak to ourselves as the psalmist did, not denying what we're dealing with but declaring all the while, "*I shall* again praise Him. I may not be in praise mode right now, but I declare that *I shall again* praise Him!" With that mindset, the Lord will connect with our expectation and intervene to cut short or circumvent what could otherwise prove disastrous.

Let's take one more glimpse at the way that depression or lows can seek to overtake the man or woman of God as we explore the importance of self-care. Often leaders experience lows after great spiritual victories or highs. Many pastors and leaders take their Mondays as days for no calls and use this time for rest and an opportunity to unwind. This is wisdom and a great way to attend to self-care. In the Old Testament, we read an account regarding Elijah the prophet in 1 Kings chapters 18 and 19 where he challenged the prophets of Baal regarding whose god would answer by fire as they built an altar before the people. You can take time to read it in its entirety, but it happened that Baal's prophets called upon Baal from morning until the time of evening sacrifice and received no answer. Elijah mocked them and stated that maybe their god was on a journey, maybe he was asleep or talking to someone else, etc. We know in the end, Elijah placed a sacrifice on the altar and had the sacrifice along with everything around it doused with water three times. After he called upon the God of heaven, the scriptures tell us that God answered by fire and all the people who were around fell on their faces and declared, "The Lord, He is the God; the Lord, He is the God."

Elijah had all of the false prophets of Baal brought to the brook of Kishon, and they were slain there. Ahab went back and told all of this to Jezebel, and she in turn sent a messenger to Elijah saying that he would be slain by the next day because of what he had done to the prophets of Baal. Now Elijah had just experienced a great spiritual victory, but when he received this threatening message from Jezebel, his response was to run away. He hid under a tree and prayed to die. After a great high, a great victory, he was now facing a spiritual low, and I said all of this to say that no matter how high the man or woman of God may go in the things of God, there is no guarantee that he or she won't face the retaliation of the enemy and those whom he uses to negate the mighty things that God chooses to do in, with, and through us.

You see, we must remember that it was God who sent fire from heaven. It was God who showed up and made a declaration regarding the fact that He is the true God, yet the enemy, through Jezebel, pursued the prophet and unleashed a spirit of fear against him and caused him to run until he was exhausted and prayed a prayer asking to die. This is real, my brothers and sisters! This man of God was ready to die after such an overwhelmingly great victory. Watch what happens. This is the reason why we simply must wait on God from a place of expectancy.

The scripture says that God took care of Elijah by sending an angel to feed him twice. This is not a fable; it's an account of what happened, and it shows that even those who are strong in the Lord can suffer lows or deep valleys, but we must remember that our God will restore us. We must allow him to restore us and not act as though all is well when we know that we are in a low place where the enemy is pursuing us and attempting to make us faint and draw back. The Lord will restore our souls. Our God is a God of restoration. Whatever you do, don't give up! For those in leadership, sometimes it's difficult to trust and to acknowledge that perhaps the Lord has sent others (typically a select few) to help restore your strength and to minister to you wanting nothing in return. He will reveal who those individuals are; however, we must be willing to allow them to minister to us as we have ministered to others.

The closer we get to anyone in Christian leadership, we should see glory, we should see mercy, we should see grace, we should see the power of forgiveness. Yes, there may be an image that draws us, but as we get closer, we need to see less of the person and more of Christ, the hope of glory. You see, when we portray false images, when we're not transparent, when we refuse to acknowledge the existence of valleys in our lives, we rob others of the opportunity to experience the reality of the word of God. The word of God is not just written words on a page. We're living this word. We need to pull from the pages and understand that this word is meant to be lived and experienced. David said, "Yea though I walk through the valley of the shadow of death." There were valleys in his life and in the lives of most of those whom we read about in the word of God. Each of us will have valleys too, but since the Lord is with us just as He was with David, Elijah, Joseph, Esther, and others, we don't have to fear any evil. We have to be real about the valleys, just as we want to shout and dance about the mountaintop experiences. Leaders show the way by exemplifying balance. We have ups and we have downs; we rejoice but we also experience disappointments.

As we show the way, let's always seek to portray one who walks through and comes out only by the grace of God and because the Lord is with us. This is a powerful image and one that all others can find courage and confidence in because the Lord is the same today, yesterday, and forever. If He did it for your brother or sister, He can do it for you. In the words of the late songwriter Andraé Crouch, "The Lord chooses and uses ordinary people." Yes, He still does!

Know the way, go the way, and show the way! That's not only about *doing* things, but it's about living. The ability to live a life of integrity is strengthened by the power and might of the true and living God. To some this sounds foreign because we've gotten far removed from seeking the Lord first in our lives and allowing Him to be the One who guides and orchestrates our lives and ministry decisions. A quote by Christian writer Max Lucado says, "A man who wants to lead the orchestra must turn his back on the crowd." If you're going to lead, turn your back to distractions, those who walk out in the middle of your assignment or task, the harsh faces, and instead fix your eyes upon Jesus. Move to His cadence and rhythm. In this fast-paced world, it's just easier to make snap decisions and to come back later and ask the Lord to bless the decisions that we've made or to ask Him to clean up our messes. We must make a conscious decision that we will no longer operate in this manner because we'll go farther faster when we go with the Lord.

Prayer: Lord, thank You for the example that You've shown to us regarding humility, submission, and always giving honor and praise to the Father in all things. We realize that any image that we show to the world must be a reflection of the love and grace that You have extended toward us in taking our faults and sins upon Yourself as You died on the cross. Let us always lead men and women to You and be mindful to tell of Your saving power that has been extended toward us. This

is the most powerful image that anyone who knows You can ever hope to display. In the Name of Jesus I pray. Amen.

God's Wonderful Women

Scripture: Psalm 139:14

NKJV: "I will praise You, for I am fearfully and wonderfully made; Marvelous are Your works, And that my soul knows very well."

NLT: "Thank you for making me so wonderfully complex! Your workmanship is marvelous— how well I know it."

I can recall an awesome time of fellowship and sharing of the word at a women's conference in Stafford, Virginia, at the Victorious Overcomers Church of God in Christ. The theme was "Wonder-full Women" since the intent was to explore the fullness of life, liberty, and power that we have in and through Christ. Having been called to inspire and equip women of God makes it a pleasure for me to fellowship with and to pour into women who have a desire to fulfill their purpose and to do more for the Kingdom.

Wonderful is defined as, "Inspiring delight, pleasure, or admiration; extremely good; marvelous. Knowing the great truth that our God can make something from absolutely nothing, we're going to move forward with what the Lord wants to share with us and speak into our spirits.

My desire and intent are to fan the flame that is burning down inside each and every one of you. I want to stir you up to realize once again just how special, how powerful, and how significant you are in the Kingdom of God right now. So let me establish that there's no one reading these words who does not have purpose in your life.

Take time to say to yourself, "My life has purpose." We're going to talk about the "wonder" of who God has created you to be and how He has purposed and prepared you to navigate through this life. We're also going to talk about the fullness that is ours, the very weight of the glory of God that causes every woman of God to affect everything that she touches with the transforming power of the living God. I'm a firm believer that our foundation in Christ lies in knowing what the word of God has said about us. Yet we must go farther than just standing on that foundational truth; we must build upon it. We must meditate on it until we begin not only to believe it but to allow it to become actions that we apply in our daily lives. There is so much power in the words that we speak because those words come from our thought processes and soon become actions.

Starting today, you can begin to become more conscious of the things that you think and say pertaining to yourself. If your thoughts and words are not serving to build, strengthen, and encourage you throughout the day, then those thoughts and words must be changed. It's not enough to say that we believe God's word, but then when it comes to ourselves, we're held back by negative thoughts and fears of what others may say or have said about us. We must begin to move and operate in what the word of God has declared about us. Just accepting it as truth is not enough. We must let the truth of God's word penetrate our spirits, and that alone will serve to keep us from falling victim to the lies and schemes of the world that shout to us that we're not good enough, that we have to look a certain way, possess certain things, live in certain neighborhoods, or make a certain amount of money in order to have a place of significance or belonging. That couldn't be further from the truth, yet many have bought into these lies and have become stagnant or stifled in their lives.

We're fearfully and wonderfully made. Do you believe that? The scripture reference was given for this impactful truth, yet sometimes those who call themselves Christians or believers are the hardest ones to convince that the word is true and that it applies to them and their lives. We find the wonderfulness that is everything woman throughout the scriptures.

We're not going to hang out nursing our past. We have to be willing to embrace the truth and walk in it. Your past, that thing that wants to condemn you and haunt you, has only served as a setup for you now and a stepping-stone to every one of your tomorrows. The enemy will always use our past to obscure our future, so today I want to hang out around the Wonderfulness! I submit to you that God intended for His women to set the standard and to be the example of what it means to be a woman who 1) is comfortable in her skin, 2) has found forgiveness and dares to walk in it, and 3) can unashamedly be strong, assertive, smart, savvy, and powerful or quiet, unassuming, yet confident in the world and in the Kingdom of God.

So what makes us unique? Do we have an advantage? Some of us certainly don't feel like it. Honestly, we feel quite contrary to that. I know that we come from different backgrounds and experiences, but it's important to know what the Bible has said about us. It's one thing to think we're wonderful by the world's standard, but then we have to constantly get our kudos and approval from the world and those around us. The Bible declares in Psalm 139:14 that you and I are fearfully and wonderfully made. And the writer goes on to say, and that I know right well.

Fearfully and wonderfully made. So let's talk about the wonder in all of this. While checking Wikipedia and an article on the skeleton online at Standardofcare.com and WebMD online, I came across some very interesting facts about the wonder of the human body. The human skeleton is the internal framework of the human body. It is composed of around 270 bones at birth—this total decreases to around 206 bones by adulthood after some bones get fused together. Your heart is an amazing organ that continuously pumps oxygen and nutrient-rich blood throughout your body to sustain life. It is a fist-sized powerhouse that beats 100,000 times per day, pumping five or six quarts of blood each minute, or about 2,000 gallons per day. A piece of brain tissue the size of a grain of sand contains 100,000 neurons and 1 billion synapses, all communicating with each other. All brain cells are not alike. There are as many as 10,000 specific types of neurons in the brain. All of this is quite amazing, right? Babies have big heads to hold rapidly growing brains. A two-year-old's brain is 80 percent of what it will be at its adult size.

There's so much more that we could say about the wonder of God just simply by considering our natural, physical makeup, but I want to share a bit about the wonder of how God has designed you and me. We are carriers of God's anointing with the ability to see as He sees in the Spirit. We can hear His voice and can open our mouths with power and authority that can change the course and plan of the enemy. According to the word of God, we have the power to lay hands on the sick and see them recover. We can walk in agreement with heaven and rest in the assurance that all of heaven is backing us. Just like the writer in scripture, we've got to know this right well! Being fearfully and wonderfully made has to do with more than our physical makeup, and that in and of itself is *awesome*!

The late Dr. Myles Munroe said: "Although we are all born originals, most of us become imitators." You're a force to be reckoned with and the enemy knows this!

We're taunted and intimidated when we don't know what we have or what we're made of. I know right well that I'm fearfully and wonderfully made when I can walk into a situation and discern the presence of God or the activity of the enemy (I'm not talking about paranoia). It's time to know the voice of God and stop double- and triple-checking on what He's saying to us by asking, "Is this me?" "Is this the devil?" or "Is this the result of the big meal that I ate before bedtime?" You see, there are those who will tell you that God is not speaking to you or that He doesn't speak that much, yet they are the very ones who are quick to talk about getting a word from God. Our God does speak, but all too often we brush His leading aside by saying things such as "Something told me ..." or "For some reason, I just felt like ..." We don't place confidence in the truth of the word of God, which is very clear about the Lord leading, guiding, and speaking to His people.

The Lord said, "My sheep know my voice, and a stranger they will not follow." Hear, trust, and obey! All of this is the wonder of God, the great mystery. Great is the mystery of Godliness! For this next move of God on the earth, we're going to have to be full. Not full of ourselves but full of God's Spirit and full of His power. The Lord will drive out fear, doubt, and unbelief. He'll drive out the spirits of guilt and condemnation that have kept so many of us from moving to the next level. You're not what you've done, and when we allow the Spirit of God to take up residence the way that He wants to in our lives, where we're withholding nothing, then nobody will be able to talk us out of our calling and election in Him.

What is it about you? I can't put my finger on it, but I dare to say, it's *favor*! It's the wonder of God! Favor can't be bought! It's a wonder straight from God! It's so important that we recognize and appreciate that. What a tragedy it is when we fail to recognize the favor of God that rests upon our lives. Many chalk God's goodness up to luck. We're not lucky, we're blessed; and the unmerited favor of God will cause us to experience blessings that we simply have no earthly explanation for. Everyone who is prosperous, wealthy, or healthy has not necessarily found favor with God. On the other hand, there are times when those who are favored will also suffer hardship, but we have an assurance that God will always be with us and working on our behalf. We're not immune from the struggles and pitfalls of life.

Ever wonder what it would be like if we could simply live from day to day believing that the word of God is true when it says that *all* things work together for good to them who love the Lord and are called according to His purpose? We wouldn't become worried or fearful, anxious or angry, when things seem to be working against us. There would be no good reason for it because the word of God has already declared that everything pertaining to those who love the Lord and who have been called according to His purpose must work together for good (Rom. 8:28). To live in this manner is certainly reflective of a life of sacrifice, one where we no longer try to figure everything out but we trust the Lord to orchestrate the twists and turns, hills and valleys, in our lives without our interference.

What's operating in and through you is the life-changing presence of God! You are fearfully and wonderfully made! This is the wonder of God, and God wants us and those around us to see what happens when yielded vessels allow themselves to be broken and filled with His anointing, presence, and power! There's a treasure in these earthen vessels, our bodies. Do you know why you're still here today? It was planned; our steps are ordered. No one has control over God's next move in your life.

We are fearfully and wonderfully made! When I read the scripture in Psalm 139:14, it speaks of strength, fortitude, and the reality that when God gets through with us, none of us will look like where we've come from or what we've been through!

Prayer: Father, in the Name of Jesus we come to You with thanksgiving in our hearts. Thank You for Your word, which declares that we are fearfully and wonderfully made. We must know this, and I declare now that it is so! I pull from the written word of God and profess this powerful truth over my life now. Grant me the will and strength to live a life that accepts and reflects unapologetically Your wonder, Your favor, and Your grace that has been extended to me. Amen.

Inspiration Break

Consider this: All of the power and blessings that are bound up in the Name of Jesus only benefit you if you *call* on Him. Have you called on Him and waited expectantly, patiently, and submissively in His presence?

The Spirit of the Lord has come to bring ease to those who are dealing with anxiety on any level. We rebuke fear and trepidation, along with every plot and scheme of the enemy. We are not ignorant of the enemy's devices.

During the time of the pandemic, the enemy has escalated his attack, his schemes, and his plots with an intent to instill fear, trepidation, and intimidation. These are all carnal weapons that are a part of the enemy's arsenal.

Remember that you are above and not beneath. We trust the Lord to speak comfort and contentment to you, your household, your children, on your job, in your neighborhood, in your community, and upon everything and everyone who is attached to you.

We speak peace in the Name of Jesus. Fulfillment is a part of your contentment. The word of the Lord will be fulfilled in your life. Nothing takes Him by surprise, and we declare that He will deal with every crooked and false way that comes against you and all those who are attached to you in an attempt to bring anxiety and to loose the spirit of fear upon your life.

Take courage in knowing that your outcomes don't dictate your faith but your faith dictates your outcomes.

Jeremiah 33:3 declares, "Cry unto Me and I will answer you and show you great and mighty things that you know not."

Because our God reigns and because He's still in control, we can be content. We declare that today! Declare it out of your own mouth.

Because He sees, He knows, and He cares about everything that concerns you, He will quiet the storms in your life.

We don't always understand, but we speak hope and contentment to your people, oh Lord.

The Lord is here and the Spirit of God prevails. He speaks from eternity into time, He quiets the noise and the clamor around us and says, "Rest in Me, trust in Me, for what you're experiencing now is but for a season."

Vision to Refocus Today's Church

> "If then you were raised with Christ, seek those things which are above, where Christ is, sitting at the right hand of God. 2 Set your mind on things above, not on things on the earth" (Col. 3:1,2).

God is moving by His Spirit as He calls to His church to get focused in order to take part in the shift or refocus which is on the horizon for us. As we note here in Colossians 3:1,2, the instruction in the word is to set your mind or set your affections. It's noteworthy that the scriptures use this language because our affections, our emotions, our minds have to be set or focused, otherwise they will be drawn to all sorts of distractions that call to us from our situations and circumstances. When our focus is misdirected to things on the earth, what we see in the earth realm will lie to us, deceive us, and cause us to give weight to things that merit no weight at all in light of what the Lord has done, is doing, and is about to do.

Those who are focused and moving with the Spirit of God in this shift toward a church that is being refocused are hearing a clarion call right now. God calls to the church during this time of shifting and refocus so that we will know that it is not about *doing church* or *having church* as usual. I've heard so many saying this, so what does it mean for us as people of God? What do we mean by "not church as usual"? Certainly during this time of the pandemic, which we are almost nine months into at the time of this writing, God has revealed to us that the body of Christ must shift and operate by His Spirit as never before. The scripture that was referenced in Colossians states that if then we've been raised with Christ, we are to seek those things which are above where Christ is. We declare today that we are setting our minds, our affections, on things above and not on things on the earth!

What would happen if God's people were focused? What would happen if the prayer warriors focused in prayer, all of those in ministry really focused and gave attention to receiving a right-now word from God? What would happen if we all focused on what God is saying rather than how the people might respond to the word that we're preparing to share? Yes, it's true that many prepare messages. and all the while there's a small voice that keeps interrupting with how the people will respond and what they will or won't receive. I've been there and I know that others have as well.

We're not to fear the faces of the people but rather focus on what God has said **and say that**, focus on what

God has said and **do that**, focus on what God has said. and **be that**. There is a clarion call to the remnant of God in these times to hear what the Spirit of The Lord is saying to the church and more specifically what He's saying to you. You are not responsible to bring to pass anything that the Lord has spoken over your life; however, you must believe it and your belief must cause you to live it in order for it to manifest in the earth realm. In other words, stop waiting for something to happen and simply focus on what the Lord has shown you, support it with the word of God, and begin to live like it is so. We're not waiting on a position, a title, a validation, or a piece of paper! If the Lord has spoken it, none of these things make it any more legitimate than it already is. Do you remember the saying, "God has said it, I believe it, and that settles it"? Well, keep that one in mind and just know that if it's settled, then you and I need to start living like it's already a reality.

God is clearly saying, "Focus in prayer, focus in seeking Me, in studying My word so that I can download a fresh anointing, wisdom, insight, and vision as you move forward in time while touching eternity." We're dwelling in this earth, but we're ambassadors who must stay focused on our Kingdom assignments. Our assignment is to share the agenda of the Kingdom of God and the plan of the One who has sent us. We are not our own!

We move and operate in the earth by Kingdom authority and we must rebuke and pull down the distractions that come against us and our Kingdom assignments. We must consciously refuse to be distracted by what's going on around us. What the enemy meant for evil, the Lord has shifted and caused to work for our good, although it may not always readily appear to be so. The Lord now causes the church, His bride, to refocus, to recalibrate and to become more intentional in our warfare. God-given clarity is imminent!

By the power of the living God, we can and must bind the spirit of lawlessness, racism, hatred, and variance that is so prevalent in our nation because the word of God has identified them as works of the flesh and we have power over them. We *cannot* carry out Kingdom agenda with worldly principles. The refocus, the shift, is all about Kingdom.

Who are you without your title? How do you show up? Can you function without it? God calls to us during this time of shifting and refocus so that we will know that it is not church as usual. Get ready to operate outside of the role by which you've been identified and in which you have operated in the past. There's an acceleration in the church of God for Kingdom order and manifestation. What God has planted down on the inside of us must come forth! God is calling for His church to refocus and to make a hard shift away from being impressed with anything apart from an authentic move of God, and He'll show us exactly what that is as we continue to seek Him.

As we refocus, we must understand that we simply cannot rely solely on what we see, hear, or feel. There have been so many things in our nation during the time of this writing that have come against every fiber of decency, justice, or caring within our society. So many distractions pull at us as we have witnessed the murder of numerous men of color in our streets with seemingly no regard for justice. This causes deep responses on the inside of not only adults but our children as well. It has not only affected people of color but many all around the world as the evil of personal and systemic racism, along with hatred, has lifted its ugly head, and we're seeing many who are carrying out unthinkable acts of hostility and violence toward others. The reset and refocus is vital, as we are positioned to come against these forces of evil. God has called and positioned His church (not a building but His people) to make a difference.

We simply cannot afford to become weary in well doing. As those who have refocused, we declare that we walk in discernment and keen awareness, a recognition and a knowing. Being aware, recognizing, and having knowledge of the enemy's devices is not enough. There must be action. Our faith without works is dead, as it then has the propensity to become an indictment against us. There is little respect for an individual or an institution that speaks of faith yet takes no identifiable action during times of hardship or great need. These times cry for a viable response.

As those who have refocused, we declare that we operate from a Kingdom place and vantage point that flesh and blood *cannot* regulate. God is sending a clarion call by His spirit and fine-tuning the spiritual ear of His people. We must dare to go higher and to go deeper.

We declare that we agree with God and all of heaven who have our backs. We refuse to faint, give up, or to question Him when our circumstances don't look like we think they should. Those of you who are intimate with God, the ones with whom He shares His heart and His secrets, you will see the manifestation of the power of our God. You've wept in the night because of what the Lord has revealed to you, but don't be afraid. God is pulling you from a place of obscurity. God's refocused church is not a church full of programs but full of power. You're a part of the shift; move with the shift! Stay focused!

Prayer: Father, in Jesus's Name, I thank You for your written word, which declares that as your children, we have been risen with Christ. Keep us from every distraction as we refocus and accept a shift in our relationship with You. Stir within me the desire to draw closer to You and to become more sensitive to Your voice and the leading of Your Spirit. Give me the boldness to speak when situations warrant a response. Please give me the strength and wisdom to remain silent when I would otherwise be quick to speak but slow to hear Your voice. Amen.

Recognize Your Flame Fanners!

2 Timothy 1:3–7,13,14

³ I thank God, whom I serve with a pure conscience, as *my* forefathers *did,* as without ceasing I remember you in my prayers night and day, ⁴ greatly desiring to see you, being mindful of your tears, that I may be filled with joy, ⁵ when I call to remembrance the genuine faith that is in you, which dwelt first in your grandmother Lois and your mother Eunice, and I am persuaded is in you also. ⁶ Therefore I remind you to stir up the gift of God which is in you through the laying on of my hands. ⁷ For God has not given us a spirit of fear, but of power and of love and of a sound mind.

¹³ Hold fast the pattern of sound words which you have heard from me, in faith and love which are in Christ Jesus. ¹⁴ That good thing which was committed to you, keep by the Holy Spirit who dwells in us.

Timothy was the **son of a Greek father and a Jewish mother**. He was with Paul during one of Paul's later missionary journeys, and in a passage of scripture in 1 Timothy 1:2, Paul addresses Timothy as "my true son in the faith."

Timothy was a young man probably no older than late teens or early twenties when he joined Paul, yet he was seen as faithful and the elders took note of him. Timothy's mother and grandmother had been flame fanners in his young life, preparing him to recognize the Christ, the Messiah, when he would come. Paul notes in 2 Timothy 3:15, "And how from infancy you have known the Holy Scriptures, which are able to make you wise for salvation through faith in Christ Jesus."

There were two letters written to Timothy, and in the first one, Paul advised him on leading the church. He exhorted Timothy not to let others look down on him because of his youth but to set an example for other believers "in speech, in conduct, in love, in faith and in purity" (1 Tim. 4:12). Paul advised Timothy to be devoted to reading Scripture, exhorting, and teaching, and not to neglect the gift that he had been given.

The enemy doesn't care much about you excelling naturally in this world. That's what many people are after. Even in the church, there are those who are looking for others to push them to the next position or title. On any level, we can benefit from those who encourage, push, or help us to maintain forward momentum. We'll call these "fanners."

But just as Paul warned Timothy, and I'm para-phrasing, you'll have haters and resisters inside and outside of the church. As I've said many times before and I'll say it again, so let me establish that each and every person has purpose in his or her life and there are absolutely no mistakes. We have a choice to make regarding whether or not we'll live out our God-given purpose or if we'll live our lives our own way, but your life has purpose and God's intent is that you would fulfill that purpose.

We're talking about flame fanners, and I want you to consider that there is a flame within you that comes from God and it has been placed there as a means to ignite you for your Kingdom purpose and assignment.

Let's establish that what has been placed within the believer for Kingdom purpose is of God and not of ourselves. Within each of us is at least one God-given gift that is intended to be identified, developed, and used for the purpose of expanding and building the Kingdom of God. It is God-given and not of man; we don't choose it, but we must identify it and begin to operate in it because this is where the flame within us resides.

The Holy Spirit of God gives power and ignites the gifts of the Spirit that reside within us. That flame within those who are born again is not ignited by simply sitting in the midst of good teaching or preaching or being around those who are anointed. Timothy was surrounded by godly women who had the gift of faith. The gift is in us, but we have the responsibility to stir it up. The apostle Paul wrote to Timothy, "For this reason I remind you to fan into flame the gift of God, which is in you" (2 Tim. 1:6). We must have a desire to stir it up and to become flames in the Kingdom that cannot be easily extinguished.

We're talking about flame fanners, not flame starters because God has already imparted to us but what we have is in a state of potential, the operative word being *potent*, meaning "powerful."

This flame does not function by natural means. It is really sad to see people trying to operate in the things of the Spirit by their own power, will, and volition. Those who fan are fanners by way of the Spirit of God. They connect with the spirit of God within you and help to bring clarity, increase, and challenge to your walk. You can readily recognize a flame fanner because their presence seems to stir something in the Spirit. The Spirit of God within you seems intensified as they pray, preach, exhort, teach, or connect with the power of God in any way. They inspire while at the same time exposing areas in our lives that yearn for greater depths than what we have dared to allow ourselves to experience.

As we take a look at Timothy's life here in the scripture passages that have been given, he was young in the ministry. He was one of Paul's sons in the gospel, and his heritage was rich. Note that although he had a rich heritage, as he was greatly affected and influenced by women of faith in his family—his mother and grandmother—Timothy was still being admonished by Paul to understand that what was in him required *his* attention. It had to be his decision and his alone to place a demand on it in order for him to become all that God had designed for him to be and to do. Paul was a flame fanner!

Paul hadn't come to start the flame, but he instructed Timothy to tend to the flame that was within him and to stir the flame, just as we are to do. We were never meant to stay in a state of potential. There are those around you who are content with themselves and content to see you remain the same, but know this: nothing touched by fire can remain the same. I'll say that again: nothing touched by fire can remain the same. Even the heat from the fire changes the makeup and the character of anything near it. Stand close enough to a fire and your clothing may become hot, the temperature of your skin will change and become warm or hot to the extent that you may have to back away, and if you get too close, you run the risk of something catching on fire.

In the spiritual context when we speak of the flame, the light of the flame reveals, exposes, draws, changes, causes a stripping and a transformation. Anyone who has ever dealt with a natural fire knows that if we don't attend to the flame, and if there's nothing around the flame to feed it or in other words to cause it to continue to burn or to spread, it will eventually go out.

Flame fanners are those who feed your flame; they apply the kindling. There are those who cause your flame to burn hotter and brighter so that the fire of God can be applied to life's situations that you will encounter. As a flame fanner, Paul had to call out some of those things that he knew Timothy was contending with. You need someone who sees what you can't see, like Paul with Timothy. Stay away from those who can't or who refuse to see. The fanner fans the flame so that what needs to be burned off can be burned off before the next level, before the next move of God in your life.

Paul told Timothy to "Stir it up!" He told Timothy to devote himself to reading the scriptures, to preaching, and to teaching. He admonished him not to neglect the gift that was given to him through prophecy and laying on of hands of the elders. He made sure to advise him to be diligent about these things and to give himself wholly to them in spite of the fact that he was a young man, so that everyone would be able to see his progress. Paul was in the role of a fanner when he told Timothy to watch and be mindful of his life and doctrine and to persevere in them so that he would not only save himself but also his hearers (1 Tim. 4:13–16). He told him how to conduct himself with elders, never to rebuke them but to treat them as fathers. My, how this teaching is needed today! He went on to share that the elder women are to be treated or seen as mothers and the younger women as sisters with all purity. In other words, he was to treat the young women with the utmost respect and not become common with them (1 Tim. 5:1,2).

Paul shared a powerful truth with this young Timothy in 2 Timothy 1:7: "For God has not given us the spirit of fear; but of power, and of love, and of a sound mind." It was as if he were saying, "Timothy, I know you're wrestling or will wrestle with being young, and the reality that some may not want to hear or receive from you. Timothy, you may be dealing with fears, but I don't want you walking in resentment or getting distracted by attacks on your mind, so let me take the liberty in the spirit to fan you right here." Of course, I've added my backdrop to this; however, it seems apparent that Paul took the time to pour into Timothy in order to help him realize that he could rise above the obstacles that he would encounter by applying himself to study and developing his own unique relationship with Christ. This quote by the late Dr. Myles Munroe bears repeating: "Although we are all born as originals, most of us become imitators." We all need those flame fanners in our lives who will continually nudge and sometimes push us toward the unique space that has been carved out for us within the body of Christ.

I say to you today, get around those who can fan you in the spirit, those who demand more, those who help you to see more. Sometimes it's through your fanner that the Spirit of God will bring things to your remembrance. Just as Paul was there for Timothy and so many others and his word still inspires us today, there will be those who are sent to our lives to fan the flame of God that is down on the inside of us. When we're going through, they remind us of truths in the word of God that cause us to triumph, such as, "All things work together for good to them who love God and who are the called according to His purpose" or "Greater is He that is in you than He that is in the world."

Flame fanners speak truth; they're not "fans" as in followers who will say whatever they think will stroke our egos and make us feel good. No, they're fanners of the flame that God has placed in us by the Holy Ghost and they are tasked with being bearers of truth as well as light. Speaking truth to us is not always about quoting a bunch of scriptures, but sometimes it's simply about helping us to see where we've chosen to step out of the race or where we've given over to the enemy that which was purposed for us to have. God has something for you and me to do in the Kingdom, but if we walk in a place of continual resistance or a mindset of thinking that we can walk this walk on our own, we're wrong. We're dead wrong!

Somebody must speak truth, and this is the role of a fanner. Not your truth, not my truth, but God's truth. Everyone wants to speak his or her own truth, but at the end of the day, the only truth that exists and that matters is God's truth.

Let's talk God's truth—

> ➢ **It doesn't matter where you've been**
> ➢ **It doesn't matter what you've done or what they've said about you**
> ➢ **It doesn't matter what they said you could never become**
> ➢ **You can do all things through Christ who strengthens you**
> ➢ **You're above and not beneath**
> ➢ **You're the head and not the tail**
> ➢ **Behold if any man be in Christ Jesus, he or she is a new creature/creation**

Flame fanners remind us of God's truth!! They won't allow us to wallow in our false narratives and distractions. They remind us when we're low, when we're struggling, and when we're grieving that God's still here, He hasn't left you, He won't leave you, and He's strengthening you! Then our flame starts to rise!

Flame fanners don't have control over God's next move in your life. As you avail yourself to fanning and to fanners, understand that you may be fanned into adversity, opposition, and various trials. These come to make your flame stronger, for it takes more to keep it burning as you advance in the Kingdom—more kindling, more logs. Remember that a good, strong fire must be fed. We place something on that fire or allow the air or wind to blow on it in order to ensure that it burns bright. I've come right back to the point where the Lord requires that we become living sacrifices. It seems that there is just no way around it if we are to truly reflect the image of Christ in our lives. God pleads with us through His servant, Paul, in Romans 12:1 to present ourselves, our bodies, as a living sacrifice. If we present our bodies, then no part of us is withheld. We want flame fanners but we have to tend to our own flame. We have to fan the flame that is within ourselves and stir it up just as Timothy was admonished to do.

We must be willing to become the sacrifice. Remember that **nothing** touched by fire remains the same. The mystery of becoming the living sacrifice has several layers. First of all, it's a choice because a living sacrifice can get off the altar and out of the fire at any time. We must trust God to make the flames as hot as He chooses and to allow them to burn as long as He deems necessary. Our trust and our faith in Him keep us on the altar of sacrifice because we realize that when we have allowed the flames of God to consume our lives, we will remain unscathed, yet everything about us or in our lives that's not like God is burned up or consumed.

Sometimes people make living a Christian life seem next to impossible. It's really about surrender. We must surrender our will and believe that God has a divine or perfect will for our lives. Well, how do we surrender our will? After we accept Jesus as Lord over our lives, we take time daily to ask Him to lead and direct our lives so that our will lines up with His will. Our agenda is never placed ahead of His. The teaching in the Bible about becoming a living sacrifice has to do with understanding that each day you and I have a choice to either do things our own way, without considering or consulting the Lord, or we can live our lives as though every decision requires His direction and approval. This type of lifestyle is easier to write about than to live because our nature as humans is to be selfish and to want things our own way. We don't want anybody telling us what to do. Yet scripture teaches us to acknowledge Him in *all* of our ways, and it's then that He will direct our paths. To live in this way, consistently open to His direction and leading, is foundational to becoming a living sacrifice and walking in surrender to the will of God.

As living sacrifices, it's a choice to allow God to burn away all that's not like Him—the hatred, jealousy, envy, adultery, pornography, withholding of our praise, our worship, our prayer life. I can recall many times in my Christian walk when I would withhold my praise from God because of things that were going on in my life that I simply did not like. If there was friction in my marriage and things weren't going well, I held the mindset that to get to the church and to sing and praise as if nothing was going on was being hypocritical on my part. I felt like I had nothing to praise God for since everything around me seemed to be in shambles. But you see, that's just not true. We never have a reason not to praise God or not to be thankful. I really had to learn this over time. It's not about what we may be experiencing at the time, but the reality is that the Lord is always worthy of our praise. He is the Creator of all things, our Redeemer, our Lord, our Guide, and our Friend. He's all that and so much more. Beyond all of that, He's worthy of praise not because of what He has done or is doing in our lives but because of who He is.

No longer can we refuse to be changed. So many want to carry the flame, the fire, the anointing of God but not allow it to change us. What's in you is the life-changing presence of God! As your flame is fanned, it's not about others patting you on the back and agreeing with the agenda that you've set for your own life.

We're all in different places in our walk of faith. We can be fanners and we can be fanned, but we are not to be burning like wildfires, wreaking havoc and destruction among everything and everyone around us. A lot of time has been devoted here to talking about fire and flames, but we know that fire can also be a destructive force if not properly maintained. The Holy Spirit fell as fire, the scripture speaks of us being as a city set on a hill, the light of the world with reference to the flames that burned in the city causing all to take note of it. Flame fanners are the ones who help us to stay in a place of renewal, accountability, and growth. A flame that burns brings light, hope, and warmth. That same flame also has the potential to draw, spread, and consume.

You might ask, "Then how do I maintain my flame in the face of opposition and adversity?" This takes us back to the advice that Paul gave to Timothy regarding the need to be disciplined in his Christian life. We must determine to study more, to pray more, and to quiet ourselves in order to listen for the voice of God in the midst of all that we may be dealing with. Get intimate with God and find out how He speaks to you. It could be through impressions in your spirit, He may show you things, or He may give you dreams. There's a real issue with those who claim that God doesn't speak whenever it's someone else who claims to have heard God, yet on the other hand they're constantly talking about what God has said to them. So the reality is that they hold the position that God speaks to them but not to anyone else. This is a fallacy.

God's word declares that His sheep know his voice, and that's for a reason. Plain and simple, the reason is because He speaks to us! We have an all-seeing, all-knowing God, and what sets Him apart from all false gods or idols is that He's alive and there would be no need for us to know His voice if He did not speak. So many walk around saying they don't know what God wants them to do, they've never heard His voice, and on and on and on. More than likely that mindset prevails because we haven't taken the time to quiet ourselves and to spend time with Him. Even in the natural sense, you only get to know a person's voice when you spend enough time with them and become acquainted with them. It's only then that they cease to have to tell you who they are when they speak to you. You know who they are because you know their voice. It's the same with God, and no one can tell you how He's going to speak to you, but the reality is that He will and He does speak.

Many times I hear people saying, "Something told me." They refuse to give credit to God. This takes away from our capacity to hear. Give Him credit for speaking. There are times when you will have a strong inclination or unction to do a certain thing, to call someone, to stop in the middle of what you're doing, and to simply begin to pray. Practice being quick to follow these promptings and you will find that you will become more discerning and sensitive to the voice of the Spirit of the Lord and His leading. Maybe you've already experienced this as you've strongly felt the urge to phone someone only to hear them say, "I was hoping that you would call" or "This is right on time! I needed someone to talk to." Life with Christ and walking in His Spirit isn't designed to be difficult, but it does require daily application, faith, and a willingness to follow His lead.

Now, back to dealing with how we maintain our flame in the face of opposition and adversity. Both opposition and adversity are real. If we've been around for any length of time, we are all very aware of this. The sense of rejection and isolation can sometimes be very real even within Christian circles, but we can hold on to our drive and will to move forward even in the face of these obstacles. Maintaining our flame is not always about jumping about and being the most vibrant coal on the pile. Have you ever stirred a pile of coals that seemed to have been totally burned out only to find that underneath, there were some that were still red and hot. They're unassuming, and yet the fire still burns hot within those coals. I like to think of this as experiencing the flame while basking in the presence and peace of God. Actually it's sometimes during those moments of just basking in God's presence and pulling away from all of the hustle in life that we really begin to experience that "fire" that is shut up within us and that causes us to go ahead when we might otherwise have been inclined to give up.

Consider that you're experiencing the presence and peace of God as a means to enable you to:

> Become a flame fanner—what you've gone through has only served to add more fuel to your fire;
> Become your own first fanner, the one who is determined to stir up what is on the inside of you;
> Fan the flame of someone who's now walking where you've walked—they're dealing with

spousal abuse, the shame and guilt of abortion, rejection, fear, intimidation, a negative diagnosis or prognosis;

➢ Discern the pain and disappointment of another who is about to give up. You have the power, opportunity, and responsibility to fan their flame!

Prayer: Father, in the matchless Name of Jesus, help me to pull from Your divine word and apply to my life the reality and ability of stirring every gift that is within me. Help me to recognize those who have been sent to fan the flame of Your Spirit within me and cause me to be a flame fanner for others as I seek to build them up in the most holy faith. I choose not only to read Your word, but I acknowledge it as truth and I will live each day to apply it to my life in Christ. Amen.

Inspiration Break

Oftentimes the Spirit of God will alert us and cause us to become aware of things before we have the understanding of what has actually happened in the spirit realm. You and I are spirit beings having an experience in a natural body.

Our spirit receives messages from God and begins to cause us in the natural to become excited about something that we may not be privy to with our natural senses or our natural mind.

Have you ever had those times when you begin to feel excited and you just know that the Lord is up to something? What has happened is that He has uploaded information into your spirit and you have not become aware of exactly what it is before it is revealed in the natural realm.

Since we have come outside of the four walls of the church, the Lord has begun to deal with so many in ways that He never has before. We've been pulled away from programs and rituals to a place of dependence upon Him and His voice. You can't take what you've done before and try to apply it to where the Lord is taking you.

The Lord is giving us a "newness." He's doing a new thing, and it will spring forth according to the word of God at the appointed time. You will know it! The Spirit of the Lord will let you know that all things have become new.

You don't know all of the intricacies of it, but the Lord is doing something and awakening something within you. He alone has the ability, the wherewithal, and the power to make that place where you dwell brand-new, and you don't even have to physically move. The new thing will be evident to the enemy and everyone around you. They will know that it is of God.

Let's agree and declare that your prayer life is new, your gifting is new, you're doing new things in God and operating on another level now. Your vision is new, and clarity is coming where things were once out of focus.

The Lord is about to show you things that you've never seen before, and He is doing a new thing in you. He is opening up streams in the desert and doing miraculous things through His people, even during a pandemic.

New means *new*, and you are entering into a new place in God.

It Ain't Over!

Genesis 37:18–20

¹⁸ Now when they saw him afar off, even before he came near them, they conspired against him to kill him. ¹⁹ Then they said to one another, "Look, this [b]dreamer is coming! ²⁰ Come therefore, let us now kill him and cast him into some pit; and we shall say, 'Some wild beast has devoured him.' We shall see what will become of his dreams!"

Someone else is tied to your ability to hold on, to exercise patience, and to have a resolve to continually move toward your purpose—and it may not be who you think. The scripture reference takes us to a very familiar story, but I want to take time to pull out a few excerpts that speak to the fact that even when everything points to the end, it ain't over! We know this isn't considered proper English, yet sometimes we just feel like taking a position even in our declaration that lets the enemy know that we mean business and that we're taking a stand. This chapter title kind of does that for me.

Joseph had ten older brothers and he was favored by his father, Jacob (whom God later named Israel) because he was the son of his old age. Jacob showed his special love for Joseph by making a coat of many colors for him. This act solidified in the hearts of his brothers that their father loved Joseph more than all of them. Genesis 37:4 (AMP) states, "His brothers saw that their father loved Joseph more than all of his brothers; so they hated him and could not [find it within themselves to] speak to him on friendly terms." This fueled the jealousy of Joseph's brothers, who were sons of other wives of his father. His brothers hated him and could not speak peaceably to him. Then Joseph had a dream. Now mind you, we don't determine what we dream, and Joseph was given a prophetic dream.

Joseph was actually given two dreams, and he decided to share his dreams with his father and brothers. In his first dream, he and his brothers were binding sheaves of grain stalks when suddenly his sheaf stood upright and the sheaves of his brothers surrounded his sheaf and bowed down in respect (Gen. 37:6,7). Sheaves are bundles of wheat that people would gather and tie. After sharing this dream with his brothers, they hated him even more than at the beginning. We really don't know what Joseph expected in terms of a response from them, but they asked him, "Are you actually going to reign over us? Are you really going to rule *and* govern us as your subjects?"

Joseph dreamed another dream and shared that one as well. In the second dream, the sun, moon, and the eleven stars made obeisance to him or bowed in respect to him. This time he shared the dream with his brothers and his father. His father rebuked him and asked, "What is this dream that you have dreamed? Shall your mother and I along with your brothers come and bow down before you?" His brothers envied him but the scriptures state that his father "observed the saying," meaning that he took careful note of what Joseph had shared. Some have come away from the text with the description of Joseph as a favorite son who was arrogant and self-absorbed, but we see nothing in the scriptures that would indicate such a description. Our focus will be on the fact that what God chooses for our lives and the wonderful things that He shares with us will not always be understood, accepted, or celebrated by those around us. Joseph had no control over what he dreamed, and he certainly had no control over how what he saw in those dreams would come to fruition in his life. The hatred that his brothers had toward him because of the dreams could not prevent the content of those dreams from unfolding in all of their lives.

One day Joseph's father sent him out to check and see how his brothers were faring in the fields as they were feeding the flocks. He went looking for them in Shechem, but a *certain man* told him that he had overheard them say that they were going to move on to Dothan, which was about a day's journey from where he had hoped to find them.

As Joseph made his way to their location and they saw him off in the distance, they began to plot his death. Nothing good can come from allowing jealousy, envy, and unforgiveness to rest in our bosom and to take up residence in our heart. No doubt, Joseph knew that his older brothers didn't like him; he was aware of how they treated him and how they always spoke to him using unkind words. But I would venture to say that it probably never entered Joseph's mind that they would try to kill him. They began to say to one another as he came toward them from far off, "Behold, this dreamer cometh. Come now therefore, and let us slay him, and cast him into some pit, and we will say, Some evil beast has devoured him: and we shall see what will become of his dreams." They thought that they could kill the dream by killing the dreamer, but it wasn't Joseph's dream. God had given the dream.

The oldest brother, Reuben, convinced them to throw him into a pit alive rather than to take his life because his secret motive was to come back later and save Joseph in order to get him back to their father (Gen. 37:22). Unfortunately, Rueben's intentions were foiled. The scripture is not clear regarding where Reuben went, but for a period of time, he was apart from his brothers and they sold Joseph to Midianites who were passing their way. When Reuben returned to the pit to rescue Joseph, he wasn't there because his brothers had sold him for twenty pieces of silver. Reuben tore his clothes as a sign of grief and despair. How could this have happened? It was Judah who suggested selling Joseph into slavery instead of killing him, and thereby they could profit. How selfish and hard-hearted of these young men to take their brother's coat and dip it in the blood of one of the baby goats in order to bring it before their father with the lie that Joseph had been killed. Jacob mourned and none of his sons or daughters could comfort him as he declared that he would go to his grave mourning for his son. How hardened their hearts had become in order to be able to watch their father mourn the loss of their brother while they hid a horrible lie all in an attempt to do away with this hated brother who now carried a dream.

The Midianite merchantmen brought Joseph into Egypt and sold him into Egypt unto Potiphar, an officer of Pharaoh's and captain of the guard. Joseph was around seventeen years old when he was sold into Egypt. By the time he was thirty years old, he was made overseer over Potiphar the Egyptian's house and over all that he had. The word of God clearly states that Joseph was a goodly man and well favored, for Genesis 39:2 notes that "the Lord was with Joseph and he was a prosperous man." As a testament to the favor of God that was upon his life, we are told that the Egyptian was blessed because of Joseph as the word of God says that the Lord blessed the Egyptian's house for Joseph's sake. You see, sometimes the blessings upon those around us are a direct result of the favor that rests upon our lives. Joseph had so much favor until Potiphar withheld nothing from him except his own wife.

Soon Potiphar's wife began trying to seduce Joseph and became angry with him when he refused to sleep with her. Many of you are very familiar with this story, but we are laying it out because it is so important for all of us to realize that in spite of all the plots and schemes of the enemy and those around us, it ain't over until God says it's over. Some of you may be walking through some very difficult times in your life right now, but just know that God has a plan and your focus must remain on Him. Joseph's way was not made easy. Potiphar's wife falsely accused him of attempted rape, and since she had the clothing item that he left behind when he ran from the house, it seemed that she had him right where she wanted him. She was intent on punishing him for rejecting her advances.

We must never let our guard down by trusting in the arm of the flesh, positions, or the status that we've been blessed to obtain. It was evident that Potiphar's wife sought to destroy him. She had him thrown into prison, but take a look at what happened when Joseph was thrown into prison. Even there favor showed up, and the keeper of the prison committed everything to Joseph's hand because he could see that the Lord was with him. Understand, man or woman of God, that somebody is tied to your persistence and your determination to stand in the face of adversity although it may be hard and may seem as though you're standing alone. The application in our own lives from what we read and glean from Joseph's story is all about being our authentic selves in Christ no matter what situation we may find ourselves in. The gifts that the Lord has entrusted to us are not just for use within the four walls of the church or among those who are just like us. This man's gifts and integrity were evident in whatever arena or circumstance he found himself. It should be the same with us.

As we move forward in his story, we'll find that the text screams of the truth that we read in Proverbs: "A man's gift makes room for him and brings him before great men." This is so very powerful! All of us must remember this because God has placed a gift or talent in each of us, and room will be made for it/them in this world. It was the gifts that operated in Joseph that consequently allowed him to fulfill his God-given vision, and it's the same for you and me. Room is made when we dare to exercise the gift and not hide it, waiting for the moment or place that we think is appropriate for it to come forth. Our spiritual gifts are a part of our spiritual makeup, and they operate by the spirit of God. Become familiar with what God has placed on the inside of you, then accept and embrace it.

God not only dealt with Joseph through dreams, but Joseph also possessed the gift of interpreting dreams. While in prison, he became acquainted with the butler and baker of Pharaoh. Both of them had dreams that Joseph interpreted. All he asked was for the butler to remember him and to make mention of him to Pharaoh upon his release, but the butler forgot about him. At the end of two full years after the butler's release from prison, Pharaoh had a dream, and all of a sudden the butler remembered Joseph.

As we're pulling from the written pages, please allow me to admonish you to stay persistent and to realize that you cannot escape the favor of God. The anointing and favor of God was upon Joseph's life, and in spite of all that he went through, he could not escape it. He entered Egypt as a slave, yet everywhere he went, people realized that there was something different, something special, about him. In the midst of adversity even to the extent of being falsely accused and locked up, Joseph kept moving forward and operating in his gifts. He had experienced the pain of rejection from the time that he was a young boy, and to make it worse, that rejection came from those of his own household, his brothers, his father's sons. As much as his father loved him, Joseph still had to wrestle with hurt from his brothers, who took every opportunity to speak negatively to and about him. They finally took occasion for the ultimate act of rejection and betrayal by selling him off to Egypt although their initial plan was to take his life. I'm sure that on some level, Joseph said within himself, "There's got to be more to my life than this!" Have you ever said that? "There's got to be more!"

His brothers must have thought that they were finally rid of him when they sold him, but right where you are, can you just say "!t ain't over!"? I can't help but think that there were times when Joseph didn't know whether he was coming or going, but God was in the midst and He was working His plan! What has God shown you? Weeping may endure for a night, but joy will come in the morning.

I'm sure there were many times when Joseph wept. While in the pit, perhaps he wept. While in the caravan with total strangers after being sold by his brothers, I'm sure he wept. After being thrown into prison after doing all the good he had done only to be falsely accused by Potiphar's wife, I'm sure he wept.

Joseph's life was far from easy, and yet he was favored. You may say, "Yes, but everything was in his hand to do with as he pleased while he was in Egypt." What we must remember is that there was a process that he had to go through before he got to that point, and the process didn't begin in the pit or in Egypt. Joseph carried something that no one saw. He carried the pain, rejection, separation, hurt, and longing for acceptance that he had dealt with from the time when he was a young boy. Anybody who is part of a family wants to feel accepted by that family, and he just didn't find that fit among his brothers due to their jealousy of his father's love for him. Yet as we follow his story, we find that he operated in his God-given gifts and abilities even while confined in prison. It was his character and integrity that caused him to flee from the clutches of Potiphar's wife, which subsequently resulted in his incarceration.

If he was anything like most of us, he must have struggled with what God had shown him. On some level, he might have tossed around questions such as, "Did the dream come from God?" "Why did I share it?" "Why did I think for a moment that they would understand or maybe accept that it was from God and rejoice with me?" "What was I thinking?"

In life, we will endure difficult and trying times. Sometimes those hardest and most perplexing seasons in our lives seem to come as a result of what God has said or what He has shown to us. Temptation doesn't come from

God. James 1:3 states, "Let no man say when he is tempted, I am tempted of God: for God cannot be tempted with evil, neither tempteth He any man." Temptation is always intended to make us fail or to fall.

Testing, on the other hand, builds us and can prepare us for what is to come. Your test is the backdrop to your testimony! It's during the test that pruning may take place. Whatever is in our lives that is not of God, He cuts away. It is pruned. It doesn't feel good, but it's for our good.

Somewhere down inside, Joseph must have said, "It ain't over! There has to be more to my existence than this!"

In my first book, *Essentials for Frontline Living*, there's a chapter titled "It's Not Your Dream" that recounts the story of Joseph and the dreams that he dreamed. It speaks about how God will orchestrate and set into motion what He has imparted to our spirits because, whatever it is, it's not ours; it's His.

As we fast-forward, Pharaoh had two dreams and needed someone to interpret them. He sent for all the magicians and wise men in Egypt, but when he shared his dreams, none of them could interpret them. It was then that the butler remembered Joseph and told Pharaoh how Joseph had interpreted his dream and that of the chief baker while they were in prison. He added that everything that the young Hebrew told them had come to pass just as he said. Pharaoh sent for Joseph and had him brought out of the dungeon. Joseph shaved and changed his clothing before coming before Pharaoh because the Egyptians were a very clean people who did not believe in having hair on the face. When Pharaoh informed Joseph that he had been told that he was able to interpret dreams, Joseph was very quick to answer that the ability was not in him but that God would be the one to give Pharaoh an interpretation that would bring peace.

After the dreams were shared and Joseph told him that the two dreams were, in fact, one, he gave the interpretation regarding seven years of great plenty and seven years of famine that would follow those years. The famine was to be so great that everyone would quickly forget the years of plenty that they would be afforded to enjoy. Joseph explained that the dream had been repeated twice to Pharaoh because that was God's way of indicating that this thing was established by God and would come to pass shortly (Gen. 41).

Joseph then advised Pharaoh to find and select a wise, discerning man and to set that person over the land of Egypt. As Joseph began to advise on what would be needed, it was apparent that God had imparted wisdom to him that would secure the land of Egypt during the time of plenty and that would keep them from utterly perishing during the great famine that was to follow. Pharaoh and all of his servants knew that the advice was sound; it seemed good, and Pharaoh's statement regarding the appointment of Joseph speaks to the fact that he recognized that the Spirit of the Lord was with Joseph. Pharaoh responded, "Can we find such a one as this, a man in whom is the Spirit of God?" He declared to Joseph that it was God who had shown him all that he had spoken of and furthermore that there was no one as discerning or as wise as Joseph in the land. With that declaration, Pharaoh placed Joseph over his house and declared before everyone that the people would be ruled by the word of Joseph and that only in regard to the throne would the Pharaoh be greater than Joseph. Pharaoh set Joseph over all of the land of Egypt. How is that for one's gift taking him or her before great men? How is that for one's gift making room for them on the earth?

Pharaoh took his signet ring off his own hand and placed it on Joseph's hand, had him clothed in fine linen garments, and put a gold chain around his neck. Joseph rode behind Pharaoh in the second chariot and the people cried out before him, "Bow the knee!" By Pharaoh's instructions, no man in Egypt was to lift his hand or foot in the land of Egypt without Joseph's permission. He was given authority over all the land of Egypt. Pharaoh changed his name to Zaphnath-Paaneah and gave him a wife who was a daughter of the priest of On. Joseph was thirty years old at this time.

Time passed and the seven years of plenty came and the seven years of famine began to come just as Joseph had foretold. Famine was all over the face of the earth, but due to the wisdom that God had given to Joseph as an administrator, there was bread in Egypt. The word of God tells us that all countries came to Joseph in Egypt to buy grain because the famine was so very severe elsewhere.

God was orchestrating everything that he had shown to Joseph years ago in his dreams. I will assert that the gifts that we possess have been given by God and are intended to be used to glorify Him and to benefit those around us. Everywhere that Joseph went, others were able to see that God was with him although they could not quite explain what it was that was different about this young man. When we walk with God and adhere to His plan, He has a way of causing others to declare His presence and His power just as He did in the case of Pharaoh. Joseph's brothers, Potiphar's wife, those in prison, the Pharaoh, and all those around him were all tied to Joseph's story. They were tied to his persistence, his perseverance, and his patience whether he or they knew it or not. God was at work.

Needless to say, Joseph's family was touched by the famine just as others were, and Jacob, his father, told his sons to journey to Egypt in order to buy grain so that they could survive and not die. Jacob did not want to send his youngest son, Benjamin, because he was the only other son that he had by his wife, who was also Joseph's mother. Benjamin and Joseph shared both parents, unlike the other brothers. Jacob was determined not to lose this child of his old age as he had lost Joseph. So they made the journey from Canaan to Egypt to buy food. Since Joseph was governor over the land and the one who sold to all the people of the land, they found themselves before Joseph and bowed down before him with their faces to the ground. Although they didn't recognize Joseph, he recognized them immediately but acted as a stranger toward them and spoke harshly to them. Joseph remembered the dreams that God had given to him and accused them of being spies. I believe that God was giving him a plot to obtain access to his father and younger brother. Joseph was around thirty-nine years old when his brothers first came to Egypt (it was the second year of the famine, or nine years after he had been made overseer in Egypt). That seems like an awfully long time to be separated from his family, more specifically his father and the life that he once knew. The reality is that he didn't even know if they were still alive. God was working something in Joseph. He wasn't ready to see his brothers until God set it up. Somehow in the midst of all the pain, anguish, disappointment, and trauma of separation, life kept propelling him forward. Maybe it was those flickers of hope or those times of success that caused him to continue persisting and remembering that the God whom his father worshipped must be real.

Pause for a moment and consider that somebody else is tied to your persistence, your perseverance, and your patience just as we are seeing it play out in Joseph's life.

I'm reminded of the scripture in 1 Thessalonians 5:24: "Faithful is He who calleth you, Who also will do it." Joseph had to face his brothers again after all of those years. He could have done them harm by just speaking a word. He could have sought revenge. You are strongly urged to read Genesis 42, where you will find that Joseph had his brothers put in prison for three days, and I'm sure that they rehashed all that they had done to their brother, although at this time they had no idea who Joseph was.

What is compelling and is also telling of Joseph's character is that he kept his God at the center. When he brought his brothers out of prison on the third day, he said to them, "Do this and live, for I fear God: if you are honest men, let one of your brothers be confined to your prison house; but you, go and carry grain for the famine of your houses. And bring your youngest brother to me; so your words will be verified and you shall not die." Joseph's brothers believed that they were falling upon hardship because of what they had done to Joseph years prior. For Joseph, the hurt was there, the memory was there, and his memory served him correctly.

As his brothers began to recount in their language all that they had done to Joseph and how God must be placing judgment upon them because of that, they had no idea that Joseph understood what they were saying. He had to turn away from them and find a place to relieve his pain. He wept because that tender place was still there in his heart. Here his brothers were before him, the ones who had sold him into slavery and had actually had a plan to kill him. He had the power and authority within his position to have taken revenge upon them on the spot, but he didn't. He had to be open and patient for divine leading. Remember that we're looking at all of this, as we do with all of scripture, in past tense, and it's easy to see everything as it's unfolding.

Yet with Joseph, he was there in the middle of his pain, anguish, and the decision as to whether or not he should reveal who he was at that time. No, it wasn't time for that yet. He wanted to see his younger brother and he wanted to see his father, whom he had learned was still alive. He had to remain patient, as God had not given the release for him to divulge his identity. All of those whom he had left behind in Canaan were tied to his patience and his ability and willingness to wait on the timing of God. Somebody is tied to your patience! The trying of our faith worketh patience, but the scripture says that patience must have her perfect work. Why would you need patience if nothing else is on the horizon for you? Patience for what? Tests indicate that a testimony is on the way!

Refrain from acting too hastily in those situations where it seems that you have an opportune time to get revenge. Vengeance belongs to the Lord, and He has unique ways of allowing situations to play out in our lives if we will keep our hands out of it and allow Him to handle it.

God was preparing Joseph, and He's preparing you and me. It's easy to just throw up our hands and throw in the towel when everything seems to be stacked against us, but there's more to our story if we'll just hold on. You can't even move to the next level in school until you've been tested and have passed the test in order to prove that you're ready for the assignments that will be given at the next level! Some things that have come your way were intended to destroy you, but thanks be to God, you're still standing! It's only a test.

All things have been made to work together for our good. All of our assignments and every single part of those assignments have served to push us toward our purpose, and somebody is tied to our persistence, perseverance, patience, and purpose. It ain't over! When we come out, others are coming out with us! During times of testing, hold on even when you don't understand.

Your test will surely work out to be your testimony!

As the will of God would have it, Joseph's brothers came back to Egypt a second time, as they needed more food during the severe famine. The brothers knew that they could not return without their youngest brother, Benjamin. So after a lengthy discourse with their father, they finally convinced him that the only way that they would be permitted to see *the man whom they had spoken to before* (Joseph) was if they had their younger brother with them. Jacob, also called Israel, made sure that they took the best that he could offer with them on their journey: fruits of the land, balm, honey, spices, myrrh, pistachio nuts, and almonds. They also took double money, which included the money that had been returned in the mouth of their sacks on the first journey.

When Joseph's brothers made it to Egypt and stood before him, he had his steward take them to his house and prepare food in order for them to dine with him. Joseph's brothers gave their gifts to him and bowed down before him to the earth, and the word of God goes on to say that they prostrated themselves before him. When Joseph looked up and saw his mother's son, his brother Benjamin, his heart was overwhelmed. He speedily left their presence and went into his chamber to weep. Then he washed his face and gathered himself before coming out and giving direction for them to be served. They ate separately since Egyptians could not eat food with Hebrews, as it was an abomination to the Egyptians to do so. However, Joseph made sure that Benjamin's servings were five times that which was given to the other brothers.

The next time that the brothers departed to head back to their homeland, Joseph had his cup planted in the sack of his younger brother, then had them accosted as they left Egypt to head home. They were brought back before him and pleaded their case until Joseph could no longer restrain himself. He put everyone out except his brothers, and it was then that he wept out loud and revealed to them who he was. He wept so loudly that the Egyptians and the house of Pharaoh heard it. He fell on his brother Benjamin's neck and they both wept. He kissed all of his brothers and wept over them, after which they all talked with him.

When the report came to Pharaoh's house that Joseph's brothers had come, Pharaoh sprang into action. He ordered that the brothers' animals would be loaded for their journey back to Canaan. After getting there, they were to bring their father and all of their households back without concern for bringing any of their "stuff." Pharaoh assured them that they need not be concerned about their goods because the best of all the land of Egypt was theirs. When Jacob's sons told him of all that had transpired and that Joseph was alive, the scripture says that he was "revived." Genesis 45:28 says: "Then Israel said, 'It is enough, Joseph my son is still alive. I will go and see him before I die.'"

We don't understand all that happens in our lives. Others may not like or appreciate how God has given you to walk out your assignments, but every step is moving you closer to fulfillment of your purpose. All that happens is not right or just and can sometimes be quite painful. That doesn't mean that God is pleased with the evil that comes our way, but He has a way of turning it around for our good. Keep praying, keep worshipping, keep giving and sowing. Above all, be willing to release hurt and unforgiveness.

Jacob/Israel worshipped before going to Egypt and he received word from God to go down. Jacob was able to see the blessing of the Lord in the land of Goshen, where his people were allowed to dwell, and he gave commandment to his sons regarding his burial as it should happen at the time of his death. After Jacob died, Joseph's brothers became fearful because they thought that maybe now would be the time that Joseph would seek to repay them for their evil toward him and that he would actually hate them. So they sent messengers to Joseph with words that they said had come from their father before he died commanding that Joseph would forgive their trespass, their sin, and the evil that they had done toward him. The passage of scripture found in Genesis 50:19–21 is one that resonates with many of us as a word that brings peace and consolation in times of great distress and hardships sometimes at the hands of others. Joseph stated to his brothers, "Do not be afraid, for am I in the place of God? But as for you, you meant evil against me; but God meant it for good, in order to bring it about as it is this day, to save many people alive. Now therefore, do not be afraid; I will provide for you and your little ones." And he comforted them and spoke kindly to them, which was something they had never done toward him.

He realized that the preservation of the lives of many people was tied to his suffering. The rejection and all that he had endured did not define Joseph or his story. Instead it worked to make him and to take him before great men as it ultimately positioned him to provide for many people during a time of great distress all because God's hand was upon him and He intended Joseph's circumstances for good.

What will you determine to do in your present situation and circumstance that will bring glory to God although it may seem difficult to you? No matter what it looks like, God is at work in your life. Do not give up!

Say God intended it for good! It ain't over!

Prayer: Father, in Jesus's Name, I want to pause and thank You for all of the examples that You've given to me in Your word that speak of Your faithfulness and desire to bring me through the hardships of life so that I can be a blessing to others and in turn bring glory to Your Name. You are sovereign and You know my end from the beginning. Although the enemy may plot against me, sometimes those of my own household,

You are more than able to establish and settle me so that I can see Your great plan unfold not only in my life but in the lives of others around me. Help me to wait on Your timing, and please help me to forgive while I wait. This I ask in Your matchless Name. Amen.

Stretch!
"Being Pulled beyond Our Comfort Zone"

There was a season when many ministries were teaching from a series on being stretched by God. No matter what aspect of stretching was being dealt with at the time, it was made clear that God has a plan and purpose for stretching His people beyond our human capacities, capabilities, and areas of comfort in order to bring us to a place of experiencing more of His supernatural power in our lives. What might stretching or being stretched look like in our lives?

How many of you know that sometimes when you're in the middle of the stretching, it doesn't make sense and it seems that the hand of God certainly can't be in it? We've explored Joseph's story and so many others in the Bible that are true and have been written for the strengthening of our faith. God stretched Joseph and others who walked with Him in every sense of the word. But my question to you is, "How are you being stretched?" It could be in any number of areas, including having your patience constantly tried at your job, in your home, in your relationships, money struggles, emotional or health challenges, unexpected losses, and various other issues or situations where it seems that we have simply been depleted. When there remains nothing that we can draw from within ourselves, when we don't have the wherewithal to pull ourselves up and out of these snares of life, we can consider that we're being stretched!

The thing about being stretched is that we seldom get the revelation or enlightenment while we're in the midst of it, but hindsight, as it is often said, is always 20/20. Joseph was stretched in so many areas of his life, but as you may recall, there was a point in his experience when he made a statement in what seemed to be total despair as he cried out, "I've done nothing that they should put me into the dungeon." It made no sense. He was wondering how he ended up where he was. Remember that the word of God has to become applicable to our lives or we're destined to remain the same. In actuality, there's no way that we can allow the word of God to become a part of us and at the same time remain the same. That simply can't happen. God's living word changes us, stretches us, and transforms us. As we pull the life lessons from the written pages of scripture, I want to make a few points that can certainly apply to each of us.

One of the first places where we may find ourselves being stretched is in our thinking. It has been noted many times that the greatest battles are waged within our minds, and the danger of warring there is that others are not privy to our battles unless we choose to share with them, and therefore they're unable to help us as we resist the enemies that come against our mind. What we think, do, and say originates in our minds, so to be stretched and elevated in that area is so vital to a productive, successful, and victorious life. The Lord is calling all of us to a higher realm of thinking and being in this world that we find ourselves navigating through. We're in the world but not of the world, which is a reminder that while we're here, we don't have to allow ourselves to become entrapped or ensnared by the ways of the world. It's really a stretch for us when we consider that God's ways are not our ways; neither are His thoughts our thoughts (Isa. 55:8,9). Many times in our faith walk, we will be led in directions that take us outside of our comfort zones as we learn to trust the Lord while navigating through this life.

If we are content with doing what we've always done, we'll continue to get what we've always gotten. I'm sure that you've heard that before, and it's true. When we allow the Lord to stretch us, we'll find ourselves in areas that have always resonated deep within our spirits yet we were powerless to arrive there. Everyone wants "sweatless victories" where they have no struggles, no issues or obstacles to overcome, yet there are times when we will be hard-pressed as we are led to the next great dimension of our lives. We will come away in awe of what the Lord has done in the midst of situations that seemed to be impossible to handle.

It's ridiculous for us to think that we can continue doing what we've always done and that we'll somehow come away with a different outcome or different results. The results won't be different or better. That just doesn't happen. The biggest piece to this repetitive process is that our minds have to be made receptive to the possibility that there is a different way that can yield greater results. One of the biggest obstacles for most of us is factoring ourselves into the equation. Most people in the Bible whom we've had the privilege of reading about and learning from did not start out as great individuals in the natural sense, although God always had great plans for their lives. It has continually played out that way throughout history because we serve a God who does great things through ordinary people who are willing to take His plans, work the plans, and leave the outcome to Him.

But again, that means that we must be willing to see ourselves as part of the equation. No, we won't measure up, but that's the power of walking with the Lord and allowing Him to be glorified in and through us. You can look at almost anyone who has done great things in this life, and you'll find that most of the time, their beginnings were humble, sometimes very humble. I not only gain strength from the lives of those in the Bible, but I consider individuals such as the late Maya Angelou, who was raped as a little girl and consequently chose not to speak for several years after she revealed her rapist to her brother and her rapist was later found murdered. From that point, she was convinced in her mind that her words could kill and that her words had killed this man. Consider the fact that as a child who did not speak, she was referred to and looked upon by many to be "crazy" or "mental" and was seen as someone who would never be able to learn or to speak. She was stretched as the Lord used her grandmother to speak positively into her life on a consistent basis and also used a woman by the name of Mrs. Flowers, who challenged her to read books and poetry. We all know that she later became one of the best poets, and she was a memoirist and a civil rights activist who published seven autobiographies. She wrote three books of essays and has been credited with a list of plays, movies, and television shows that spanned more than fifty years. This dynamic woman received more than fifty honorary degrees (Wikipedia).

Dr. Martin Luther King Jr., a young Baptist preacher whose steps were ordered by the Lord, found himself thrust right into the middle of the civil rights movement as its most visible spokesman and leader from 1955 until his assassination in 1968. He was consistently stretched as he remained committed to nonviolence in the face of a very violent society and evil opposition. The marches, boycotts, and nonviolent protests that he led served not only to stretch his reach and influence but to cause others to stand in the face of real danger, injustice, and sometimes deadly force as they felt the pull toward something much greater than what they were experiencing during the time in which they lived.

Take a look at yourself. You are constantly moving toward something that is much greater than what you're experiencing right now and becoming who you were created to be. How do you feel about it? Well, the truth is that it really doesn't matter how we *feel* about our destiny, the question is whether or not we will choose to embrace it. What inspires you? Typically our inspiration comes from those things or people whom we consider to be extraordinary. There must be something about the object or person that elicits awe. I submit to you that there is something, or should I say Someone, within you who is working out something that is awe-inspiring. Whatever the Lord chooses to do in and through our lives is great in and of itself. It doesn't matter whether or not others or even we see His move in our lives as great; the fact remains that since we have been touched by Him and our steps are ordered by Him in a lost and dying world, that is something great.

What change are you continually seeking while doing the same thing over and over? It won't work. Sometimes we can actually lose sight of who we are and where we are called to function in this life, especially when we're being stretched. We can feel so out of place and out of sorts. Most of us don't really push ourselves much farther than a place of initial discomfort, although we've probably heard "No pain, no gain." That doesn't only apply to physical exercise. It's so easy to get used to doing things in a certain way and not pushing ourselves beyond what we consider to be sufficient or comfortable. That can continue for months and even years without being tested or tried until something out of the ordinary happens to disrupt our "normal" course of life and causes us to shift. This is how the stretch often takes place. We pray for enlarged territories, greater dimensions, etc. but have you ever stopped to consider that the only way to encounter either of these is to be willing to move beyond where we are? That's not always an easy thing to do. The stretch from the pit to the palace wasn't something that Joseph asked for, yet his borders were definitely enlarged and he found himself not only in a position to feed the brothers who hated him but also a nation that was starving and in need. God knows who you are and He knows where you are.

To be stretched can mean that you're now being confronted with something that is causing you to spend more time seeking the face of God. Ideally it shouldn't be circumstances that drive us to the face of God; however, the truth is that it happens that way all too often. We may fall into routines of reading, praying, and attending worship; although, if we're honest, we're often quite negligent when it comes to our private prayer and study time. When the pressures of life are turned up and we find ourselves being pulled toward the Lord and to a deeper place of communion and fellowship with Him, this is a place of stretching. The season that we find ourselves in may reveal that those whom we thought were so very close to us are really not so close, and what we thought was solid is actually shifting all around us. What do you do when you find yourself in a stretch? What do you do when nothing seems to be working in the natural sense and there's no one who is in a position to come to your aid? Some of us have perhaps never been there, but consider that there could also be another side to this coin where you simply find yourself yearning for something deeper, something greater, and the material things just don't seem to satisfy anymore.

Typically, when something is being stretched, there is a resistance involved in the process. It's the stretching process that brings about the desired results. The resistance serves a purpose because the desired results are accomplished. For example, resistance exercises can help to build stronger muscles. They certainly don't feel good, but they serve a great purpose. Stretching exercises hurt when we begin to do them, but with time they become easier and we become more flexible. God is stretching us, and His intention is not to break us or do us harm but rather to cause us to become more flexible in His hand and more pliable to His plan.

There's something that was designed for you, but maybe because of the havoc and chaos it's caused, you've rejected it. You're carrying something that's greater than you. Each day you're given a brand-new batch of mercy to help you to face and deal with whatever will be presented to you on all levels. Allow the Lord to stretch you although it hurts and it may seem that you're nowhere near where you should be in terms of being pliable. Refuse to allow others to make you despise what's been entrusted to you. It's so easy to lay aside what the Lord has deposited within us simply because we don't feel accepted by those around us. Consider that others may have a mold that they want you to fit in order to help them feel more comfortable, but let's allow God to stretch us to the point where we will throw caution to the wind and simply trust His promptings even when what we're being stretched to seems downright impossible.

The Lord has come to stretch our faith! Stop trying to make your faith conform to what men will allow. When Jesus performed His first miracle of turning water into wine in John chapter 2, his mother was there, and what she spoke to the disciples in that moment on that day actually carries weight not only for that occasion but for every disciple who would ever come after Jesus and seek to be in close proximity to Him. John 2:5 says, "Whatever He says to you, do it!"

In that situation in John 2, there was no time for the disciples to ask, "What does filling water pots with water have to do with our present dilemma?" We don't know when or how it happened, but the water was turned to wine sometime between the time when those pots were filled and when the contents of the pots were served.

When we're being stretched, we're often challenged to move against customs and traditions. It was spoken that the custom was to serve the good wine first, then the bad, because by the time the bad was brought out and served, the people would be so wasted they wouldn't know the difference. They wouldn't care.

"Whatever He Says, Do It!"

The anger and opposition that comes against you is not about you. It's about the hatred against the One who loves you and who has clothed you with His anointing and favor. You can't see it; you don't recognize it. Jesus said, "If they hated me, they'll hate you." So why are you surprised? Why are you troubled?

It's about the favor. It's not about you. It's about His presence. It's not about you. The reality is that you take God's favor and presence with you wherever you go, but the enemy's mission is to make you:

➢ Hate what you have,
➢ Try to minimize what you have,
➢ Hide what you have, and
➢ Apologize for what you've been given.

But the Lord Says, "I'm Stretching You!"

God will set you up! You're being stretched for a reason. There's purpose in your life. We carry answers and solutions to the world's dilemmas and issues. God has something for you, and that's why He placed something of great significance within you. You're somebody's answer!

God is setting up His next move in our lives. Yes, it's a setup! God is not absent in our stretching! He's working it out for our good. Others may have evil in mind, but God is working it out for our good (reflect on Joseph's, Esther's, and so many others' stories in the Bible). Others may not like or appreciate how God has given you to walk, but your assignments are given to move you closer to fulfillment of purpose. The enemy generally comes to lie to us through our circumstances and through our senses—what we hear, see, or perceive. But what we discern is much different. What we see in the Spirit is much more real than what is presented to us in the flesh or in the physical/natural realm.

We're living our lives based on promises that can only be realized or come to manifestation through faith. It was no different for anyone who we'll read about in scripture, and it will be the same for all of those who come after we're gone.

Continue to walk in integrity even when they say that you're not the one. Walk in integrity and continue to pray when they lie on you and say all manner of evil against you. There is an all-sufficiency of God that each of us must become acquainted with. He is stretching us to a point where we know and recognize that He is a God who needs no help, His word needs no supporting texts, because if He said it, He'll make it good.

Typically circumstances dictate what is not true because what is going on in the physical realm is incapable of giving the true reflection of what is happening or has happened within the Spirit realm. Activity within the spirit realm is revealed to those who are willing to receive what natural eyes cannot see and natural ears cannot hear (1 Cor. 2:9,10). "But just as it is written [in Scripture],

'THINGS WHICH THE EYE HAS NOT SEEN AND THE EAR HAS NOT HEARD, AND WHICH HAVE NOT ENTERED THE HEART OF MAN, ALL THAT GOD HAS PREPARED FOR THOSE WHO LOVE HIM [who hold Him in affectionate reverence, who obey Him, and who gratefully recognize the benefits that He has bestowed].'"

"For God has unveiled them *and* revealed *them* to us through the [Holy] Spirit; for the Spirit searches all things [diligently], even [sounding and measuring] the [profound] depths of God [the divine counsels and things far beyond human understanding]" (1 Cor. 2:9,10, AMP).

It's so very sad that most Christians take this wonderfully inspiring and powerful passage of scripture and will choose to overlook verse 10, which clearly states that God will reveal through the Holy Ghost those things that our natural eyes and ears cannot see or hear. So it's true that our natural eyes can't see and our natural ears can't hear the things that are revealed by His Spirit to the children of God.

Our circumstances often lie to us about what God is doing, has done, or will do. Our circumstances lie to us about who we are, what we're capable of, what we possess, and what is truly ours. There's so much more to you than meets the eye, my friend.

Trust God and stay in the stretch!

Take the time now to make declarations to God regarding your willingness to allow His precious Holy Spirit and the gifts that are within you to flow and come forth. It's your turn to pray from your heart to God since this time of stretching in your life is very personal and requires a personal commitment from you that resonates from your heart.

Inspiration Break

You can't say everything that you think, nor can you run and tell everything that you see, especially when you're walking closely with the Lord.

He wants to share things with us that often have an appointed time for divulging or sharing. Sometimes we're not to share them at all but just to be partners with the Lord as He works them out or as He reveals them in His time.

As we maintain a relationship with Him, He will share things with us. When we see Him make good on His word, it becomes confirmation to us. That confirmation builds our faith.

It's not always about telling others what He has shown to us or told us but knowing that it was He who said it so that we can move farther and deeper in the confidence that we have in Him as we traverse this life.

We know that He is real and He reveals Himself daily in our lives as we look for Him, anticipate Him, and commune with Him.

What is communion? It's more than wafers and wine that we have at appointed times in religious services. The Lord wants us to commune with Him so that we may know Him in His sufferings and in the power of His resurrection.

Consider now the sufferings of this world, the plight of man, the lost, the disenfranchised, the poor, the sick, the lame, the blind, and the unsaved. All of this greatly affected the heart of Jesus as we walked this earth. Every time He saw those who were sick, He healed them. Those who were physically sick, sin-sick, sick in their thought life, sick in their habits, He healed them. How do we feel about them? What is our response to them?

Right now, He speaks to our hearts to reflect compassion and not to grow cold in this self-centered world. God calls us to be discerning and aware of those who are bleeding and dying while others walk by and look past them or look down upon them.

That bleeding and dying one was not only the one in the Bible that the Samaritan found on the Jericho road, but I submit to you that it was you and me before the Lord came along in our lives.

Right now, the Spirit of the Lord is ministering to you if you're that one who has felt like you're alone and beaten down while everyone is walking around you and no one is stopping to help. Some are looking past you and some even look at you, but they have no response to your desperate situation.

There is One who has come today to attend to your desperate situation. He now pours refreshing oil into every wound and He nurtures those broken places in your heart and your life. This healing that He brings is not only for a moment, but He has promised to sustain you and to make provision for you in every area of your life. You will suffer no lack! Rejoice in Him!

The Kingdom Ain't Fair!

When people ask if God is fair, they are often asking from a human perspective if God deals with people in the way that they deserve. God is often not considered fair by our standards, but He's right (righteous). Fair would have demanded our death, which is the penalty for sin; however, God decided to give us mercy and not judgment.

Seeking fairness causes us to operate outside of Kingdom principles. Do we really want God to be fair? If He were to be fair, there's no way that He could or would have forgiven us. Justice required that we die, that we pay the penalty for sin. Of course, we know that the only One who was truly able to atone for the sins of all mankind is the Lord Jesus Christ. He is the perfect sacrifice for sin once and for all.

Is it fair that Jesus, who knew no sin, became sin for us? Is it fair that sinners can now become the righteousness of God and joint heirs with Christ? If we're honest, we have to admit that none of this seems "fair," but it's the

---

grace of God in action toward us. Many think that God should deal with all of us in the same way, but even natural, earthly parents don't do that. God has made provision for everyone, everywhere with regard to salvation through Jesus Christ and eternal life, although all of our lives, the paths that we take, and the relationship that we experience with our Savior are very different. It's been said so many times that children can grow up in the same household but experience totally different parents. I am the third of three girls, and I can't tell you how many times my sisters have told me or have told others that I was able to get away with things that they could never get away with. Well, with the Lord it's quite different because He has all wisdom, insight, and foresight, unlike our parents, who parented us based on what they thought or perceived to be right.

The fact that my parents were somewhat more lenient with me or pushed me in certain areas such as music, etc., was no indication that they loved or cared for my sisters any less than they did for me. Parents see certain things in their children and do what they can to meet those needs and to develop what they see as the talents that exist in each particular child. After becoming a parent, and even more so after becoming a grandparent, I realize that although the love of a parent or grandparent is deep, it is not pure in the sense that the Lord's love toward us is pure. Matthew 7:9–11 reads, "Or what man is there among you who, if his son asks for bread, will give him a stone? Or if he asks for a fish, will he give him a serpent? If you then, being evil, know how to give good gifts to your children, how much more will your Father who is in heaven give good things to those who ask Him!" God has the foresight and knowledge regarding all things, and He guides us, corrects us, and loves us from that perfect place, which sometimes seems quite "off" and sometimes "unfair" to us. As I write this, I realize that those situations that are abusive must be pulled out of and excluded from this sort of comparison because abusive parents don't always have the best interest of the child or children in mind.

By comparison, there are times within Christian circles when we may look upon others who seem to have more material wealth or are graced with more spiritual gifts or talents, and this may make it appear as though God favors them more. Our conclusions in this case would be based upon our experiences in the natural, with our natural families, friends, and acquaintances. God created all of us, and each of us has been given what will be needed for the purpose that we are called to fulfill in this life. Sometimes people use their gifts and talents to build the Kingdom of God and to bring glory to His name, and there are numerous others who choose to follow after the dictates of the world for money, fame, or various other reasons. Whether it seems "fair" to us or not, all gifts come from God, and He rains on the just as well as the unjust.

We can't judge our walk with God based on another man or woman's relationship with Him. The truth is that God has been more than fair in His dealings with all of mankind. In spite of our sins, He has made provision for forgiveness (1 John 1:9). Eternal life is offered to all who will believe in His Son Jesus, the Christ (John 3:16). He may not be fair (by our standards), but He's right. God operates from Kingdom, and the Kingdom of God is not a democracy where everyone has a say and the majority opinion dictates what is fair or what will be done.

Now, please understand that when it comes to the earthly system that we're very much influenced by and have an obligation to bring correction to, we are to stand for justice and equal treatment of all people. We have been placed here as stewards on earth who constantly reflect the mind and will of God as it pertains to the affairs of men. There is a contrast in the operations of the systems and kingdom of this world and the Kingdom of God. This is why the Bible speaks of the people of God being in the world but not of the world. In the book of Revelation, there is a reminder that the kingdoms of this world will become the Kingdom of our Lord and of His Christ. So although we're not of this world, we have every right to call on the forces of heaven to intervene in the affairs of men in order to see justice and mercy prevail. It has only been the prayers of the righteous that have sustained this world. Jesus taught us to pray "Thy Kingdom come, Thy will be done on earth as it is in heaven."

Men's hearts are desperately wicked, and it doesn't take long to realize that, but the prayers of the righteous avail much and can hold back the forces of evil that have been loosed in this world. Evil will always be with us, but prayer keeps many otherwise insurmountable obstacles in check. Prayer can change our lives and our world. Alone we are no match for the evil forces that are at work around us, but we have the assurance that God is greater as the scripture declares in 1 John 4:4: "You are of God, little children, and have overcome them, because He who is in you is greater than he who is in the world." He who is in you is the Spirit of God, who is God Himself.

I committed my life to Christ while living in Korea, and one thing that I experienced and greatly appreciated while living in other parts of the world and fellowshipping with believers from other cultures was the deep hunger for God and for His Spirit among those who otherwise had so little. After returning to live in the States, it became obvious quickly that there would be many distractions and a fast-paced life that requires a discipline of making time to maintain a relationship with God and to keep a proper biblical perspective on who He is. Because we are flooded constantly with messages from various sources of media that call to us to spend more, want more, do all that we can to get more, it makes it a challenge to live a life of contentment wherein we can just take pause and appreciate the goodness and blessings of God.

It seems that our Western Christianity has been infused with an attitude or belief system that says that we can tell God what to do. In some circles people have taken the position that we simply command God and He is to follow through on what we have commanded. He is not obligated to treat us as we wish or in ways that we "feel" are fair. God is not our butler or genie who is waiting at our every beck and call to perform as we desire. The problem with that belief system is not only that it is erroneous, but there's every possibility that things won't work out the way that we want or the way that we think they should. In those cases, many become disappointed and walk away from Christianity with the conclusion that it *doesn't work* or that God is not fair or not real. He is sovereign and He knows the end from the beginning, which makes Him more than able to orchestrate not only our lives but the universe. He works all things together for good to those who love Him and are called according to His purpose as part of His perfect plan (Rom. 8:28). We can rest in this truth.

What we consider to be bad things can happen to *all people*! If we're honest, we have to admit that it is hard when we've done all that we know to do in order to stand in faith, for instance, as we pray for a friend or loved one who is facing a severe illness only to have them die. This can be devastating. I've heard people speak of questioning their faith after experiencing the loss of a loved one for whom they had prayed.

It was so very hard for me when my mother passed away of multiple myeloma cancer after I had committed so much time in prayer for her and with her. She was living in Kentucky, but I brought her to the Washington, DC, area and we attended services where others who believed in healing could lay hands on her and pray for her. I had witnessed others who had received their healings in these ministries, some of whom I walked very closely with, so their healing wasn't a matter of hearsay. Without a doubt, she wanted to live. Nevertheless, she died. Was that fair? It hurt so badly! My heart was broken and I just couldn't figure out what had gone wrong.

All too often Christians play the blame game and say that the person praying or the person who needed healing just didn't have enough faith. Although I must admit that I went through a season of anger, I never spoke it openly because I'm aware of the Christian culture and I felt that sharing those thoughts and feelings wouldn't be a safe thing to do. I was not about to allow my faith to be put on trial by others around me. The Lord was gracious toward me, as He allowed me to grieve, to question, and to cry many bitter tears. Over the months following her passing, He comforted my heart and spoke to me. What I had to realize is that He is a good Father, He is the good Shepherd, and the Creator of all things. He can actually be touched with the feelings of our infirmities, and when we weep or hurt, it touches His heart deeply. The reality is that He knows our end from the beginning and His plan is always righteous, although it may not seem fair.

Our vision is so very limited. We can't answer the whys. If we are to come out of our places of pain and disappointment, we must always find ourselves coming back to the powerful truth that our God is Sovereign and that He can do as He pleases without consulting with us. There is no way that I loved my mother more than the Lord does. She belonged to Him before she ever became a part of my life. As I began to heal from the pain of losing her, I became so very thankful to God for allowing me to have my parents for the time that I was able to experience their love on this earth. I began to shift my prayers to thanking Him for their many sacrifices that were made to give me and my sisters a good life. I thanked Him for the way that they kept any of the burden of the hardships that they faced away from us as children growing up, although there had to have been many. They were decent, loving people who kept us connected to family, friends, and caring people within our community. The Lord allowed me to lead both of my parents, my sisters, and others in my family to Him, and for that, I am forever grateful.

The memories and lessons learned from those times I've spent on foreign soil, when I was afforded opportunities of deep prayer and worship, have helped to sustain me during my times of loss and grief, and through various struggles over the years. There were many nights in Korea when some of us American Christians gathered with our Korean brothers and sisters in a small Korean church with a floor that was heated by charcoal blocks that were placed under it. We would sit on the floor and sing hymns (they sang in Korean and we sang in English); we prayed, cried, and worshipped as the sweet Spirit of the Lord would sweep through our meeting place.

What are some of your fondest memories as you reflect on your First Love? I'm speaking of the Lord as the scriptures have identified Him. Do you recall how precious it was to simply spend time with Him, how eager you were to learn something new from His word or to get an answer to a prayer that simply blew you away? He's still that same dear, loving, caring, and trustworthy Lover of your soul. A firm foundation in Christ and in His word is necessary because there will be seasons of testing, seasons of questions to which men have no answers, yet God will prove faithful even when it seems that He's not fair. Through the tears and hurt, what I've come to realize is that my life has been so richly blessed and that God always understood and cared about my pain. In times of deep despair, we need to run to Him, not from Him.

We won't always understand His plan and purpose, but that speaks to why we must live a life of faith. It also speaks to why so many are reluctant to fully surrender to the Lord. They refuse to give up control of their lives in order to trust the Lord and to begin to live a life of faith with God being the head and with Him being in control. The Kingdom of God does not function as the kingdom of this world. In the Kingdom of God:

- ➢ **God alone rules,**
- ➢ **Everything belongs to God (we are managers and stewards),**
- ➢ **The Kingdom is not a democracy, and**
- ➢ **God works all things together for our good but according to His plan, not ours (Rom. 8:28).**

No one will have a valid excuse for unbelief because God has made Himself known through His creation (Rom. 1:20).

Within the Kingdom, all is an act of the will and must be governed by faith. The Lord never forces anyone to accept Him, although the Father draws us. He doesn't make us pray or obey His word, although this is clearly how we have the most fruitful and powerful life as His disciples. It is His desire that we would long for and appreciate the times of communing with Him because we love Him, not because we're forced to do so.

Let's make some things crystal-clear as it pertains to the Lord and His sovereignty. We praise God and bless His Name as an act of our will, not because we have to. The Lord alone is worthy of our praise; however, we don't have to direct our praise or worship toward Him. Each of us was created to worship, so worship comes naturally to us. This is why we see people who worship the stars, the moon, the trees—they trust horoscopes or they worship themselves, their jobs, or other people, etc. All of this is an act of the will and is based on the principle that man's basic purpose is to worship. Mankind was created to worship his creator, not the creature or the thing that has been created. Many people talk about looking to the "universe" or submitting their prayers to the universe, but the universe was created by God and has no power to change or influence our lives. The universe belongs to God and is governed by Him. "The earth is the Lord's and the fullness thereof, the world and they that dwell therein" (Ps. 24:1).

As we live by the standards and principles of the Kingdom of God, we must come into agreement with God. He owes us nothing. We must understand that everything belongs to Him—in heaven, on earth, and under the earth. Man has been given dominion, which means that we are stewards and managers who own nothing. Accepting accepting that reality can actually make it easier on us and we won't take it so hard when we lose things that we acquire because we realize that we are only stewards over them anyway. Things can be replaced. Everything that we see and those things that we cannot see belong to God, including ourselves. This sometimes seems too much for our finite minds to grasp. Grasping this is a Kingdom mindset, which allows us to handle this world and all that is in it loosely because it is fading quickly. Everything here is temporary, but we can rejoice in knowing that our God is eternal. Life on earth is certainly a temporary assignment.

How will you pull from the scriptures and apply this to your life? How will you begin to reflect that God is right and He is just? You can start right now by repenting and deciding to move forward while acknowledging that you've actually been angry with God on some level (if that's you). He knows about your struggles and He cares. Just begin to thank Him for the power of forgiveness and the ability to start over again. There are many of us who have been in situations when it seemed that God just wasn't being fair or that He had certainly abandoned us, but that can never be the case. He will never leave or forsake us, and no matter what it looks like, it's working for our good. There's so much more waiting for you on the other side of this season in your life.

What will you pull from this chapter, and how will you seek to apply it in your life? Trust God now to help you make it happen.

Prayer: Father, in the Name of Jesus, I humbly submit my will to Yours and boldly proclaim that You alone are God. You are righteous and just. Help me to trust the great plans that You have for my life even when I don't understand the paths that I must take. You're right, I'm wrong; and I ask Your forgiveness for often considering Your ways to be unfair due to my lack of understanding. Help me to trust You more. In Jesus's Name. Amen.

Withholding Nothing

Let it go! Whatever it is, stop withholding it and let it go! Let it go in order to go to your next level. Let it go in order to have a more intimate relationship with the Lord. Let it go so that you can be free to trust Him.

We act out of character and live beneath our privilege and purpose when we don't know who we are and when we don't know who He is. What a great privilege we have been afforded. We are seated in heavenly places in Christ Jesus according to Ephesians 2:6. God raised up Jesus and seated us with Him in heavenly places. In order to receive this, we must know that this is our position in the spirit realm. The apostle Paul spent much of his writing in the letter to the Ephesians trying to explain the magnitude of what has been done for us as children of God. The Lord communes with our spirits. He desires to show us many things that can only be perceived and received through the spirit because our natural man cannot receive the things of God. The Bible says that the things of God are foolishness to the natural, carnal man or woman (1 Cor. 2:14).

None of us should want to hold back anything from the Lord. I just want to talk briefly about what advantage the enemy has when he can get us to withhold from God. The devil is not a figment of your imagination; he is not a made-up character that is used to scare people into doing right. He's real and he has a mission. John. 10:10 (NKJV) states, "The thief does not come except to steal, and to kill and to destroy. I have come that they may have life, and that they may have it more abundantly." The thief is the devil. He was our enemy before we were saved and he's still our enemy. We need to know that. The devil has not been destroyed, eliminated, or annihilated. If we take him out of the equation, we will continue to fight shadows and we'll continuously overlook what's really afflicting us and wreaking havoc in our lives. We're not wrestling against flesh and blood.

Some of the devil's chief works are:

> ➤ **to destroy your ambition for destiny,**
> ➤ **to kill your influence in the Kingdom,**
> ➤ **to steal your dreams, desires, and zeal and appetite for the things of God.**

The spirits that we toyed with before coming to Christ are not loyal. They are deceptive and destructive. 1 John 3:8 says: "He who sins is of the devil, for the devil has sinned from the beginning. For this purpose the Son of God was manifested, that He might destroy the works of the devil." It's the last part of that verse that I want to bring emphasis to. Jesus came to destroy the works of the devil—"the works," not the devil, but "the works" of the devil. We're going to find out why it is so powerful and needful that we move forward in our walk from this day forward withholding nothing.

Why surrender? Because literally a whole new world awaits us when we decide that we will stop withholding from God. Think of starting each waking day with the decision that we will no longer withhold any part of ourselves from the will and power of God but will allow Him to be manifested in and through our lives. When nothing is off-limits to the Holy Spirit in our lives, what is it that He can't do? The Spirit of God will help you to push past your fears. Dare to open your mouth and release your praise, your worship that has been withheld for far too long. God says, "It's Mine." The Spirit longs to worship, and we're grieving the Spirit when we won't worship. Actually it's only through the Holy Spirit that we're even able to worship because worship is about declaring the worth of God and only the Spirit of God can declare that in truth. That's why the word of God states that God is a Spirit and that those who worship Him must worship Him in spirit and in truth, for these are the ones whom He seeks to worship Him (John 4:23,24).

I shared the story before of how I came into church service after an argument with my husband on the way to church. Because of my attitude and the state of mind that I was in at the time, I was determined to sit on my seat, not raise my hands or open my mouth. That was withholding my praise from God, and the Spirit of the Lord convicted me of that as the Lord spoke to me during service and asked, "What have I done to you?" I wept because I knew that the Lord had been nothing but good to me and I was consciously making a decision to withhold something that belonged to Him in spite of how I felt. I was withholding my praise and my worship. Now, did we ever have arguments on the way to church after that? You'd better believe it. Actually most families, if they're honest, will tell you that the time before worship is the time that confusion tends to erupt between them, meaning that couples will have a disagreement, the children will act out, or the baby will throw up all over him- or herself after being dressed. Distractions happen, and quite frequently they happen to take our mind off praise, off times of fellowship and opportunities for communion with the Lord. But what we must be conscious of is the fact that these things happen to distract us and to disrupt our peace, so we have to determine that we will push beyond what would be our natural response by going forward in worship, prayer, praise, dance, and being open to receive the word of God in spite of ourselves. After we yield ourselves to the move of God, if the situation that we were dealing with is not resolved, we usually don't see it as important or relevant anyway. It was there to distract us, and the more that we begin to push past these types of situations in order to yield to the Spirit instead, then the enemy sees that he can't block our praise and those attacks or distractions become fewer or at least far less significant to us.

It doesn't matter what yesterday looked like; you can decide today to give all of yourself and say to the Lord, "Use me in any way that You choose." Let the Lord deal with your naysayers. Jesus said that every tongue that rises against you in judgment shall be condemned. There's so much power in a *yes* that is directed to the Lord. Our adversary knows that, and therefore he continues to seek ways to cause us to withhold various areas of our lives from full surrender to the Lord. Anything that the Lord said His disciples would do and could do includes you and me if we are His disciples. We too can do it! His promises apply to us.

The first step after saying yes is to avail yourself and resist holding back. Believe me, I know that this can sometimes seem easier said than done. We can say yes but then never make ourselves available to carry out the plan and purposes of God. The biggest culprit is fear, so start right now saying to yourself, "It's not about you!" Yes, say that to yourself. There's nothing wrong with talking to ourselves and getting our natural man to quiet down and come under subjection to what the Spirit is trying to do in our lives. Talk back to the enemy; talk back to those negative thoughts in your mind that come to tell you that you'll never measure up. We can all agree with the statement that we'll never measure up, but that's what makes us stronger and more qualified for the tasks. None of us can heal, deliver, or set anyone free. That's a work of the

Spirit, and thank God that we can choose to yield to the Spirit of God and allow Him to work through us. So the next time that negative thoughts come to you to keep you from responding to situations according to the word of God—i.e., "You don't know how to pray for that person," "No one wants to hear what you have to say," or "You're not all that!"—simply respond with, "I can do all things through Christ, and it's He who does the work; I don't have to. It's all a work of the Spirit, and we walk in the Spirit. Do you recall that I told you a little while ago that we forfeit so very much when we don't know who we are or the privileges that we have in Christ? It's a must that we search the scriptures and use them in times when negative thoughts come our way in order to keep us from moving forward. It worked for Jesus and it will work for us. He is our example, and His response to the lies of the devil was always, "It is written."

Many churches are heavy into titles, positions, and connections that can be used to make people feel significant. What the Lord has given to you and deposited in you is valid, so ask Him to help you to avoid all such traps. Many are held back because of titles and positions because this can prevent us from flowing outside of what that title of position represents. For far too long, too many have listened to what boils down to being no more than religious rhetoric as onlookers say, "God can't use you like that," "God doesn't use women," "You're too young (or too old, etc.)," "Not like this, not like that, can't do that or be that." There are no limits with God, so anything that comes to place a limit on our faith is not of God. His word is clear that He's able to do exceedingly abundantly above all that we could ever ask or think. It also reminds us that there is nothing too hard for God, and the word gives us an opportunity to weigh in and agree with this truth when it asks in Jeremiah 32:17, "Is there anything too difficult for me?" Of course the answer is a resounding "No!"

You may ask, how it is that we can surrender all to the Lord and withhold nothing? We do it one day at a time. Be honest in your times of prayer and ask the Lord to cleanse you from all unrighteousness; confess the things that torment your mind and your flesh because you know what those things are better than anyone else. There is a hymn that we used to sing in the Methodist church (we sang lots of hymns), and the chorus went like this: "Ask the Savior to help you, to comfort, strengthen and keep you. He is willing to aide you. He will carry you through." I've found this to be true. Cry out to Him and just ask Him to help you, ask Him to comfort you and strengthen you as no one else can. I'm a witness that He will come to your rescue, or as the songwriter says, "He will aide you" and you will be astonished at how He will carry you through whatever you're facing. Try Him and get to know this truth firsthand. Remember that we're talking about withholding nothing. That's about being open and honest with ourselves and confessing to God that we can't do it on our own. We need His help and guidance in all things.

When all you have to hold on to is your faith, you're in the best place because it's your faith that will give substance to what you hope for or else your hope is simply wishful thinking. Believe that you've been forgiven by God, and with that, reverse the practice of withholding forgiveness of yourself and others. The Lord says, "Give me that story and don't try to clean it up." He is the one who makes all things new and cleanses every stain in our lives. He is the One who causes us to have lives that look nothing like where we've come from or what we've been through. We have to come as we are and allow the process to happen in our lives as we make this marvelous journey to connecting with our destiny.

Psalm 84:11: "No good thing will He withhold from those who walk upright." It's imperative that we stop competing for the throne of our lives. The Lord is not going to share the seat of the throne of your heart and your life with you. He doesn't share the throne. He alone has to sit on the throne, and that includes the throne of your heart because He's sovereign. The issue with many of us is that we're still competing for the throne of our lives. We're still competing against the agenda and will of God. You and I are able and must be willing to empty ourselves of anything that would separate us from the power and presence of God in order to be filled with more of Him and in order to be used by Him. Whatever we choose to hold on to and refuse to surrender is not worth it.

Sometimes our biggest issue is not those outside of us, our biggest issue is not the devil, but our biggest issue is often ourselves. Your biggest enemy can be yourself—feeling inferior when God has said that you're the head and not the tail, you're above and not beneath. Why is it so hard for us to believe that? Let's reveal some real warfare here in the way that it often goes down. God has given us authority over principalities, over powers, over spiritual wickedness in high places, over rulers of darkness. God has given us authority over every devil in hell. God has given us authority over the mind although we know that the mind is a battleground. Through the word of God, Paul admonishes the believers to "Let this mind be in you which was also in Christ Jesus" (Phil. 2:5). But we sometimes choose to sit back and think on things that are detrimental, think on things that don't have a good report, things that we know are not pleasing to God and yet we entertain them.

Some of us would rather hold a grudge and pass that along to our children and our friends like we're passing a baton and we're entrusting them to step in as part of our team and to keep moving forward in that messed-up race that leads to nowhere. But when we withhold nothing, God's word clearly points out that we are to think on things that are true, right, pure, lovely, and of a good report. Your biggest enemy is you when you allow yourself to walk around feeling inferior or less-than when the truth is that God has changed your entire story and the reality is that you're unstoppable. We have clear instructions on taking our warfare beyond flesh and blood. That's where your grudge is, that's where your hurt feelings started, that's where rejection and inferiority are seated.

Our prayers are going to outlive us. Have you thought about that lately? Our prayers and our petitions are going to outlive us. We are still living on the prayers of somebody else who has transitioned and is no longer here. In some of our cases, people prayed for us who never lived to see the results of their prayers over our lives. They prayed for our deliverance, our salvation, our barren womb, or maybe our ability to find a good mate and to walk in the favor of God. Whatever they prayed, the reality is that their prayers outlived them because prayers are wrought in the spirit and are answered in the spirit before they are manifested in the physical realm. When you're a child of God, He hears every prayer that you pray and there's an appointed time for His response. Our prayers do not go unnoticed by God. What will outlive you? Will it be your hatred? Will it be your grudge that's passed on to your children and your children's children, leaving them to often navigate years of spiritual entanglements and bondage? Oh, God, help us in the name of Jesus!

We're not wrestling against flesh and blood, not anymore, that's carnality. As we elevate our minds and move higher, we recognize those principalities that have not only sought to dominate and influence our personal lives, but we also recognize those that have a stronghold over our regions, our government, our communities, our neighborhoods, our families, and even our children. We need to use our spiritual weapons to pierce the darkness and pull down the strongholds that have warred against us for far too long. Many don't realize that we have spiritual weapons at our disposal all of the time. There are not only certain Christians who can war in the spirit and push back the enemy and the forces of evil that come to challenge us and to invade our territory. Your praise is a weapon, and you can begin to praise God wherever, whenever, and for however long you may choose to do so.

When you run out of spontaneous praise, pick up your Bible and begin to read out loud from the Psalms. You will find yourself strengthened and encouraged, and the forces of evil will lose their grip. Your prayers are definitely a weapon, and again this is a weapon that can be used no matter where you are. You can pray silently, as you drive, as you work around the house, as you relax, as you lie in bed waiting for sleep, when you wake in the morning, or on your knees if you prefer that posture and are able during the day or before retiring at night.

A great resource to help you become more comfortable with prayer and praying for various situations is a book that I think has several editions titled *Prayers That Avail Much* by Germaine Copeland Word Ministries, Inc. I own a special commemorative gift edition, and I highly recommend it for getting started and maintaining consistency in your prayer life. You will soon find yourself adding to the prayers that you read as you begin to make them personal to the people, places, and things that the Lord places on your heart. Praise is a weapon, as God inhabits the praises of His people and praise brings Him close. Your prayer is a weapon as you partner with the Holy Spirit, who makes intercession as we pray and causes us to pray in agreement with the perfect will of our Father in heaven. Dancing in the spirit, clapping your hands, and even speaking in your heavenly language (tongues) becomes a weapon against the enemy and causes you to release to the Lord and to give Him spontaneous worship.

As we learn more and more about giving up the throne of our lives, how to step away from needing to always be in control, and avoiding withholding ourselves from God, His supernatural power will begin to rule and reign in and through us. What a glorious thought! The battles that matter most aren't won in the flesh. We have the word of God, which continuously inspires us to release and to withhold nothing even when the picture may not be a pretty one because we stand firm in the truth that we are victorious in all things.

We must be cognizant of the fact that our flesh, which is our sinful nature, will act as a distraction to keep us from the things of God so that we're so busy attending to and pacifying the flesh at the expense of the spirit. For those who are not saved, I want you to know that God's best plan for your life is that you would yield, accept Christ, and begin to live for Him. To those who are saved, God is saying that it's time that you start living in and for the Kingdom. If you are born again, you have been birthed into the Kingdom of God.

God is transitioning His body, His bride, to a new level, a new dimension in the Kingdom. We must be reacquainted with the Kingdom: There is one King, and everything belongs to Him. There is no democracy. We manage and are given stewardship, but we don't own. When we seek to withhold from God, we are deceived into thinking that what we have is ours, yet we, and everything attached to us, belongs to God and will return to Him at the end of all things.

If we're living and breathing right now, we've been blessed with an opportunity to empty ourselves of any- and everything that we know is not like God. We know. It's a personal thing, but we know. You and I don't have to be Bible scholars to know what's displeasing to God because He has placed within our hearts the knowledge of good and evil. We know.

After we realize our sad state and that we have need of Him, we'll come to Him and say, "God, I'm sorry. From this point and forward, I'm withholding nothing; I'm giving it all to You. I'm sorry for how I've hurt others. I'm sorry for my rebellious spirit. I'm sorry for how I've rejected Your plan for my life and wasted precious time. I'm sorry for the times when I saw You and didn't feed You, when I turned my back on You when You were sick and I never visited You. I'm sorry." Make this time of pouring out to God your own by placing the words that are in your heart right here, right now. This is what this book is about. Let's make it real. Let's get practical.

This is not rocket science. On some level, we just need to get back to basics. God wants to deal with us now. He wants to take the spotlight off everyone else's story and help us to begin to review our own stories.

Take a few moments to reflect on areas of your life that you have been withholding from the Lord. He doesn't condemn us, but rather He wants us to see that surrender is often a process, and little by little as light is shone on our lives, we are given precious opportunities to walk in that light and to step away from those areas that have not been fully surrendered. You and I know what those areas are in our lives, and if by chance we don't, now is a good time to ask the Holy Spirit to reveal those areas that we have declared off-limits to the wonder-working power of our Savior. I encourage you to take an introspective look and take time to pray now, asking the Lord to help you to release to Him the areas that are revealed to you that you have kept under your fleshly authority rather than placing them under the authority of your King.

You're not the first one, nor will you be the last, to turn away from the Lord and seek your own way. Too many of us have pursued the blessings rather than the Blesser. Maybe we took all of the credit when He blessed us, when He opened doors for us, and we didn't give the credit to Him. We let the people think that it was us. We let others think that we pulled ourselves up by our own bootstraps and we even tried to show them how to do what we had done instead of showing them how to seek the face of God in prayer. Lord, maybe, just maybe, we've been too full of ourselves and not full enough of You!

Prayer: Father, in the Name of Jesus, I ask that You would search me and reveal to me the areas of my life and my will that I have withheld from You. I know that I should place _____ in Your hands, and now I ask You to help me to fully surrender to You in order

to be a vessel full of Your grace, power, and truth as I continue to grow and learn through Your life-giving word. Thank You for assuring me that I do not have to walk in condemnation as I allow You to work the process of complete and total surrender of my life to You. In Jesus's Name I pray. Amen.

Inspiration Break

The word of God declares that the Lord has revealed to us by His Spirit what the natural eye cannot see and the natural ear cannot hear (1 Cor. 2:9,10).

We must make it our earnest desire to :

> ➤ Develop the habit of stretching to see beyond what our natural/physical eyes can see. Do it consistently.

> ➤ Develop a keen and discerning spiritual ear by agreeing with the declaration of God's word that He has revealed to you what natural ears cannot hear.

> ➤ Develop the habit of a finisher—consistently do something toward what you were sent here to this earth to accomplish. You're not too young and you're not too old.

> ➤ Treat your body like a temple and not like a trash can. Refuse to listen to trash, eat trash, talk trash, or watch trash (1 Cor. 6:19,20).

➤ Refuse to procrastinate. Stop putting off and determine to show up every day for your life.

We speak now to the scattered mind and unfocused mind. By the power of God, we pull down and refuse to give place or to entertain vain imaginations that exalt themselves against the knowledge of God.

We bring into captivity every thought to the obedience of Christ.

By the authority of Christ, we come against procrastination, which works against the right habits in our lives.

We put off negative thoughts and negative self-talk. We declare that according to Philippians 4:8, we will think on things that are true, holy, upright, pure, of good report, virtuous, and praiseworthy.

We declare according to Philippians 1:6: "I am convinced and confident of this very thing, that He who has begun a good work in you will continue to perfect and complete it until the day of Christ Jesus, the time of His return."

"Provision Has Been Made for You"

(Jehovah-Jireh)

There's only one time when God is referred to as Jehovah-Jireh or Yahweh Yireh (in Hebrew), and that can be found in Genesis 22, where we read the story of Abraham, who was instructed by God to take his son, Isaac, to Mount Moriah and to sacrifice him there.

Genesis 22:1–5

"Now it came to pass after these things that God tested Abraham, and said to him, "Abraham!" And he said, "Here I am."

² Then He said, "Take now your son, your only son Isaac, whom you love, and go to the land of Moriah, and offer him there as a burnt offering on one of the mountains of which I shall tell you."

³ So Abraham rose early in the morning and saddled his donkey, and took two of his young men with him, and Isaac his son; and he split the wood for the burnt offering, and arose and went to the place of which God had told him. ⁴ Then on the third day Abraham lifted his eyes and saw the place afar off. ⁵ And Abraham said to his young men, "Stay here with the donkey; the lad and I will go yonder and worship, and we will come back to you."

We've heard this story told so many times, but what I want to point out is that it's so important to have a relationship and to be in a place and position in that relationship where we can hear God. We have an all-seeing, all-knowing God, and what sets Him apart from all false gods or idols is that He's alive and He speaks. There would be no need for us to know His voice if He did not speak.

Prior to the text that we're now exploring, God had spoken and promised this son, Isaac, to Abraham and Sarah in their old age. God made good on that promise. Now He was requiring Abraham to bring Isaac back to Him as a sacrifice in the face of the promise that through his seed all of the nations would be blessed.

A relationship demands trust, and Abraham, through trust in God, headed to the mountain. Most of us are familiar with the story; however, I don't want to be dismissive in case someone needs some gaps to be filled in. This was a son whom Abraham and his wife, Sarah, brought forth in their old age all due to a promise from God. So we see that God is already showing up as Jireh in their lives as they were given what was impossible for their flesh to deliver.

On this particular day, God spoke to Abraham to make preparation and to head to the mountain. What was to happen there must have gripped his heart and filled him with questions that no one else had the answers to but God. Abraham took his son, who in turn exemplifies trust and obedience as he goes along with his father toward the mountain.

Isaac, no doubt, heard his father tell the others that the two of them were headed up the mountain to worship and that they would return. All of a sudden it must have dawned on Isaac that there was no sacrifice. So quite naturally he spoke up and asked his father where the sacrifice was among all the things that they were taking on their journey to the mountain. Faith speaks up and answers: "God will provide the sacrifice."

Notice that Abraham (father of faith) had already determined that worship was going to happen in spite of the directions that he had been given. He had already had an opportunity sometime between the time when he left home and the time when he came to the base of the mountain to reason within himself that if God's promise was true and since He is almighty God, somehow this boy, this promised one, must live.

Abraham reasoned that God could raise him up and bring him back to life again. After all, He gave him out of nothing.

Hebrews 11:11; 17–19 reads:

> [11] **By faith Sarah herself also received strength to conceive seed, and she bore a child when she was past the age, because she judged Him faithful who had promised.**

> [17] **By faith Abraham, when he was tested, offered up Isaac, and he who had received the promises offered up his only begotten son,** [18] **of whom it was said, "In Isaac your seed shall be called,"** [19] **concluding that God was able to raise him up, even from the dead, from which he also received him in a figurative sense.**

Dead Sperm, Dead Womb—but God!

To hear in the moment is critical! "Lord, we know what You said then, but what are You saying now?" Had Abraham not been able to discern and hear the voice of the Lord, he would have slain his son, the son of promise. No matter what it looked like, Isaac was still the son of promise. Understand that before Abraham arrived there at the top of the mountain, the place of sacrifice, provision had already been made. As close as it was, he couldn't see it.

There was no turning back; the only remedy was intervention. Sometimes we need an intervention.

God is still looking for people who will worship when everything you hold dear seems to have been required of you, when hope seems lost. I said "seems lost" because we're never left without a hope and a future. The place where you almost lost it all can now become a place of worship. The Lord is still with you, so for that reason alone, your present place and circumstance can yield worship.

When I recall to my mind how I almost gave up, how I would have fainted, I now have hope and I worship.

I don't praise the provision, I don't embrace the thing that has been restored, but I worship the Provider, the God of restoration. Like Abraham, my response is to worship! He said the boy and I will go yonder to worship, and *we* will return. Faith had spoken and Jehovah-Jireh had shown up and made it so.

I worship Him because I realize that Jehovah-Jireh has shown up and has done it again. He has provided not simply because that's what He does but because that's who He is!

It's a Name for Him and a Name given to the place where He showed up to provide Himself a sacrifice by allowing a ram to be caught in a thicket.

Abraham called that place Jehovah-Jireh, the Lord will provide, and to this day it is said, "In the Mount of the Lord it shall be provided." In its Greek translation "Jehovah-Jireh" means "the Lord hath seen."

We must remember that God sees and He knows all things. He's already in the place that He has called us to. He's in every one of our tomorrows, the months and years that lie ahead. He has preceded us in all situations.

He's the One who provides and sustains on the journey to the place of sacrifice. He puts hope in our hearts when circumstances dictate that we should be in despair.

Jireh! He Has Done It Again!

But that must be our position before we get there. While we're on the way to the place of great sacrifice, our declaration must be the Lord will provide!

He's your provider before you see provision. Declare it now!

Your place of provision is not at the base of the mountain, the low place. We're going to have to go higher! We want to stay in the safe place, the comfort zone, and call on God to make provision there. No!

He says, Come higher! This is no indictment of those whom Abraham had to leave behind at the base of the mountain, but God's provision for Abraham wasn't there. It was at the top of the mountain in a thicket by the place reserved for Abraham to offer what was near and dear to his heart.

We want to hold on to what we hold dear in the low place, the place of comfort, when all the while we're being deceived because whatever we're holding on to is not really ours, whatever it is.

The Spirit of the Lord is saying, "Give it up!" Abraham reasoned within himself, "If I kill him, God is able to raise him up again, so however He might choose to do it, God will provide." Abraham became the father of faith. God said that through this test, Abraham proved that he would withhold nothing from Him. God assured him that because he had chosen to obey the voice of the Lord, in Abraham's seed all of the nations of the earth would be blessed. What a blessing! What a promise! We are a part of that promise, as we have been grafted in as Abraham's seed.

Whatever the Lord has called you to do, wherever He has told you to go, provision has already been made there—not where you are but *there*. Determine that you'll withhold nothing from Him. All that we have belongs to Him anyway.

Our faith without works is dead, for without works, it then has the propensity to become an indictment against us. There is little respect for an individual or an institution that speaks of faith yet takes no identifiable action to reflect that faith during times of hardship or great need. These times that we're facing now cry out and demand a viable response.

We declare that we operate from a Kingdom place and vantage point that flesh and blood *cannot* regulate. God is sending a clarion call by His spirit and fine-tuning the spiritual ear of His people. We must dare to go higher!

There is a clarion call to the remnant of God in these times to hear what the Spirit of the Lord is saying to the church, and more specifically what He's saying to you.

You are not responsible to bring to pass anything that the Lord has spoken over your life. You must simply believe it, and your belief must cause you to move. As you move, be prepared for God's manifest presence and promise to be revealed in your life. He's still Jireh! Jehovah-Jireh! Now worship!

Abraham heard, he obeyed, he declared, he worshipped, and he named the place of provision where God had seen and provided for him. Jehovah-Jireh!

Prayer: Dear Lord, I thank You for Your provision in every situation. I declare that I will cause every place that You have called me to become a place of worship and thanksgiving unto You. I declare that I will bless You at all times and that Your praises shall continually be in my mouth, for You are the God who sees, cares, and provides for my every need. Your grace is sufficient for me, and I agree with Your word and Your good plan for my life. Amen.

"Who Shall Deliver Me?"

(The Rest of the Story)

Romans 7:14–20 [14] For we know that the law is spiritual, but I am carnal, sold under sin. [15] For what I am doing, I do not understand. For what I will to do, that I do not practice; but what I hate, that I do. [16] If then, I do what I will not to do, I agree with the law that *it is* good. [17] But now, *it is* no longer I who do it, but sin that dwells in me. [18] For I know that in me (that is, in my flesh) nothing good dwells; for to will is present with me, but *how* to perform what is good I do not find. [19] For the good that I will *to do*, I do not do; but the evil I will not *to do*, that I practice. [20] Now if I do what I will not *to do*, it is no longer I who do it, but sin that Sdwells in me.

This chapter was written as a result of a message that I shared during a series that our ministry covered on addictions. A man by the name of Paul Harvey used to have a radio show that was called *The Rest of the Story*, and this show gave behind-the-scenes information for events or occurrences that people might have been familiar with but for which there was something significant that had been hidden from most listeners, or at least those who did not have the inside scoop. Mr. Harvey is deceased now, and many of you may never have heard of him. There was always something intriguing, eye-opening, or enlightening about "the rest of the story" that he would share.

As we look closely at Romans 7, we see the very candid description of a struggle that the apostle Paul was very forthcoming and transparent about. We're not told exactly what the struggle was, and somehow the text indicates that the type or source of the struggle is not as important as the struggle itself. Maybe it started out as a habit; we don't know. Many addictions can begin as habits—things that we like to do, that we do over and over again, and that bring us some sort of fulfillment. We know when a habit has become an addiction when we no longer do it but it does us. It calls to us and says, "This is what we're doing today whether you want to or not."

Whenever there is anything that has mastery over us besides the Spirit of God, the Lord can't get His best use out of us because there's always competition for our time, attention, energy, and sincere devotion. By the time the day is done, we're spent and have no time for prayer or communion with God. We can be left as Paul was, asking ourselves how we could have been used again, taken advantage of by this vice in our lives that we know is no good for us but that we just can't seem to shake. Once the enemy discovers your Kryptonite, he'll use it against you every time. He knows you're weak around certain people, places, and things, so he wants to keep you vulnerable and exposed. You can talk a good game to yourself, know that you shouldn't do what you do, but you're too weak to resist. You've come into the presence of something or someone who has a pull or stronghold over you.

When we've moved over to the area of addiction in any part of our lives, relationships, gambling, smoking, snorting, drinking, watching pornography, or other sexual addictions, we have moved into an area of being controlled and enslaved.

Let's take a closer look at Romans 7. Paul was aware of the pull, the wrestle in his life, and he was very clear about it. He didn't front as some of us do: "Oh, I can quit this at any time." He said, "It's in me to do what's right. I know what's right, I know what the law of God and the Spirit of God demand, but yet I find myself at a loss to execute or to perform what I know in my mind and heart is right to do." He said that he thought about what's right, even when he was in the midst of carrying out what he had chosen not to do. Just like with many of us, Paul discloses that he would find himself doing that thing and despising himself later. Have you ever been there? This is the type of dilemma that Paul was talking about when he shared his struggle with us.

This is not a fairy tale. This is the rest of the story. It has almost become foreign to hear the unadulterated gospel where people are told the truth of the matter. We can't get by with hiding behind clichés such as "I'm spiritual but not religious" in an attempt to resist and dismiss people who want to share the truth of God's word with us and to get them to leave us alone. If we choose to live outside of the truth of God's word, we're kept at a disadvantage. What we're dealing with here is not about a change of mind or willpower. The rest of the story has to do with what we don't see but that is having a direct impact on our lives and the lives of those around us whom we care so deeply about and who care about us. Relationships are being destroyed and people are watching as their lives crumble and fade right before their eyes as they feel helpless to do anything to stop it from happening. Paul finally came to the end of his writing in Romans 7:24,25 (NKJV) and cried out, "²⁴ O wretched man that I am! Who will deliver me from this body of death? ²⁵ I thank God through Jesus Christ our Lord! So then, with the mind I myself serve the law of God, but with the flesh the law of sin." Now let's look at this same passage of scripture in the amplified version: "²⁴ Wretched *and* miserable man that I am! Who will [rescue me and] set me free from this body of death [this corrupt, mortal existence]? ²⁵ Thanks be to God [for my deliverance] through Jesus Christ our Lord! So then, on the one hand I myself with my mind serve the law of God, but on the other, with my flesh [my human nature, my worldliness, my sinful capacity—I serve] the law of sin."

Can you identify with this on any level? Do you have even the slightest idea of what it's like to be in a place of wanting to do good or to do right and just being powerless to make that happen? Say with me, "Who shall deliver me?" We can't say that Paul was dealing with any sort of addiction per se, but what we're addressing here has to do with anything that holds us hostage in our minds, our emotions, or our physical being. What we know is that Paul was dealing with the reality of the sinful nature that we all contend with, which can lead us in many directions apart from God. That nature is a part of all of us, and we are powerless to break free from it without the intervention of the Lord. It's not a natural thing that we're talking about; this is totally spiritual. Paul realized that he was confined by death and becoming defined by death because he was unable to break free.

Have you ever noticed that after a while people begin to define you and describe your life based on your struggle or your addiction? You know, "the one who's on crack," "the drug addict," "sex fiend," "the pathological gambler," or "the liar." What happens is that all too often, people seek help from sources that compel them to forever identify with their addiction or the struggle in their life. They're advised to call themselves by and identify themselves by their addiction or area of struggle as though this somehow will help them to overcome it. Well, in Paul's case, he wasn't looking for "something." He was a scholar who was well-read, but he wasn't looking for a new book, a highly recommended class, or a support group when he cried out in desperation, "Who shall deliver me?" There's nothing wrong with any of those sources of help; however, what stands out is the fact that Paul somehow recognized that what he was dealing with went far beyond what any of those remedies could offer. He cried out, "*Who* shall deliver me?" Deliver? Deliver? What's going on here? Paul recognized that this thing that he was dealing with wasn't something mental, physical, or psychological. It was spiritual! This was something bigger than himself, and He knew where to turn.

If it was simply about his will, he had that. If it was about a decision, he tried to make the right decision, but it just wasn't working. Can you identify with that at all? Just because we choose to stop talking about it in order to avoid seeming too religious or deep doesn't mean that it doesn't exist and that it will simply go away. The spirit realm is real! Spiritual warfare is real, and it's more real than what is visible or tangible around us. This is truly a huge part of the rest of the story that all of us must contend with at some time or another in our lives.

These are people's lives that we read about in the word of God. We read many of their stories every time that we pick up the word of God, but let me remind you that any story that you read is a story about ordinary people, people whom God chose and some whom He was able to use. They're not super-saints; they were simply ordinary people who said yes to God, and every single one of them encountered spiritual warfare on some level.

Paul's story or testimony in Romans chapter 7 is a vivid reminder of the fact that our flesh is in direct opposition to the plan and will of God. The flesh and the spirit are at enmity against one another so that the things that you would do, you do not. The flesh opposes anything pertaining to God and righteousness. It must constantly be placed under subjection and kept under control by a Spirit man that has been built up and fortified in the things of God.

All things are lawful to me but I will not be brought under the control of any or become the slave to anything (1 Cor. 6:12).

Addictions open the door for demonic activity that pushes beyond what the natural man can control on his own. The definition of addiction is: "a psychological and physical inability to stop consuming a chemical, drug, activity, or substance, even though it is causing psychological and physical harm." Addictions to food, certain relationships, and others things too numerous to name here are also applicable to what we're speaking of here. I've watched episodes of a show called *My 600 Lb. Life* and heard stories of people who really have a desire to stop eating because on some level they realize that they're killing themselves, but they're helpless to get off that cycle that is leading them to destruction. It's almost like they're watching it happen but are powerless to do anything to stop it. So again, as we reflect on Paul, we're not saying that what he experienced was an addiction, but he makes us aware that although he knew that what he was dealing with was causing harm, he had no ability to break free from it. Unlike a physical addiction (which really has a spiritual side to it as well, but we won't go into that here), he realized that he was dealing with something on a spiritual level. I know that people typically push back when we begin to talk about these areas of struggle because on some level they feel as though they're being judged. Yet it's okay as long as we keep it light and I compare my stuff to your stuff and we laugh, joke, and realize, "Hey, you're in just as deep as I am," "You struggle just like I do," and the sad truth is that neither of us has the power to do anything about it.

Why talk about it when there's a possibility of turning people off or causing them to shut down? Why don't we just leave people alone? Well, if we as children of God really care about people and can identify with any level of human suffering and pain, we must often be the first ones to admit that everyone struggles with *something*. If we live long enough, life will definitely make that clear to us. It's a serious matter when we lose touch with ourselves or the self whom we thought that we knew. Don't ever say what you'd never do. If you've never gotten to the point where you've looked in the mirror and said, "Who is this?" then it may be somewhat hard for you to identify with any of this. The sad truth is that we can get to the point where we've lost touch with ourselves and can't seem to break free from what holds us hostage in order to get back to what we would consider a safe space. Substances may not be a part of your equation, and maybe you can't identify with addiction on any level. This book is about taking what we may have read about numerous times in the Bible and making a determination to begin daily application so that the word of God is no longer words on a page to us but they are our reality. Those words that we read in the Bible are spirit and they are life. They are intended to change us!

When we know what to do and we desire what's right to do but can't find the power to do it, we're living a Romans 7 situation. Again, I'll say that Paul cried out for deliverance. Why? Because it's not just a mental decision when we're battling something or someone to whom we are addicted. Deliverance is needed. Paul recognized that something greater than his mentality and willingness to change was needed. He had the desire to change, he realized the need to change, but what he lacked was the power to change or to do something different.

Paul got to the point where he was fed up with his condition. He was sick and tired of being sick and tired. He had to come clean. He said (I'm paraphrasing), "Look, I know what to do but just can't seem to do it. Inside I'm telling myself what's right to do and what the Lord requires, but in my flesh, I'm powerless to carry it out because my Kryptonite keeps showing up." He got to the point where he said, "Who shall deliver me from this body of death?" "What I'm doing, this vicious cycle is destroying me"— whatever that might have been that was preventing him from moving to the next level that he wanted in his walk with the Lord.

The answer that was given in Romans 8 verse 1 indicated that there is no condemnation to those who have decided to trust the Lord and to follow the leading of the Spirit of God rather than the pull of the flesh. We can only walk after the Spirit if we're born of the Spirit. Prior to that we have no other choice but to fulfill the lusts of the flesh. The Amplified Version of Romans 8:1 reads: "Therefore there is now no condemnation [no guilty verdict, no punishment] for those who are in Christ Jesus [who believe in Him as personal Lord and Savior]."

I wonder if you could say right now, "Lord, deliver me, change my story!" You may have reminders of your past failures, but there's no condemnation. You may have lost a lot, but there's no condemnation. Recognize where your fight, your wrestle is, and be willing to take it to another level by making a decision to let the Spirit of God fight for you. We can't just hang around the church or claim to know God and refuse to become actively involved in our own deliverance, our push for destiny, and what's ours in the Spirit. The stakes are too high. We may be outside of the four walls of the physical building, but we're still a part of God's church, His body, and He wants us to be aware and prepared to rise above our circumstances. We're a part of His victorious remnant. Too much has been paid for you, and God has declared that you will not come under the mastery or dominion of anything that is sent to destroy you or to knock you off course. It's time to agree with what the Lord has said about you. We're not wrestling against flesh and blood, so we must seek God and pull ourselves up above what flesh and blood is dictating to us and about us.

If we're still hanging around the things of God but not getting saved because we haven't made up our minds that it's time to let go, then we're not tired of it! The enemy is wearing us out, but we're not tired of it; he's destroying our families, taking our babies, causing us to deplete our seed so that we can't reap a harvest, but we're not tired of it! Who shall deliver us?

The Lord is ever present to deliver us from sin, from every addiction, affliction, and anything else that we may wrestle with. The Holy Ghost is the only one who can coach you through this one because you're in a battle with an opponent who you can't see. To break free was beyond Paul's human capabilities, and it's beyond ours. We can come together whether online or within the church building and act as though all is well while battles rage in our minds right where we sit. While the message is going forth, we can wrestle with whether or not we'll go back to that thing, that person, that high after the benediction is given. The Holy Ghost knows the enemy's next move. He's not blindsided or caught off guard. He knows!

It's time for us to get excited about Jesus's power to save, to deliver, and to set free! Get excited about the fact that Jesus is still Emmanuel, God with us. He's with you now, right where you are. Claim your deliverance! Rejoice! Jesus is here!

What the enemy meant for evil toward you and me, the Lord has turned it for our good. When others might have thought that we'd surely go under, the Lord has caused us to rise yet again and to come out with the victory in our hands. To all who will accept Him, He remains our Savior, our Deliverer, and our soon-coming King. And that, my friend, is the rest of the story.

Reflection: What's the rest of your story? How will you apply this chapter to your life? Take the time to respond to the Spirit of the Lord in whatever way He is prompting you to do so right now.

Inspiration Break

2 Corinthians 4:18 says, "While we do not look at the things which are seen, but at the things which are not seen. For the things which are seen *are* temporary, but the things which are not seen *are* eternal."

I guarantee you that the issues that we wrestle with most and that may be distracting us right now revolve around the cares of this life—things that are temporal and won't last, i.e., jobs, money, clothes, our relationships. Are they important? Yes! That's exactly why the Lord gave the assurance that He knows that we have need of these things because He knew that they could easily become distractions and sources of worry in our lives.

He said in Matthew 6:31, "Take no thought." In other words, "Don't worry." When He said "Take no thought," He was also saying, "Don't even think about it." Before you even consider spending enough time with this thing to begin to worry about it, give it *no thought*.

For the women: We're not called to be superwomen, yet we find ourselves trying to be everything to everybody, do everything for everybody, and justify it by tagging on a scripture, "I can do all things through Christ which strengthens me." Then we wonder what happened when we burn ourselves out from moving in our own strength.

We were created to be free! We are to live above and never beneath our circumstances. He whom the Son sets free is free indeed. We're not superwomen but women who can tap in to and operate in the supernatural.

Many books have been written that liken the saints of God to the eagle. One that comes to mind is *Never Give Up* by Joyce Meyer. We were first likened to the eagle in the Word of God! I won't go into great depth here, but eagles soar to great heights and they soar alone. They don't fly in pairs or in flocks. This simply means that we will often have to make and act upon decisions that separate us from the pack and enable us to reach higher heights than those around us may want us to go.

God has created you to fly high, to be bold, to live with power, and to keep circumstances and relationships in perspective; thereby you'll be able to stay strong and soar above the storms of life. Be ready at His word to mount up on wings as an eagle!

Waiting is not about lack of movement. We're waiting, but we're moving; we're always advancing. We're running, but somehow the Lord has promised that we won't become weary.

It's a different situation when you're running with a purpose than when you're running because you're afraid. When you're running in a panic, you'll become weary. The Bible says you shall run and not become weary. Why? Because the Lord is with you. You won't run aimlessly, nor will you run due to fear. You shall run with purpose!

Know Who Called You

Someone reading this right now needs to hear that it's not about what people call you or what titles they may give to you. *It's about **Who** called you.* The word of God tells us to make our calling and election sure. It doesn't say to make your title or position sure. If we rely on man to establish us in the Kingdom of God, we will always be in a position of waiting on man to orchestrate or give permission for our next move. That's not the will of God for any of us.

Because of the history that I now have with the Lord, I've learned not to give much weight to the faces of the people while ministering or sharing what the Lord has given to me in a teaching setting. Faces are often strong distractions that are used to get us off course. There have been times when I have ministered and thought that certain ones were in another zone, not interested, or not receiving the message at all. Those would be the very ones who would come forward for prayer after the message or would sit in their seats weeping. Once after I spoke on a

Sunday morning, a woman who I had never met stopped me after service and said to me, "That message really touched me, and I don't even believe in women preachers." I said, "Well, thank the Lord that He ministered to you today."

Whenever I'm about to deliver a message, a part of my private prayer (and sometimes public) is, "Lord, these are your people. They don't need an experience with me; they need an experience with you." There are times when I'm preparing messages to speak and nothing seems to be coming. There seem to be no words and my thoughts just won't seem to flow. I'm not one to try to look up messages and preach from something that I've read online, but I prefer to pray and wait for the Holy Spirit to begin speaking words and sharing thoughts with me. This usually happens in the middle of the night, I might add. There have been times when I've stayed before the Lord trying to get a word, and the Spirit of the Lord will gently say, "Just go to bed and rest." I literally go to bed with nothing... or so it seems. I've learned to keep a notepad by my bed because I'm also a dreamer and like to write my dreams. On those occasions when I've gone to bed without an entire message, the Lord will awaken me in the wee hours of the night/morning, and as the words begin to flood my mind, I grab my pad, use the light from my phone, and begin to write. By the time I get up in the morning, I have numerous notes that can be compiled, typed, and shared with the confidence that the Lord has given this word.

Understand that it doesn't always happen this way, but I want to be transparent about the fact that there are times when it has happened this way and the Lord is faithful. This takes me to the point that I'm driving at here. Before and after my opportunities to speak, I always say to the Lord, "You've never failed me." This is the truth. Things may not go the way that I thought they would, and sometimes the Spirit will shift things in the middle of the service as I'm delivering His word, but God has *never* failed me. Please note that I didn't add "yet." That's on purpose because there's no failure in Him. We must be mindful when we speak of Him that we don't speak of Him as we speak of men: "He's never failed me yet." No, no, no! Men may fail us, but the Lord never will! "He Who calls you is faithful, Who also will do it" (1 Thess. 5:24, NKJV).

Prayer: Father, in the Name of Jesus, we thank You for the call that You have placed upon our lives. We are all called first to be ministers of reconciliation. Help us to rise above the opinions and expectations of men so that Your power and grace may be exemplified in our lives. Our expectation is in You and we profess that there is absolutely no failure in You. Amen.

Take Courage and Be
Your Authentic Self

We live in a world of ambiguity and uncertainty, but the Lord has called us to live our lives in a way that exemplifies courage and certainty. Our courage is based in the pursuit of the invisible and the intangible more so than what is visible in the here and now. This is a tremendous risk because we must treasure the unseen. We realize that the things that are seen are temporal, but the things that are unseen are eternal and will endure forever. Our certainty is unwavering because of the God whom we serve and His inability to fail or to change.

In Joshua 1 God encourages Joshua before the conquest of the Promised Land, and He repeatedly gives him the word of comfort and encouragement to be strong and courageous. Read Joshua 1:5–9.

God speaks to Joshua and tells him that His servant Moses is now dead and then assures him that just as He was with Moses, He would be with Joshua. Moses had poured into Joshua, who is referred to in scripture as

Moses's minister. He rose up with Moses as he was going up to the mountain to receive the Ten Commandments from God; he was there when Moses became angry at the children of Israel after returning to the camp after receiving the commandments and finding them dancing around an idol. Moses lost his temper upon seeing this and smashed the tablets that God had written. Yes, Joshua was able to see many of the triumphs and struggles of this great leader. He was the one who Moses chose to take the lead as the Israelite army went into battle against the Amalekites. Moses had done what is incumbent upon all good leaders to do, and that is to pour into those who are to come behind them. So it happened that Moses died and Joshua would have the task of leading God's people forward to take possession of the land that He had sworn to their fathers to give to them. Joshua had seen how Moses had been used mightily by God and that the history of God's strength, faithfulness, and closeness to Joshua's mentor, Moses, must now be brought to bear in his life in a real way.

We are not going to focus on all that God accomplished through Joshua as much as we want to bring forward how important it was for Joshua to hear what the Lord was saying to him at the time when He was about to move him forward into his assignment. Joshua 1:1–3 reads, "After the death of Moses the servant of the LORD, it came to pass that the LORD spoke to Joshua the son of Nun, Moses' assistant, saying: ² 'Moses My servant is dead. Now therefore, arise, go over this Jordan, you and all this people, to the land which I am giving to them—the children of Israel. ³ Every place that the sole of your foot will tread upon I have given you, as I said to Moses.'"

What stands out for me is that God is saying to Joshua, "Moses is dead, he's gone, he is no longer here. I'm not looking for another Moses, but I'm calling you to be your authentic self, not a duplication." If you've ever observed someone who spends their waking hours trying to act like, talk like, and be like someone else, it can be rather exhausting and sometimes frustrating to watch. It certainly has to be hard for the person who is trying to live apart from who they really are. God is not calling for any of us to try to be someone who we're not. He created you and me with a specific purpose in mind. We have a destiny to fulfill that is ours alone, and if we remove ourselves from where God has intended to use us and to operate through us, we are left to walk in disobedience, which is in opposition to His plan. God had to let Joshua know that (I'm paraphrasing), "I know that you're not Moses, but there is a plan for you, and just in case you want to bring up the promise that I made to Moses, I'm still making good on My promise through you." It wasn't about Moses as much as it was about the promise that the Lord had made to His people.

I want to free someone right here. Maybe you've been trying to measure up to what you've seen in someone else, whether it's a ministry leader, a mentor, a coach, or even a parent who poured into your life. You are not them. You are unique and the Lord knew what He was doing when He made you and wrote a master plan for your life. It's your makeup, your personality, your temperament, and your gifts that uniquely fit in the place you've been called to fill in this life. Your life lessons have been preparing, and are continuing to prepare you for your journey.

I'm sure that Joshua must have thought about whether or not he was really up for the task or if the people would even accept him or follow him as he moved forward with the action that God was now requiring of him. Many of you can probably attest to what it's like to come behind a dynamic leader or even a supervisor after they have moved on or, in this case, transitioned from this life. The people had followed Moses, but would they follow Joshua?

God was reminding Joshua of His faithfulness when He told him, "Just as I was with Moses, I'll be with you." We certainly need those reminders from God because any assignment that is given to us will have its challenges along with its successes. Is there anything that the Lord can remind you of today? Do you have history with Him and personal reminders of His faithfulness and ability to come through for you when no one else could or would? Joshua was admonished several times to be of a good courage and to be strong. God knew what was before Joshua, and it was going to require that he would be able to stand strong and to remember His God and what he had witnessed as he had walked closely with Moses. What is your history with the Lord? Reflecting on your history and experiences with Him will cause strength, courage, and confidence to rise up in you. You may say, "Yes, but I blew it that time" or "I totally missed it in that situation," but even in those seasons when we may have fallen short, become weak, or felt like giving up, our story can only be that the Lord has remained faithful.

Sometimes all you'll have is what God told you because everything else won't line up. It's so important to know what He said to you. Are you walking close enough to hear Him speak? Walking in obedience doesn't mean that we know the entire plan. We walk in the light that we've been given and allow the Lord to unfold His plan along the way. Stop waiting or even expecting everyone to see what you see or to hear what you hear. Just because they can't validate what you've seen or heard doesn't mean that God hasn't spoken it or that He hasn't revealed it to you.

Remember that in Joshua's situation, twelve spies were sent out and only Joshua and Caleb returned with a different report. They were up against not only the report of the other ten spies who saw defeat, but they were also faced with the anger and attitudes of fear from all of the people who believed what the other ten spies had spoken. They had to stand firm on what the Lord had said and what He had shown, and the people of Israel fell under the judgment of God due to their unbelief. To obey God will sometimes mean that we will go against the current culture—even within the church. Becoming a faith-walker can be a very lonely and unpopular place. People may taunt you or dismiss you while you're walking it out and professing your faith, yet they will seek to align with you after the Lord brings you through and proves Himself in your place of victory.

What needs to be pointed out here is that whenever we've been called to fulfill our purpose and when we begin to move in that direction, there will always be dissenters who will object to the move of God because in their minds they think that they know what's best, and to them their way is best. Being called and appointed by God is not synonymous with being popular or accepted. What is important for each of us to understand is that the enemy will always seek to magnify the voices and actions of the few in order to distract us in life. You can have an entire room full of people chanting your name and being excited about your presence, but I guarantee you that if there are five over in a corner with constant "boos" and ugly remarks, it's the five in the corner who most of us are likely to walk away remembering. It's almost as if we've conditioned ourselves to listen to the negative narrative around us and within us as well. Most people have to really make a concerted effort to change their self-talk from negative to positive.

Some of the things that you're dealing with now or going through in your walk may seem insignificant to you at this point in time, but everything works together in our lives to bring about God's purpose. God was preparing Joshua the entire time that he was walking with Moses, yet there is no indication in scripture that Joshua was aware of the fact that he would be the one who would be chosen by God to lead the children of Israel into their Promised Land. He was just living his life as a faithful minister to Moses. If we always knew God's next move or where He was taking us, nine times out of ten we'd probably say, "No thanks; I'm good right here." The Lord will use things that may seem insignificant at the time to prepare you for what lies ahead.

You're being set up to operate from the place of knowing the all-sufficiency of God. Sometimes what may seem to be a failure from our perspective is simply God's nudge to us, which says, "Seek Me first. I could have led you around this or shown you another way." The Lord wants us to understand that we are totally dependent upon Him, because we are and that's actually a good thing. The reality is that all too often we try to live as though our lives don't depend upon Him, and that's when we begin to run into trouble. Jesus was totally dependent upon the Father and did not say or do anything that He didn't hear from the Father first.

Take a look at John 5:30: "I can do nothing on my own initiative or authority. Just as I hear, I judge; and My judgment is just (fair, righteous, unbiased), because I do not seek My own will, but only the will of Him who sent Me" (AMP). This was Jesus speaking, and if He was mindful of His need for the leading, direction, and plan of the Father, how much more should we be? Jesus became fully man so that He could experience the life that we are faced with, and He is our example.

Now let's consider John 15:5 where Jesus is again speaking and He says, "I am the Vine; you are the branches. The one who remains in Me and I in him bears much fruit, for (otherwise) apart from Me (that is, cut off from vital union with Me) you can do nothing" (AMP). So now He's talking about you and me and reminding us that just as He is totally dependent upon the Father, so are we dependent upon Him, and without Him, we can do nothing. Now whether or not we believe that is irrelevant. Truth stands whether we believe it or not. Sure, we all make decisions and go about doing whatever we do throughout the course of our day, but what Jesus is speaking of is our ability to do anything of significance or lasting effect for the Kingdom of God. There's absolutely no way to do that apart from Christ because He is the One who works in and through us as we navigate through this experience called life.

You're called to be more than what you are pursuing right now. Our wisdom, insight, and discernment are to be gained through the word of God. What do you see? We must always remember that there are more with us than with those who stand against us.

Do you remember that Joshua was among those who went to spy out the Promised Land? Moses had chosen one man from each of the twelve tribes of Israel to go and spy on the land that God had promised them. Ten of them came back with a report that put fear into the hearts of the people because they reported that the people and everything else in the land was huge and that the people of Israel were but grasshoppers in their eyes. Their report was that there was no way to conquer this land.

Joshua and Caleb, on the other hand, saw a land that was beautiful, bountiful, able to support and sustain them, and beyond that, it was a land God had promised to them

Their report was that it was certainly within their power to conquer it because God had promised and He was with them. Only Joshua and Caleb came back with a different report than the others. They looked over and saw the same things physically, but their perception of what they saw was in line with what God had said. God had promised the land that they were looking at, and no matter how big and intimidating the people appeared to be, Joshua and Caleb's report was that the children of Israel could take the land.

The people rejected their report and wanted to stone them. God decreed that the unbelieving people would wander in the desert for forty years and die there because of their unbelief, and not until the doubtful generation had died would their descendants be able to go forward and possess the Promised Land. Joshua and Caleb would live to see that promise fulfilled and Joshua would be God's chosen leader as Moses would not be permitted to enter the Promised Land, although God gave him an opportunity to look upon it from a distance. The Lord God's response was, "Because my servant Caleb has a different spirit and follows me wholeheartedly, I will bring him into the land he went to, and his descendants will inherit it" (Num. 14:24 and 30). Numbers 14:38 adds, "Not one of you will enter the land I swore with uplifted hand to make your home, except Caleb son of Jephunneh and Joshua son of Nun."

God promised to be with Joshua, and I'm sure Joshua had to remind himself of this promise many times. We know that He lives in us, that He's with us and will never leave us. This is true. Yet in spite of this truth, how many of you have experienced the spirit of fear when it's time to do what you've been called to do? Have you ever had to speak, preach, read, play an instrument, or stand before the people of God in any capacity while wrestling to silence the spirit of fear and trying to find those couple of friendly, supportive faces among the crowd? It comes with the territory, and we have to make up our minds to move forward in spite of the hindrances that are placed before us that come to distract us and cause us to stumble. God's word reminds us that if He's for us, He's more than the world against us. We are always in the majority.

Joshua 1:9 says, "Have I not commanded you? Be strong and courageous! Do not tremble or be dismayed, for the Lord your God is with you wherever you go." I take that as "Never let them see you sweat." We're not to act as though we are clueless about where our help comes from, to be dismayed, which is to be in distress or terrified. You and I have to make Joshua's story our story. The Lord wants us to see life through His lens, which always causes us to see far beyond what the natural eye presents. Remember that Joshua saw what the others saw when he spied on the land of Canaan, but his perspective was different. Everything there was supersized, yes, but that only spoke to the power of God that would have to be manifested on their behalf. It also spoke of the great provision that had been made for them in the land that was awaiting their possession.

Anyone who is saved has history with the Lord, even if that history is that He saved you and completely changed your life as recently as yesterday, and I can say that with confidence because this life that we live in Christ is all about relationships. It's the relationship that you share with Christ that will help you to stand in confidence along with what you have experienced by way of others whom the Lord has allowed you to walk closely with. Joshua had walked closely with Moses and had experienced things that only that relationship could have afforded him. He knew God had used Moses to part the Red Sea. This would be a source of faith and courage for him, as the Lord would use him in a like manner to part the Jordan River. Take note of the people, places, and things God has placed in your life. Lessons are all around us. Life is our classroom, so it behooves us to sit up, pay attention, and take notes.

One thing I've learned is that as much as I love the people of God, there's no way for me to love them more than He does. Some of them, like some of us, can be quite unlovable at times, and we're left to wonder why the Lord is so very longsuffering, patient, and kind toward us. Just as the Lord was with Joshua to bring victory to Him, He's with you and me in every situation that we may face, no matter how small or how insurmountable it may seem to be. Whether the people are with us or not is not important when the Lord has called us to a specific task. He will accomplish His purpose through that calling if we simply choose to walk in obedience. The truth is that some of those who you think are with you are really not and some who you might have never considered as those who would walk with you and have your back are the very ones who the Lord will raise up to escort you to your next level.

We are never in control. Never! Without the Lord we can do nothing. Reflect on John 15:5. Men and women are walking in deception whenever they think that they alone are responsible for the events and outcomes in their lives. The other side of that is "With God all things are possible" (Matt. 19:26).

God's promises are certain and His character does not change. He cannot lie. It is impossible for Him to lie. What He has promised will come to pass. Whether we live to see it or not, if God has promised it, it will come to pass. God used Joshua to make good on a promise that had been spoken while Moses was alive. True confidence toward God isn't bound by time. The scriptures tell us that God could swear by none greater than Himself because there is none higher; there is no greater authority in heaven, on earth, or under the earth. When He speaks a thing, anything, it will come to pass. Just as Joshua had to have confidence toward God in the face of what appeared to some to be insurmountable odds, we are called upon to do the same. He had to wait for the appointed time as God purged the people of those who were walking in unbelief. It was forty years later, but God raised up another generation who would be willing to take His word through His leader, Joshua, and move forward to victory. It's always been that way, my friend. We must learn to wait on the Lord and be of Good Courage! How long do we have to wait? The Lord alone has the answer to that question, yet our position must be that what He has promised is already established in heaven and it will come to pass whether or not we live to see it.

There's no way around this life with God through Christ without faith. Faith is the key. We must see it God's way even if we transition from this life to the next while we stand fast on His promise. When you read Hebrews chapter 11, some call this the faith chapter because it starts out by defining what faith is and then goes on to share great acts of faith that believers accomplished in their lives because of the faith that they placed in God. These weren't "super saints," but these were people like you and me whose stories are shared in scripture in order for us to take hold of faith with tenacity as we wait for victory in the middle of turmoil and adversity. That chapter speaks of many people of faith whom we read about in the Old Testament who had great confidence toward God, yet they died without ever seeing the promise of the Messiah who was to be born of a virgin and walk among men here on earth. They believed Abraham's seed would be far too numerous to count, and here we stand today. The promise is still being fulfilled. The Lord doesn't break promises and His character cannot change.

The Lord is not mad at us today and then on good terms with us tomorrow. He's not in a good mood today and out of sorts tomorrow so that we have to really think about whether or not we want to talk with Him or share our feelings or concerns with Him. Have you ever had your character insulted? We insult the character of God when we doubt Him or when we fail to trust the truth of His word. He cannot lie. He longs for fellowship with us. He longs to inhabit our times of worship and praise. We are to come into His presence with reverence, awe, and expectation, but never are we to come as though we're walking on eggshells and are afraid to share our innermost thoughts and desires with Him. These types of feelings and thoughts come from erroneous teaching that portrays God as a punitive dictator who is just waiting to find us doing something wrong so that He can mete out the punishment that we deserve. He wants us to desire time in His presence because it's in those intimate moments when He reveals His heart to us and rids us of the residue of this world that can cause the light within us to grow dim.

It takes real courage to risk everything on the promises of God. I only say "risk" because sometimes that's what it seems like to us. It seems like we're taking a big risk when in fact we're learning to exercise our faith. The tests don't stay the same, nor do they remain on the same level as we grow in our relationship and faith walk with the Lord. We like to play it safe and test the waters to see who will go along with us. But real courage is taking that risk, that step of faith, and staking your life on something that you haven't seen yet. At times it may mean staking our reputation, our titles, and our positions. Who will go along with it? What do I have to lose? Who will stand with me? This is a time when many of us are going to have to seemingly stand alone. The crowds are going to disperse. Are you ready for that? The Lord will help you as you transition to your next level in Him.

Our faith has to be tested at each level of our walk, but be courageous, don't fear, because the Lord is with you just as He was with Joshua.

Reflect on those areas of your life where you feel the nudge of God to move forward but you've held back because of concerns about what others might think, what they might do, or whether or not they will support you. It's time now to apply this life lesson and allow the Lord to use you in whatever way He chooses. We simply must begin to pull from the written pages of His word in order to experience Him in ways that we never have before. He's with you! Step out now, even if that means taking what you would consider to be baby steps. You can start by simply saying to the Lord, "Please help me. I want Your will to be fulfilled in my life, and I surrender to You right now." Go ahead and **Pull It off the Page!**

CPSIA information can be obtained
at www.ICGtesting.com
Printed in the USA
LVHW081914170921
698109LV00010B/245

9 781662 817250